Absolutization

Middle Way Philosophy
Series Editor: **Robert M. Ellis**, Middle Way Society

Middle Way Philosophy is a cross-disciplinary project developed by Robert M. Ellis over more than 20 years, to develop a consistently pragmatic approach to the justification of human judgement. It follows through the implications of the Buddha's Middle Way, rejecting absolute beliefs of a negative as well as a positive type, in the light of the developing modern understandings of uncertainty, scientific method, mindfulness, embodied meaning, neuroscience, cognitive and developmental psychology, systems theory, Jungian archetypes, and democratic political practice.

Diagnosing the central problem of absolutization that interferes with the justification of human judgement, it then seeks to identify the most effective responses to that problem. It does this through the rigorous application of pragmatic philosophy, drawing on a wide variety of evidence. Overall it thus offers a detailed normative ethical philosophy based in the conditions of psychology, and an overall framework to show the relationship of a variety of practices (from mindfulness to critical thinking) to the universal goal of improving each human judgement.

This is the first book in the series. For the full list of titles see page 270.

Absolutization
The Source of Dogma, Repression, and Conflict

Robert M. Ellis

SHEFFIELD UK   BRISTOL CT

Published by Equinox Publishing Ltd
UK: Office 415, The Workstation, 15 Paternoster Row, Sheffield, South Yorkshire S1 2BX
USA: ISD, 70 Enterprise Drive, Bristol, CT 06010

www.equinoxpub.com

First published 2022
© Robert M. Ellis 2022
All rights reserved. No part of this publication may be reproduced or transmitted in any form or by any means, electronic or mechanical, including photocopying, recording or any information storage or retrieval system, without prior permission in writing from the publishers.

British Library Cataloguing-in-Publication Data
A catalogue record for this book is available from the British Library.

ISBN-13 978 1 80050 205 5 (hardback)
         978 1 80050 206 2 (paperback)
         978 1 80050 207 9 (ePDF)
         978 1 80050 247 5 (ePub)

Library of Congress Cataloging-in-Publication Data

Names: Ellis, Robert M., author.
Title: Absolutization : the source of dogma, repression, and conflict / Robert M. Ellis.
Description: Bristol, CT : Equinox Publishing Ltd, 2022. | Series: Middle way philosophy ; volume 1 | Includes bibliographical references and index. | Summary: "This book puts forward a theory of absolutization, bringing together a multi-disciplinary understanding of this central flaw in human judgement, and what we can do about it. This approach, drawing on Buddhist thought and practice, philosophy, psychology, neuroscience, embodied meaning and systems theory, offers a rigorous introduction to absolutization as the central problem addressed in Middle Way Philosophy, which is a synthetic approach developed by the author over more than twenty years in a series of books. It challenges disciplinary boundaries as well as offering a substantial framework for practical application"-- Provided by publisher.
Identifiers: LCCN 2022011191 (print) | LCCN 2022011192 (ebook) | ISBN 9781800502055 (hardback) | ISBN 9781800502062 (paperback) | ISBN 9781800502079 (epdf) | ISBN 9781800502475 (epub)
Subjects: LCSH: Concepts. | Knowledge, Theory of. | Categorization (Psychology) | Buddhist philosophy.
Classification: LCC BF443 .E45 2022 (print) | LCC BF443 (ebook) | DDC 153.2/3--dc23/eng/20220715
LC record available at https://lccn.loc.gov/2022011191
LC ebook record available at https://lccn.loc.gov/2022011192

Typeset by S.J.I. Services, New Delhi, India

Contents

List of Figures and Tables	vii
Foreword to the Middle Way Philosophy Series *Iain McGilchrist*	viii
Preface	ix
Acknowledgements	xii
Introduction	**1**
1. Early Buddhism	**12**
a. Mental Proliferation	12
b. Craving, Hatred, and Delusion	18
c. The Absoluteness of Negations	23
d. Excluding the Options	29
2. Systems Theory	**39**
a. Reinforcing Feedback Loops	39
b. Assumed System Independence	48
c. Fragility	53
3. Embodied Meaning	**61**
a. Representationalism	61
b. The Denial of Embodiment	70
c. Discontinuity	79
d. Interpretation	84
4. Philosophy	**89**
a. Metaphysics	89
b. The Absoluteness of Deductive Logic	99
c. Foundationalism and Circularity	105
d. Infinite Rationalization of Experience	110
e. The Claim that Metaphysics is Inevitable	116
f. Inflation of Metaphysics and Logic	120
5. Psychology	**129**
a. Repression and Conflict	129

	b. Projection	139
	c. Confirmation Bias	144
	d. Substitution	149
	e. Group Binding	155
	f. Archetypal Function	161
6.	**The Unity of Absolutizing Phenomena**	**164**
	a. The Blind Synthesist	164
	b. Clarifying the Relationships	167
	c. The Use of Synthesis	171
	d. The Practical Arguments	176
7.	**Criteria for a Response: Practicality**	**182**
	a. What is Practicality?	182
	b. Embodiment	188
	c. Responsibility	194
	d. Effectiveness	201
8.	**Criteria for a Response: Universal Aspiration**	**208**
	a. Top-down and Bottom-up Universality	208
	b. Normativity	212
	c. Systematicity	220
	d. Universality across Groups	224
	e. Universality across Space	228
	f. Universality across Time	232
9.	**Criteria for a Response: Judgement Focus**	**236**
	a. Judgement as the Cutting Edge	236
	b. Diversions from Judgement Focus	242
10.	**Criteria for a Response: Error Focus**	**248**
	a. Falsification and Error Focus	248
	b. Refining Shadow Avoidance	253
	c. Emotionally Positive Context	257
Conclusion: Criteria for the Middle Way		260
Appendix		267
The Old and New Middle Way Philosophy Series		269
Bibliography		271
Index		279

List of Figures and Tables

Figure 1.	Dimensions of absolutization	8
Figure 2.	Reinforcing and balancing feedback loops	43
Figure 3.	Substitutions that occur in the denial of embodiment	71
Figure 4.	What is practicality?	186

Table 1.	The conditions of emergence of the 23 dimensions of absolutization	168
Table 2.	Four criteria for the Middle Way	177
Table 3.	Features of evil correlated with dimensions of absolutization	254
Table 4.	The 23 dimensions of absolutization	267

Foreword to the Middle Way Philosophy Series

Iain McGilchrist

The 'Middle Way' Ellis argues for so cogently is far from being a simple compromise between existing polarities, but a departure at right angles to typical thinking in the modern Western world, which looks to me like the path to ancient wisdom.

The perception that objectivity is neither an absolute, nor any the less real for that, is central. Ellis argues for an approach that is incremental and continuously responsive to what is given, rather than abstract and absolute. This is the difference, as he notes, between the pragmatic, provisional, nuanced, never fixed position of the right hemisphere in the face of the absolutism towards which the left hemisphere always tends.

The need for certainty must inevitably lead to illusion, whether in philosophy or in the business of living, and here too Ellis makes clear – as far as I am aware for the first time – the connections between the cognitive distortions known to psychology and the fallacies identified in the process of philosophy.

This is an important, original work, that should get the widest possible hearing.

Dr Iain McGilchrist is the author of The Master and His Emissary, *fellow of All Soul's College, Oxford and a former psychiatrist.*
This foreword was originally written for the old Middle Way Philosophy series.

Preface

Most people who pick up this book will probably not need convincing that 'extreme' thinking (or dogma, repression, and conflict) is a bad idea. But what constitutes extreme thinking? It is obviously not just what our particular group considers conventionally 'extreme', so what are the common elements across groups? In this book I set out to answer that question in a thorough fashion, by drawing together a variety of disciplinary perspectives. I am also doing so with the longer-range practical aim of equipping us for an effective response to such 'extreme' thinking.

I aspire to do genuine interdisciplinary work, which synthesizes different perspectives whilst critically questioning some of their limiting assumptions. In my experience, it has been difficult to get such work off the ground. Nevertheless, I have been committed to such work for around twenty years, since I completed the unusually broad Philosophy PhD in 2001 that set the agenda for my work on the Middle Way. That work has been through two more distinct stages of development since that PhD, to form first what I now call the 'old' Middle Way Philosophy series (2012–15), followed now by the new one of which this is the first volume. I'm immensely pleased to be able to start publishing the much improved and updated third incarnation of the project with Equinox.

I perceive most academics as being forced by socio-economic constraints into an over-specialized system. That system may suit relatively discrete objects of investigation (such as mosses or metal stresses), but has been disastrous for the systemic understanding of our own process of judgement. There philosophers, psychologists, neuroscientists, linguists, and religious practitioners (among others) are (to apply the Buddha's parable) just different blind men making claims about different bits of the same elephant, often apparently oblivious to the ways the same issues are approached quite differently elsewhere. I have been fortunate enough to be able to ignore most of those specializing pressures, and to continue to work in a way that doesn't just branch out from one discipline (for instance, much 'interdisciplinary' work is actually social science based), but critically engages with the assumptions of opposing perspectives. I have published most recently on the Middle Way in relation to Buddhist and Jungian themes, largely in order to get published on something, but my interests are very wide.

There is, of course, an opposite trap for those with wide interests: vague generalization, New Agey waffle, and false synthesis. Let me assure those who approach this book with suspicion on that score, that I am just as much aware of those dangers. Synthesis is the life-blood of thought, because creativity comes from previously isolated ideas being brought together. However, each new synthesis also needs to be subjected to critical scrutiny, and empirical claims need evidential support. My approach is that of critical universalism, not of naïve assertions about universality. I am rigorously focused on the Middle Way as *a principle of judgement*, not as any kind of metaphysical claim about the universe or top-down assertion about human nature. One of the aims of this book is to try to establish much of the basis of that principle.

Generally speaking, I have reached my current understanding of these issues by an extended process of checking one perspective against others, so as to gradually develop an increasingly adequate account of what the Middle Way consists in. It is not merely Buddhism, nor is it only to be understood philosophically or psychologically or neuroscientifically. Nevertheless, all these perspectives can illuminate each other. My prime criteria throughout have been practical: in other words, the most important question has always been 'Can this help anyone?'. The 'helping' may in some cases be very long-range, but it is precisely by insisting on a wider perspective that we can be *more* helpful, not less.

The need to begin this new presentation of Middle Way Philosophy with a focus on the problem, in the form of a book on absolutization, has only quite recently become apparent to me. It's important to start with a focus on the problem in order to develop a fully relevant solution. It is not only practical problem-solvers who will recognize that point, but also Buddhists, who will be used to the way in which the Buddha's 'Four Noble Truths' begin with practical problem and diagnosis before proceeding to solution and prescription. Buddhists may thus recognize in this book a (highly unorthodox) exploration of some of the insights in the First and Second Noble Truths of the Buddha. Another reason for adopting this approach, however, is a gradually increasing recognition on my part that different specialists in other areas only seem to have partial views of the problem, and that these do not generally connect up to each other.

There are five major perspectives represented in the starting points for the first five sections of this book, and my challenge is to make those who start with one of these perspectives connect it adequately with the others. After my introduction, I begin with Buddhist ideas about proliferation – the hindrance to mindfulness, and the insights of the Buddha's Middle Way into the sources of polarized thinking. If you are aware of these, have you connected them with limiting non-embodied understandings of meaning, as pointed out in so-called 'cognitive linguistics'? I then talk about systems theory. If you were aware of the property of fragility in systems (very much brought to our attention of late in relation to the tipping points of the earth's climate), have you connected this to the fragility of absolute *belief*? In section 4 I discuss metaphysical beliefs in philosophy: if you were aware that these might be criticized because they are beyond all human experience, have you connected those beliefs to bias in psychology? If I achieve nothing else in this book, I hope that I stimulate you to make a few more connections of this kind.

Beyond this, though, is the need for a more adequate understanding of absolutization due to its practical effects. The interconnections between dogma, repression, and conflict mean that we cannot succeed in addressing any of them adequately by doing so piecemeal without a fuller interdisciplinary perspective. We also need to do so in a way that addresses the situation of judgement of every human being, not merely offering further causal explanatory theories or analyses. This book will have still better achieved its aims if it helps you to reconsider absolutization as you have found it in your own experience.

Acknowledgements

This book is an entirely new presentation of the phenomenon of absolutization, but is also built on much previous work on Middle Way Philosophy. So I'd like to thank all the people who have either supported and encouraged me along the way, or have commented on one issue or another so as to help this work reach its present form.

Amongst many others, those particularly include my wife Viryanaya, and also my friends and associates in the Middle Way Society, such as Barry Daniel, Jim Champion, Susan Averbach, Nina Davies, Julian Adkins, and Peter Goble. I'd also like to thank Iain McGilchrist, who is a patron of the Middle Way Society, for the foreword, and Dan Nixon and Rodrigo Caceres Riquelme for some very helpful comments on the manuscript of this book.

Introduction

> *Even by the barbaric standards of Islamic State, the murder of the captured Jordanian pilot is particularly gruesome. The 26-year-old is paraded around the site of an alleged coalition airstrike, presumably to witness its effects first-hand.*
>
> *He is then placed in a metal cage and set alight. The scenes are harrowing, the screams of anguish unimaginably horrific....*
>
> *IS believes in a principle known as 'qisas' which, in its broadest terms, is the law of equal retaliation. Put another way, it is the Islamic equivalent of 'lex talionis', or the doctrine of an eye for an eye.*
>
> *As a pilot fighting with the Western coalition, Lt Kasasbeh would have been associated with dropping incendiary bombs – so burning could be seen by them as appropriate retaliation.*[1]

In this news report from 2015 about the activities of the 'Islamic State' group, we have just one of a myriad of possible examples of absolutization, from across the globe, across cultures and religions, and across history. I am not referring to anything specific to Islam or Islamic State here, but to a more general question of how human beings can enter a mental state in which their beliefs require them to do things like this.

Although my arguments in this book are *not* specifically about Islamism, the example quoted above is an especially clear one. The executioners act as they do because of a principle that they believe in and have clearly articulated. They can give further justification for it, from the Qur'an and its tradition of interpretation. This principle is one that completely determines the actions of Islamic State members in that context, not one that is weighed up against other principles in any way. It is completely isolated from all contextual values or considerations. The people who oppose it are demonized. The people doing this *believe they have the whole story.*

1   https://www.bbc.co.uk/news/world-middle-east-31129416   (accessed November 2020).

This is my immediate and imprecise definition of absolutization: *the belief that we have the whole story* (I do not attempt any comprehensive definition at this stage, because a wider understanding of the concept needs to emerge for the reader through synthesis, not strict definition). Used in this sense, the term 'absolutization' is not exactly a coinage, but perhaps a specific new development of the previous use of the term. There do not seem to be any equivalents elsewhere.[2]

As a phenomenon, absolutization is not specific to any culture, religion, location, or time – it is a feature of human belief in general. Apart from extreme instances like that of Islamic State, we could also cite very ordinary and trivial ones. Supposing in conversation with a friend, I claim that Lagos is the capital of Nigeria. This is a result of out-of-date information, as the capital switched to Abuja in 1991, and the friend soon shows this to be wrong with reference to online information sources. However, I won't admit that I was wrong, and keep claiming that the capital of Nigeria is *really* Lagos 'in the ways that matter', because it is still the largest city. So here I am starting to indulge in *ad hoc* or 'moving the goalposts' argument, because *I can't let go of the idea that I have the whole story*. None of us can plausibly claim to be totally immune from absolutization in these less serious forms.

Absolutization does not *merely* consist in dogma, bias, fallacy, metaphysics, repression, certainty, projection, or addiction, though it can be responsible for all of these phenomena. To understand it as a whole, we need to understand how these phenomena are linked, and thus a multidisciplinary approach (what is sometimes described as a 'transversal' approach) is demanded. That's why in this book I draw together approaches to absolutization from Buddhism, Western philosophy, psychology, neuroscience, linguistics, and systems theory. I find that there is still a great deal of resistance from academics and others to genuine interdisciplinarity that synthesizes approaches from different disciplines, and some of this itself may be due to absolutization, in the form of implicit assumptions that a given discipline *tells the whole story*. So it is impossible to separate my topic from the issues involved in understanding it. In our understanding of complex systems in the world, just as in a

---

2   The nearest predecessor I have found is Alfred Korzybski's concept of 'allness': Korzybski (1993).

functioning constitution, effective checks and balances are needed: to understand a complex phenomenon, we need to be able to use one kind of disciplinary perspective to check the assumptions in another.

What does this multidisciplinary approach have to say that previous academic investigations into, say, bias, or conflict, do not? The key thing I will suggest is practicality. My thesis is that absolutization, as a general, enveloping phenomenon with some clear determining features, is *the biggest underlying problem facing human beings*. It leads us to sabotage many creative and helpful undertakings, whether these are related to personal health, relationships, careers, studies, organizations, ideological beliefs, states, or our dependence on the world environment.

Absolutization sabotages our undertakings by distorting our *judgement* at each point. Thus, we can respond to it effectively by maintaining a focus on *judgement in experience*, without distraction from cosmic claims or speculations that are themselves usually absolutizations. The practical value of gaining a general understanding of absolutization, then, is to help us identify an effective response to it that incorporates the widest possible understanding of the phenomena involved.

That's why the account of absolutization in this book is not an end in itself, and is not attempting to be merely descriptive. An account of absolutization forms the first half of this book, but the second half will consist in an attempt to identify the defining features of any response to it that effectively addresses its multiple interdependent features. These criteria for an effective response in turn offer a starting point for the larger focus of my whole work on Middle Way Philosophy, and I am expecting this book to be the first volume of a new and more rigorous exposition of Middle Way Philosophy as a whole, that will improve on the previous versions.[3]

The first half of this book will introduce absolutization using 23 interdependent features of it that I have identified. These are roughly grouped into five disciplinary areas that are the primary ones where we are most likely to find these features explained, modelled, and evidenced. Using these five disciplinary areas will, I hope, provide some way in for readers who have an interest in or familiarity with

---

3   See 'The Old and New Middle Way Philosophy Series' listed before the bibliography in this book.

at least one of them. However, you must also be warned that the treatment of these disciplinary areas is not watertight, and I will also be using insights from one area to challenge the assumptions in another throughout this book. For instance, the perspectives offered to me by Buddhism and systems theory mean that I do not accept the still-dominant academic assumptions about representational meaning and metaphysical philosophy, nor the excuses often made for bias. The first section labelled 'Early Buddhism' for instance, is not solely about Buddhism – Buddhism just provides an identifiable starting point. You will need to expect constant interweaving and comparison of different kinds of sources throughout this book.

The first section starts with Buddhism only because it is from Buddhism that, in my own personal progression of understanding, I first recognized the importance of putting practice first, and tackling abstract conceptual issues in a way that is consistent with long-term practical experience. I am no longer a formally committed Buddhist, however, and recognize influential elements of the Buddhist tradition that do not effectively prioritize a practical perspective in this way. For that reason, I now describe myself as a practitioner of the Middle Way (which is not a Buddhist monopoly) rather than a Buddhist. My earlier book, *The Buddha's Middle Way*[4] goes into more detail on the distinction between the Middle Way and Buddhism. Here, then, I limit myself to some key insights on absolutization that I get *primarily* from early Buddhism: the experience of mental proliferation (which any meditator will recognize); the interdependence between craving, hatred, and delusion; the absoluteness of negations (that is the recognition that denying an absolute view just gives one another absolute view); and the restriction of options (also known as false dichotomy, or dualism). These are insights that can be gained from the teaching and exemplification of the Middle Way in the Pali Canon, as long as one interprets it sufficiently in a practical context.

These four points are insights that drew me on from an early stage in my investigations to try to understand absolutization better from other kinds of sources. They are thus expressed and symbolized in Buddhist sources, but this does not mean that they are restricted to them. Indeed, one could give a fair justification for them without any particular reference to Buddhism. Mental proliferation can also

4   Ellis (2019).

be understood using psychology and systems theory; the relationship between craving, hatred, and delusion can be similarly based in psychological observation; and the avoidance of false dichotomy or restriction of options is long-established in the Western critical thinking tradition. Perhaps the absoluteness of negations is the point least understood and almost never applied in Western discourse: but it can also be readily justified through arguments that involve no appeal to Buddhism or Buddhist tradition.

The second area is systems theory, an interdisciplinary approach that has been steadily transforming a whole range of disciplines in recent decades, by recognizing the greater degree of objectivity that can be developed by treating phenomena as systems of relationships rather than fixed objects. Systems theory identifies two kinds of recurrent feedback loop that can be found in all kinds of organic and inorganic systems: the reinforcing and the balancing. One of the basic features of absolutized beliefs is reinforcing feedback loops, meaning ones that indefinitely repeat the same pattern of assumptions. In systems theory it is also clear that no system is in practice independent of other systems, yet absolutized beliefs assume themselves to be so. Absolutized beliefs are also *fragile*, meaning that they lack resilience, and are likely to be completely destroyed by a large disruption. The writings of Nassim Nicholas Taleb are highly informative on the extent to which beliefs that continue in the same pattern of assumptions can become disastrously ill-adapted to their context.

The third area I draw on is embodied meaning theory, the revolutionary approach to meaning developed by George Lakoff and Mark Johnson since the 1980s, yet since then often under-used by theorists who have appropriated it to other approaches rather than followed through its radical implications. This appropriation is particularly clear from the fact that it is often referred to as 'cognitive linguistics', when it is neither exclusively cognitive nor exclusively linguistic.

Embodied meaning provides a standpoint from which we can particularly identify the meaning assumptions that create absolutization: those of representationalism. Representationalism assumes that meaning arises from the relationship of language with potential reality, rather than being developed from bodily experience. This is a key feature of absolutization, which operates on the constant assumption that absolute claims get their meaning from a relationship with independent reality.

The denial of embodied meaning in absolutization in turn is an indication of a wider denial of embodiment and its implications. The perspective of the body, backed up by the neuroscience of the brain hemispheres, is a *continuous* one, but the absolute perspective is readily distinguishable for its *discontinuity*. The body providing the basis of every kind of meaning in human experience, though, also means that the meaning of words must always be judged in relation to that bodily context. We thus have to be careful in our judgements about what is an example of absolutization and what is not, that we do not attribute the final meaning to the assembled words alone.

The fourth area for discussion of absolutization is that of (Western) philosophy. Absolutized beliefs in philosophy have taken the form of metaphysics: that is, of beliefs about what is ultimately the case rather than what merely appears in our experience. These ultimate beliefs are not just discussed in philosophy, but much applied – for instance in religion, politics, ethics, or even when interpreting science. I will explain why metaphysical beliefs are unavoidably absolute. Since metaphysical beliefs cannot be justified through experience, they rely on claims about ultimate sources of 'knowledge' of some kind, and these are taken to be foundational.

To draw further conclusions from metaphysical beliefs, we also adopt the assumption that deductive logic provides an absolutely valid link between one 'truth' and another: but embodied meaning undoes this assumption. Philosophical tradition also gives us evidence of all the ways that absolutized beliefs can be made compatible with any new observation whatsoever – think, for instance, of the way that any amount of suffering can still be judged compatible with the existence of a loving God. Although empirical philosophy has started to offer challenges to some aspects of absolutization, it has not done so effectively, because it has continued to be appropriated by absolutized beliefs.

Philosophy also provides the resources for some of the most widely used defensive arguments that try to maintain absolutization when it is challenged, by making it apparently non-negotiable. Prime amongst these is the claim that metaphysical belief is inevitable, and that anyone arguing against it must be hypocritical, because they must be using metaphysical beliefs themselves. I shall be arguing that this kind of defence again assumes a basically disembodied view of human experience, denies the very possibility of provisionality as an alternative to metaphysical belief, and fails to apply a criterion of practical relevance to the metaphysical beliefs we are assumed to hold.

Further defensive moves may inflate the scope of 'metaphysics' and 'logic' in ways that confuse the issues. Metaphysics may be associated with religious experience or with profound insight in general, for instance. 'Logic' may be used in many remarkably vague senses, including the attribution of the faults in both formal and informal fallacies to faults in 'logic', when it is primarily practical criteria that actually make them problematic. I argue that more careful (and practically motivated) distinctions in how we use these terms can resolve these kinds of issues.

I then draw on aspects of psychology and psychoanalysis to discuss repression and projection, which are both psychological aspects of absolutization. Repression, whereby an absolutized belief tries to 'win' against its rivals, is the basic reason why absolutization is the source of endless conflict. If we did not assume that we had the whole story, there would be no problem with resolving conflict, either within ourselves or more widely in socio-political power relationships. The identification of projection with absolutization also gives us a clear understanding of why absolutization is delusory: it leads us to attribute the properties to people and things that fit our needs, as opposed to the ones they actually have.

Cognitive psychology can also make an obviously important contribution to our understanding of absolutization, through its exploration of the phenomena of bias. I will argue that being deceived by a bias (or alternatively reacting against it) is absolutization. However, there are some approaches to psychology that defend bias in ways that parallel the defence of metaphysics in philosophy – defences that in both cases involve distractions from their negative practical effects.

The most basic process of bias, as identified in the work of Daniel Kahneman and Amos Tversky, is that of substitution, whereby we adopt easier 'fast' thinking in the place of harder and more energy-consuming 'slow' thinking. I argue that this substitution process is also characteristic of absolutization as a whole. This ease of use is what makes absolutization such a tempting shortcut for group binding, with all the attendant socially negative effects of absolutization as a tool of power.

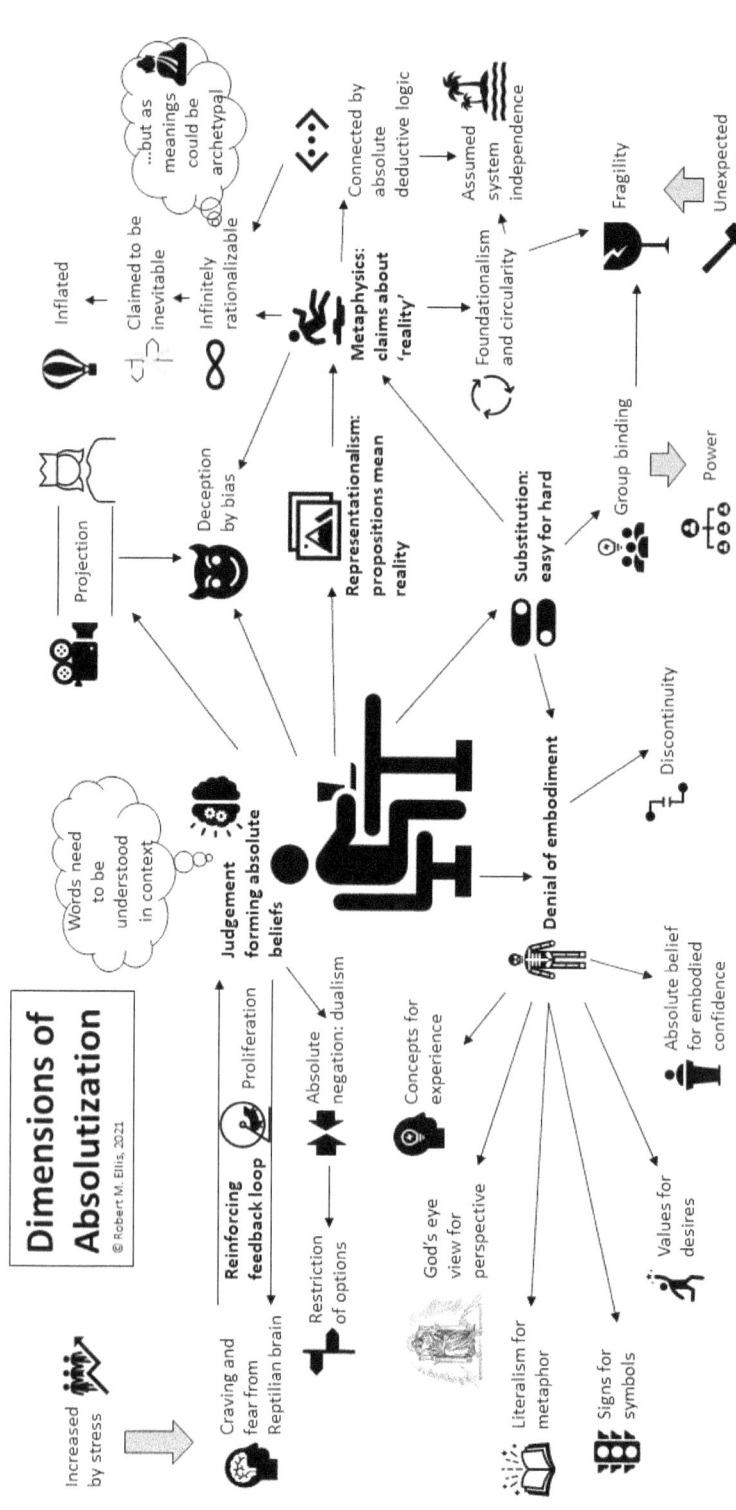

Figure 1. Dimensions of absolutization.

Finally, however, it must be acknowledged that absolutization is only negative in its effects when it is clearly put into a context of ultimate reinforcing feedback loops, representationalism, metaphysics, repression, projection, and substitution. It is quite possible to make use of the same words and symbols that we use for absolutizing purposes and make them helpful sources of inspiration by giving them a larger practical context. This, drawing on Jungian psychology, can be seen as the *archetypal* function of absolutes.

These features of absolutization are illustrated here in relation to each other in a diagram (**figure 1**). They are also summarized for reference in a table in the appendix, along with their main sources and a brief indication of the evidence and implications discussed. In section 6 I argue that they are interlinked by implicitly implying each other, not through an *a priori* equivalence, and are obviously evident at different times dependent on the conditions in which they appear. Given the particular conditions for the emergence of each dimension, though, I posit that it will appear. The argument for the relationship between the dimensions is also a synthetic one (gaining greater strength from the number of perspectives from which it can be observed) and a practical one (gaining greater strength from the ways it can be applied).

Following this account of the dimensions of absolutization, the second half of this book then offers four criteria of response. These criteria grow directly out of the account of absolutization itself as creating certain basic requirements for how we can address it effectively. The value of offering these criteria as a starting point for the Middle Way is to distinguish it as a connected approach from the many partial existing approaches. Existing approaches, I will argue, are hampered by a failure to appreciate one or other of these four criteria: these range from traditional religious and philosophical approaches to new forms of psychotherapy or other intellectual movements. If it can be recognized that their limitations are due to an insufficiently comprehensive response to the multifaceted and self-defensive nature of absolutization, it should become clearer why the distinctive approach of the Middle Way is necessary to respond to absolutization effectively. This is by no means intended to offer a blanket rejection of other approaches, but rather a basis for assessing and improving them, so that their energies can be channelled most effectively.

The four criteria that I will be discussing are practicality, universal aspiration, judgement focus, and error focus.

Practicality is the first requirement, shown primarily by the inadequacies of purely philosophical responses to absolutization that ignore psychology. Practicality involves not only considering our mental states as well as the content of our beliefs, but working with them over the long term, using techniques that take the conditions into account and try to improve our judgement. A wide range of techniques can potentially do this, so the main challenge is not to develop new techniques, but to integrate the ones we already have in a framework of practice that is fully justified.

However, 'practicality' is unfortunately often associated with short-termism or parochialism, and the second criterion of *universal aspiration* is required to make sure we keep stretching our outlook to wider adequacy so as to be able to face new and perhaps unpredicted conditions. The Middle Way holds this universal aspiration in creative tension with a recognition of the particularity of all our judgements. Approaches to absolutization that merely react to the failure of positive absolutes by adopting negative ones (for instance, relativism) do not help us to avoid absolutization.

The third criterion, *judgement focus*, is a corrective to our tendency to excessive or irrelevant theorizing about conditions that do not affect how we actually respond to conditions. This includes not just metaphysical speculation in philosophy and religion, but also scientific diversion onto excessive concern with explanatory theory at the expense of effective response to the absolutization. We need a principle of theoretical economy to avoid getting caught up in trying to explain things that we do not need to explain – a process that can rapidly take us back into absolutization.

The final criterion, *error focus*, refers to the specific type of error involved in absolutization. It argues that this type of error is much easier to identify than any correct positive principle that we can have complete confidence in. Although we do need inspiring positive symbols and intermediate goals for our development away from absolutization, our beliefs about how to develop need to primarily focus on what we need to avoid, rather than what we need to positively achieve. It is probably much easier for us to consistently unite, both as individuals and as a species, around the need to avoid absolutization, than it is to all, for instance, agree to gain enlightenment, follow God's will, identify the true facts of nature, or any other positive formulation of the kind that usually divides rather than unites us.

These four criteria will define the basic requirements for the approach to understanding the Middle Way (the path avoiding absolutization) in further books of the planned series succeeding this one. The structure overall, then, is one of problem followed by a solution. This is not to underestimate the unfathomable size of the problem or the extreme difficulties of the solution. However, it is to try to face up to all the ways that merely partial accounts of the problem prevent us from reaching an adequate understanding of appropriate solutions.

1. Early Buddhism

1.a. Mental Proliferation

> *Summary*
>
> Mental proliferation consists of energy continually directed down the same mental and neural channels to produce repetitive thoughts and feelings. The energy applied is continually trying to remove the same obstacles to a goal, but the obstacle is part of a complex system and is not so easily removed. This proliferation is the *papañca* mentioned by the Buddha, and can also be directly experienced in mindfulness practice. It connects desire and belief in maladapted patterns.

Suppose, Malunkyaputta, a man were wounded by an arrow thickly smeared with poison, and his friends and companions, his kinsmen and relatives, brought a surgeon to treat him. The man would say, 'I will not let the surgeon pull out this arrow until I know the name and clan of the man who wounded me;... until I know whether the man who wounded me was tall or short or middle height;... until I know whether the man who wounded me was dark or brown or golden-skinned;... until I know whether the man who wounded me lives in such a village or town or city;... until I know whether the bow that wounded me was a longbow or crossbow;... until I know whether the bowstring that wounded me was fibre or reed or sinew or hemp or bark;... until I know whether the shaft that wounded me was wild or cultivated;... until I know with what feathers the shaft that wounded me was fitted – whether those of a vulture or a crow or a hawk or a peacock or a stork; until I know with what kind of sinew the shaft that wounded me was bound – whether that of an ox or a buffalo or a lion or a monkey;... until I know what kind of arrow it was that wounded me – whether it was hoof-tipped or curved or barbed or calf-toothed or oleander.'

All that would still not be known to that man and meanwhile he would die. So too, Malunkyaputta, if anyone should say thus: 'I will not lead the holy life under the Blessed one until the Blessed One declares to me "The world is eternal" or "the world is not eternal"; "the world is finite" or "the world is infinite"; "the soul is the same as the body" or "the soul is one thing and the body another"; "after death a Tathagata [Buddha] exists" or "after death a Tathagata does not exist"...' that would still remain undeclared by the Tathagatha and meanwhile that person would die.[1]

1   *Majjhima Nikaya* 63: Ñanamoli & Bodhi (1995) pp. 534–5.

In this famous analogy, the Buddha shows us directly what mental proliferation is like: an uncontrolled flow of obsessive speculation completely irrelevant to its practical context. The sheer excessiveness of the wounded man's endless detail is somewhat reminiscent of a bore in a bar who carries on with his story despite the negative body language of his listeners, or the door-to-door missionary who carries on using the same abstract language of salvation regardless of its lack of impact on his listener.

What is particularly interesting about this passage is that it also links mental proliferation to metaphysical speculation. The context of the quotation is the *Shorter Malunkyaputta Sutta*, in which the Buddha is pressed by a man called Malunkyaputta for answers to speculative questions. Malunkyaputta even threatens to leave the Buddha's order if he does not get answers to them. These questions are whether the world is or is not eternal or infinite, whether or not the soul is separable from the body, and whether an enlightened person exists after death. The Buddha steadfastly refuses to answer any such questions. When pressed, the Buddha then offers this simile.

It is in the Pali Canon accounts of the Buddha's life and teaching that we find the concept of mental proliferation (*papañca*), along with others that I will be discussing here: the relationship between craving, hatred, and delusion, and of the Middle Way. The standard Buddhist teachings on these things require critical reflection and comparison with other sources, rather than wholesale adoption on the basis of the authority of the tradition we find them in. Nevertheless, they offer us some important initial indications of what absolutization is and why it is a problem.

The idea that craving (interlinked with hatred and delusion) leads to a cycle of negative effects, which then help to perpetuate craving, is a central insight in the Buddha's teachings. One can find this idea to some extent almost everywhere in expositions of Buddhism, but here is one example from the *Honeyball Sutta*:

> *Bhikkhus, as to the source through which perceptions and notions tinged by mental proliferation beset a man: if nothing is found there to delight in, welcome and hold to, this is the end of the underlying tendency to lust, of the underlying tendency of aversion... of the underlying tendency to ignorance; this is the end of resorting to rods and weapons, of quarrels, brawls, disputes, recrimination, malice, and false speech; here these evil unwholesome states cease without remainder.*[2]

2   *Majjhima Nikaya* 18:8: Ñanamoli & Bodhi (1995) p. 202.

The source of craving, hatred, and delusion here involves 'mental proliferation' (*papañca*). Without an object that stimulates this mental proliferation, the Buddha asserts, consequent craving, hatred, delusion, and conflict are avoided. The difficult questions are those of exactly what this mental proliferation consists in, and how it relates to desire and belief.

The above quotation from the *Shorter Malunkyaputta Sutta* shows the way mental proliferation is supported by metaphysical beliefs (beliefs about things that lie beyond experience). The avoidance of metaphysical beliefs involves finding the practical Middle Way. The Middle Way requires us to reconsider the whole context and framing of metaphysical beliefs. In the context of the analogy, that means cutting the man's obsession with whether beliefs about things that lie beyond experience are true or false, and him focusing instead on an immediate concern about life and death. This puts abstract speculation in a bigger and more urgent context, so that it can fall away, because it is readily seen as less important than that bigger context. The circular and repetitive pattern created by the reproduction of such obsessive beliefs has a maladaptive effect, preventing us from prioritizing and addressing the practical situation.[3]

An immediate insight into mental proliferation can also be aided considerably by the experience of mindfulness practice, central to the Buddha's practical teachings. In mindfulness practice, one starts off with the intention to focus on a simple aesthetic experience, most typically the breath, aided by a process of bodily relaxation and adjustment. However, anyone who has tried this practice will be aware that it is constantly diverted by proliferating 'distractions' or hindrances: that is, streams of thought and emotion accompanied by a loss of awareness of one's wider goal. When we are in this state of diversion, our current focus and assumptions are taken to be complete, yet the anchoring effect of the practice can nevertheless enable us to regularly 'surface' into an understanding of how limited that state is, by putting it into a wider context of awareness. It is this state of hindrance, understood in a wider context, that can offer an experiential starting point for understanding the nature of craving and absolutization.

---

3   Also see Ellis (2019) pp. 109–13 for much fuller discussion of the arrow simile and its implications.

The dynamic of proliferation, as one can encounter it personally in mindfulness practice, depends very much on the way that energy is continually applied to a set of thoughts motivated by craving, hatred, or anxiety. We represent to ourselves an intransigent obstacle needing to be overcome, so we apply a burst of energy to overcome it. That energy is directed at removing the obstacles that are blocking our path and preventing us from reaching a perceived goal. In some practical situations, this is a strategy that works: for instance, an intense heave may enable us to shift a door that is stuck, or to move a heavy object at the edge of our strength. However, it's more likely that such an effort will fail when we are dealing imaginatively with a situation not actually present, or one actually present that is complex and long-term. For instance, in our imaginations, we can end up telling our enemy what we think of them over and over again, because they are not present either to admit to their faults or to put them in any bigger perspective. In the complex long-term issues created by relationships, the workplace, or politics, too, one effort from us will not be enough to fix things. So when our effort fails, we try again, and again, and again. The energy flowing in the direction of the obstacle proliferates, and as it does so it is *not* applied to a more complex understanding of the situation that would help us to direct it more effectively. Our energy gets caught up in a narrow but deepening channel, so that even if we succeed in diverting it for a while, some small trigger in future may well re-open the dam and set the energy flowing again down that same narrow channel.

This understanding of proliferation can easily be made compatible with a basic understanding of brain function, which offers an external perspective that can complement (not supplant) the internal experience. Our brains have trillions of synaptic connections through which electrical impulses flow, and that are reinforced by usage. In the words of Donald Hebb, pioneer of neuroscience, 'what fires together, wires together'.[4] So, whenever we have one kind of response to one kind of represented object, the repetition of that response becomes slightly easier, as the associated synaptic routes are strengthened. At the same time, repeated usage of one set of routes makes it slightly harder to take alternative routes (to think differently).

4   Hebb (1949).

An obvious example of the above process that can be readily recognized both in experiential and neuroscientific terms is the loop of addiction. Here is how Marc Lewis, a former drug addict turned neuroscientist, describes it:

> *The way we experience things shapes our biological matter, and those biological changes shape the way we experience things subsequently. In other words, changes in brain structure make that way of experiencing things more available, more probable, on future occasions. This can take the form of a self-reinforcing perception, an expectancy, a budding interpretation, a recurring wish, a familiar emotional reaction, a consolidating belief, or a conscious memory.... There's an important addendum to this big picture, and it's fundamental for understanding addiction. When our experience of the world is fraught with strong feelings – whether of attraction, threat, pleasure, or relief – brain change takes on extra momentum. What drives this momentum? Emotions focus our attention and our thinking, and particular emotions (in response to something), call up particular thoughts and behaviours, thereby fuelling the same feedback cycle every time that something is encountered. When those emotions recur over and over, with each repetition of the feedback cycle, our overly focused brains inevitably change in a particular direction, entrenching a certain emotional experience a little more each time.*[5]

Lewis here particularly brings out the basis of the relationship between mental proliferation as an immediate experience, and the ways in which our experiences over the long term can create an increasing vulnerability to the re-igniting of the same obsessive desires or anxieties in response to a range of triggers. Clearly the two interact, with long-term development and immediate proliferation each making the other more likely.

The experience of mental proliferation is a good place to begin (though, of course, not the only possible one) in understanding absolutization, because it helps us to relate to what it feels like to be in its grip. However, it opens up a number of other features that are also discussed in early Buddhism. One of these is the way that the proliferating state unites aspects of desire and belief: we are neither aware of the possibility of looking beyond the hindrance while we are in it, nor are we motivated to do so. Desire and belief are what we may think of as emotional and cognitive states, or values and factual claims. One of the strengths of Buddhism is that it is not obsessed by the false distinction between cognition and emotion that has so much shaped the Western understanding of this whole

---

5   Lewis (2015) pp. 30–1.

area. It will be important to adopt a framework that is *not* dominated by this distinction to interpret the Western philosophical and psychological contributions to our understanding of absolutization helpfully. This area will be the focus of 1.b.

Mental proliferation as a compulsive flow of energy also requires a target to be assumed: the obstacle we are trying to shift, whether that is a thing or a person. As we summon up more and more energy to bombard this obstacle, our conceptions of it become more and more rigid, and it fills our awareness to the exclusion of everything else. However, if we are finally forced by circumstances to suspend this compulsive view of it and cease to attack it, the way in which we have been compulsively thinking about it may well then lead us to simply switch to a positive rather than negative view of it, without reconsidering the narrowness of the whole way we have conceived it. Thus religious or political conversions can involve a dramatic switch between one perspective and its opposite, because we are only framing our understanding in the terms of that opposite. This is the phenomenon of the *absoluteness of negations* that I will take up in 1.c, and where the Buddhist conception of the Middle Way can be extremely helpful.

If we focus so much on the contrast between our own view and its negation, we will also be excluding other possible views. The more we pour our energy into one channel, the more we prevent it from flowing down other channels, and the more likely these are to become less accessible through disuse. So a further feature of absolutization, the *excluding of options*, also follows from the Buddhist Middle Way, and will be developed in 1.d.

1.b. Craving, Hatred, and Delusion

> *Summary*
>
> Buddhism identifies the interdependence both between craving and hatred (which is frustrated craving), and between craving and delusion, in the extremes avoided by the Middle Way. This interdependence is confirmed by neuroscientific evidence, but defies the weight of assumption in Western thought.

The relationship between craving, hatred, and delusion is central to most Buddhist teachings, and is symbolically depicted in the centre of the Wheel of Samsara ('Wheel of Life'). There, a cock (for craving), a snake (for hatred), and a pig (for delusion) all chase each other round in a circle.

The relationship between craving and hatred is easy to explain, since hatred is simply frustrated craving: we try to remove something that blocks our way. However, the relationship between craving and delusion is more complex, and is indicative of the wider relationship between desire and belief, feeling and cognition, values and factual claims. The insight on absolutization that we can get from Buddhism requires us to trace its operation in *both* desire and belief.

The interdependence of desire and belief, both of which we find simultaneously constrained in our distracted states, is a central insight of the Buddha's teachings. For instance, in the Buddha's Noble Eightfold Path, right view (belief) and right aspiration (desire) are interdependent elements. These in turn interact with our states of mind in the three elements of the Eightfold Path concerned with meditation (right effort, concentration, and mindfulness) and the morality of our actions (right action, speech, and livelihood).[1]

However, it is the concept of the Middle Way that most crucially focuses the links between desire and belief, with the Path being understood as lying between two opposing extremes of belief that are also closely associated with states of desire. One extreme of belief in the context of the Buddha's life is known as 'eternalism' (*sassatavada*), and includes belief in a cosmic moral system that provides inevitable rewards for meritorious practice. This extreme is also associated with the ascetics that the Buddha joined for a while in

---

1   See Ellis (2019) section 5 for more detailed discussion.

his early life-history, trying out their extreme practices of self-denial and self-torture, which were believed to create merit according to the cosmic system of karmic reward. The other extreme of belief is known as 'nihilism' or 'annihilationism' (*ucchedavada*), which denies both the cosmic system of merit and the continuing existence over lives that would be required to benefit from it. This extreme is also associated with a state of desire – the conventional and self-indulgent world of the palace in which the Buddha was said to have been raised, prior to the dramatic 'going forth' from that context that followed his recognition of its limitations. Traditionally, the lack of control over our desires is associated by Buddhists with a lack of accountability for those desires when it is believed that we do not continue to exist over many lives.

It is important not to take the Buddhist version of these relationships between belief and desire at the extremes as universally prescriptive or necessary ones, but nevertheless they provide an important symbolic *indication* of the relationship. The beliefs on both extremes claim to be total ones, offering a complete and final view of the truth about the world. In the palace this is the view that a class-hierarchized society provides a complete explanation of the relative duties of each individual, and that we should not look beyond the constraints of that society. In the forest it is a 'religious' view claiming universality on the basis of beliefs that go beyond experience. The story also shows the patterns of motivation that accompany this assumed totality: exclusivity, complacency, and indulgence in the palace, but strenuous wilful effort accompanied by obsessive focus in the forest.[2] We cannot conclude from these patterns that these kinds of motives *always* accompany these kinds of beliefs (religious believers can be self-indulgent and secular conventionalists can be ascetic[3]), but nevertheless there is an insight about the ways that beliefs that claim totality are likely to be accompanied by narrowly-focused types of motive.

Exactly how we should understand that narrowly-focused motive – craving – is not always clear in Buddhism. There are two widely-employed interpretations of it, both of which have the disadvantages of being absolute and discontinuous in their implications. The Abhidhamma tradition of the Theravada interprets craving as

2   Ibid. 1.b–1.e.
3   Ibid. 4.d.

a particular sort of unhelpful desire, to be separated from ordinary desire,[4] but an alternative Buddhist tradition, based on the Buddhist cosmology of the *Agañña Sutta*,[5] treats all desire as craving and craving as the basis of human existence.[6]

The assumption that all desire is craving leads us rapidly into the belief that the whole of human life (which is, of course, motivated by desire at every point) is somehow ultimately bad because of this, and that our goal should be to move beyond that life entirely. This leads us into the body-denying dogmas of karma and rebirth, in which 'craving for existence' (*bhava-tanha*) is taken to be the cause of rebirth.[7] For 'craving' to mean all desire is also inconsistent with the basic practical recognition that our helpful development is motivated by desire.

On the other hand, for there to be 'good desire' and 'bad desire' (craving) also creates great difficulties in practice, because in many cases we have no way of differentiating good from bad desire based only on our experience of the desire.[8] Is my desire to buy another book, for instance, good or bad? Without a basis for experiential judgement, claiming that good desire 'leads to enlightenment' is not good enough, because enlightenment is a remote and absolute goal that we cannot even justifiably assume to exist, let alone use as a yardstick to judge our present desires.

Our experience of desire is much more ambiguous than that. Some desires feel very sticky and can be readily identified with 'craving' – for instance, an addict's desire for heroin. Other desires seem very obviously innocuous – a desire to drink water, a desire to urinate. In between such examples, though, it seems that the helpfulness of a desire can only be helpfully judged in relation to the beliefs that frame it. I might think that buying another book is good because it provides a new resource for study and personal development, or bad because it takes money away from other needs and creates another possession to be concerned about. The desire by itself is just energy directed towards a particular goal. Some Buddhist scholars have thus agreed that craving (*tanha*) cannot be understood in complete distinction from delusion (*avijja*).[9]

4   Bodhi (1999) II.3 (6), p. 82; Payutto (1994) ch. 2.
5   *Digha Nikaya* 27: Walshe (1995) pp. 407 ff.
6   Morrison (1997).
7   Ellis (2019) pp. 210-11.
8   Ibid. 6.c.
9   Morrison (1997) note 18.

Regardless of the degree of confusion within Buddhism on this point, however, a central insight remains. That insight is that craving and hatred cannot be distinguished from the delusion that frames and directs them. Similarly, delusion cannot be distinguished from the energy that actuates it and makes it relevant to a specific organism in a specific context. When we add in the oppositional structures between absolute desires and beliefs that I will discuss in 1.c and d, this leaves us with associated unhelpful desires and beliefs that are interdependent with each other on either side of the more helpful Middle Way. Although the relationship between craving and belief remains contingent in the ways that specific *objects* of craving do not necessarily imply specific beliefs (or vice-versa), the concept of absolutization helps us to identify the key respect in which *conflicting desires imply absolute beliefs* (and vice-versa) – the relationship between craving and absolute belief that we have already seen operating in the phenomenon of mental proliferation. The conceptual shift needed here is from desires that are good or bad according to their objects, to desires that either conflict with each other or do not, depending on whether alternative options are absolutized.

This involves a shift from a *repression model* to an *integration model*. Repression is an aspect of absolutization that I will discuss further in 5.a below, but it consists in internal conflict. When we employ a repression model, we assume that we can impose our will of this moment on our recalcitrant other desires. In the radically different integration model, though, we have to *make peace* between our desires, recognizing all their interests and persuading them to adopt compatible goals. The use of an integration model adds a very helpful new dimension to the interpretation of Buddhism.

Unfortunately, though, we have a long tradition of entrenched thinking in contradiction to that insight in much Western thought. Not only does Western tradition separate desire from belief in popular morality (by ignoring the beliefs that accompany transgressive desires, and the desires that accompany morally superior beliefs), but the same duality is imported into academic discussions that separate 'facts' from 'values' and 'rationality' from 'emotion'. One influential early argument for this is Hume's claim that facts do not imply values and vice-versa:[10] this is an argument made in logical

---

10 Hume (1978) pp. 457–8.

terms that are entirely abstracted from the context of facts and values in human brains and bodies (see 3.a and 4.b below).

As I go on to consider the contributions made by systems theory, embodied meaning, philosophy, and psychology in the next few sections, it should become gradually clearer that this pervasive Western tradition is not the only possible way of understanding the issues, that it is very unhelpful practically, and that it both results from and perpetuates absolutization. For the moment, though, let me just note that substantial psychological and neuroscientific evidence supports the Buddhist insight into the interdependence of desire and belief. For instance, Justin Storbeck and Gerald Clore write

> *The concepts of 'cognition' and 'emotion' are, after all, simply abstractions for two aspects of one brain in the service of action.... The study of emotion and cognition should be integrated, because the phenomena themselves are integrated.... Emotions emerge from a combination of affective and cognitive processes.... Emotion can be studied using cognitive paradigms. Both laboratory findings and everyday observation suggest a unity and interrelatedness of cognitive and affective processes, and that trying to dissect them into separate faculties would neglect the richness of mental life. We suggest, like others, that the interconnections found within the brain provide no obvious basis for divorcing emotion from cognition.*[11]

This point will need to be followed through consistently (not just paid lip-service to), as we consider the evidence on the *equally* 'rational' and 'emotional' nature of absolutization, and similarly the *equally* 'rational' and 'emotional' ways that we need to respond to it. It is better to purge from one's vocabulary at the outset such appeals to facts and rationality (habitual though they are to many commentators) and instead think anew about the models we should use for understanding absolutization.

---

11   Storbeck & Clore (2007).

1.c. The Absoluteness of Negations

> *Summary*
>
> The negation (in the sense of affirmation of the opposite) of an absolute belief is equally absolute, and this needs to be distinguished from a mere failure to affirm it. This point is the basis of the Middle Way in Buddhism, and can also be supported by neuroscientific and psychological evidence of the interdependence of craving with fear in representations that support both. This is also the basis of the link between dualism and absolutization.

In the story of the Buddha's early life, Gautama was said to have been a prince in a palace, a totally enclosed and rigidly conventional world. When he started to become aware of the world beyond the palace, this can be used as a symbol of our first questioning of absolutization. The story goes that he went on a chariot ride and encountered old age, sickness, death, and the religious life – all possibilities that had not previously impacted on him, and that forced him to think more broadly. So he then 'went forth', leaving the luxury of the palace (along with his family ties) and taking up the religious life of a homeless wanderer.

In the course of this new life he learnt from two different teachers, and also spent time with a group of ascetic practitioners, who believed that they could be karmically rewarded in future for inflicting pain and hardship on themselves. Both the teachers and the ascetics also lived in an absolutized world, but this time one shaped more directly by supernatural beliefs about processes beyond their current experience. In the case of the ascetics, this had the result of leading them into damaging practices based on self-conflict, whilst the teachers were subject to the delusion that they had reached a final state of knowledge. The Buddha's achievement in discovering the Middle Way was to 'go forth' a second time, recognizing that this second set of absolutizations, too, was inadequate.[1]

The importance of the insight thus symbolized can hardly be over-stated. It comes down to the recognition that a *two-stage* process is needed to avoid absolutization. We do not need to simply

---

1   Key early sources of this story are *Majjhima Nikaya* 4, 26, & 36 (Ñanamoli & Bodhi 1995), and *Digha Nikaya* 14 (Walshe 1995) (with Gautama's role transposed to Vipassi). Ashvaghosa's *Buddhacarita* (Johnston 1972) provides a later elaboration. See Ellis (2019) section 1 for fuller discussion.

identify undesirable beliefs, contrast them with desirable ones, switch, and assume that we have then got it right. Instead, we have to adjust our course down a strait, first to avoid one set of rocks and then the other. Traditional wisdom in many places contains this idea: for instance, in classical mythology, Odysseus had to steer his ship between the monster Scylla and the whirlpool of Charybdis, whilst Phaethon was tasked to drive the sun-chariot through the sky at a level that avoided either consuming 'the mansions of the sky' or scorching the land.[2] In these images, the two absolute alternatives have *equal status*. They are the symbolizations of beliefs that are equally absolute.

The 'Middle Way' in the context of Middle Way Philosophy refers to a practical path of judgement that avoids absolutization. However, the very idea of this path is rooted in a more basic recognition of a feature of absolutization: namely that the negation (affirmation of the opposite) of an absolute claim is just as absolute as the original claim.[3] At the same time, absolutization is not inevitable (see 4.e below), so the alternative to absolutization does not lie in any negation of absolute claims, but in the Middle Way between positive and negative absolutizations. Such a 'Middle Way' does not and cannot consist just in compromise (since compromises do not necessarily question the assumptions behind a conflict), but rather in a reframing of our understanding of the conditions with which the opposing absolute beliefs were concerned, in such a fashion as to remove the absolutization.

There are two importantly distinct ways of saying 'no'. 'Negation' here must be understood in terms that clearly distinguish assertion of the opposite from a mere failure to affirm a claim. A failure to affirm a particular claim may be motivated by agnosticism and by a rejection of the way in which the belief is framed, rather than any affirmation of the opposite. Negation in the sense of affirming the opposite, on the other hand, reinforces belief in the framing of both the rejected and accepted beliefs. For example, a rejection of materialism (in the sense of a belief that everything can be understood reductively in terms of the smallest possible particles), does not entail a belief in non-material entities such as supernatural gods or Platonic souls. Instead, one can fail to accept the framing of *both*

---

2   Ovid, *Metamorphoses* 2:137.
3   i.1.e & h; II.1. (See 'The Old and New Middle Way Philosophy Series' listed before the bibliography in this book.)

opposed sets of beliefs, which similarly assume the composition of the phenomenal world from determinate elements, independent of us, that could be identified by humans.

Dualism (in the sense of a general assumption that we can understand the world by accepting or rejecting opposed beliefs) is thus an implication of absolutization.[4] Any absolute belief will have an opposite that consists of its denial within the same framing. In some cases, dualists are so attached to their absolute framing that they will unite in unholy alliance with those who advocate the opposite view, to ensure that the much more dangerous long-term challenge posed by questioning of their framing gains no headway. Thus, for instance, once they have given up trying to appropriate or demonize agnosticism by defining it in the terms of their absolute view, theists and atheists can unite to misrepresent and ridicule it.[5]

In the early Buddhist context, this point is made through examples of opposing dualistic beliefs, rather than stated in a way that is neutral as to the content of those beliefs. However, the most wide-ranging example involves the opposition between 'existence' and 'non-existence', and the recommendation of a non-metaphysical approach that lets go of both.

> 'All exists': Kaccana, this is one extreme. 'All does not exist': this is the second extreme. Without veering towards either of these extremes, the Tathagata teaches the Dhamma by the middle....[6]

> This world, Kaccana, for the most part depends upon a duality – upon the notion of existence and the notion of non-existence. But for one who sees the origin of the world as it really is with correct wisdom, there is no notion of nonexistence in regard to the world. And for one who sees the cessation of the world as it really is with correct wisdom, there is no notion of existence in regard to the world.[7]

This approach is later developed in the Buddhist tradition by Nagarjuna. Almost any metaphysical belief can be interpreted as being about 'existence' as opposed to 'non-existence' in some way. Nevertheless, putting it like this tends to focus attention on the specific content of the opposing claims, rather than the psychological context of the beliefs and the role they play in practice. As I've

---

4   But see 6.b below for the precise sense of 'implication' here. See also iv.3.g; II.1.
5   iv.4.f; II.4, VI; Ellis (2020b) 1.i.
6   Nidanasamyutta, *Samyutta Nikaya* 12.15. Bodhi (2000) p. 544.
7   Ibid.

discussed elsewhere,[8] it would also be contradictory to take 'seeing the world as it really is with correct wisdom' in contrast at face value. Early Buddhism thus gives us powerful symbols, and a context of practice, in which some of these opposing absolutizations are recognized and avoided, but it lacks a clear or comprehensive account of what the opposed dualities consist in and what the alternative most generally looks like. A scholarly quagmire also opens up if one tries to argue for what a text like the one above 'really intends to say', of a kind that usually involves implicit appeals to the absolute authority of the texts and a narrow focus on one interpretation, rather than a more balanced policy of seeing the texts as only one source of information for a practical issue. To clarify it usefully, rather than arguing speculatively about texts and historical contexts, I think we need to supplement Buddhism with the other kinds of sources I will be using: systems theory, embodied meaning, psychology, and philosophy.

An understanding of absolutization as creating dualism is consistent with the Buddhist understanding of the interactions between craving, hatred, and delusion discussed in the previous chapter. We deludedly absolutize in negations as well as in our initial positive views because of the nature of craving (as absolutized desire) in relation to hatred (as absolutized anxiety). There is never an entirely *single* focus in absolutization, but rather a combination of desire and fear to various degrees. When we focus on one view that will help us fulfil our goals in the limited and short-term way that we can envisage, there is simultaneously some degree of fear that we will not fulfil those goals as conceived. If, on the other hand, we focus on avoiding the undesirable, there is always also some degree of wanting the desirable. Believing in one absolute positive view thus always to some extent implies belief in the avoidance of the opposite.

This relationship between the fear and craving that bind opposed absolute views together can also be supported in neuroscientific terms. Although fear and craving are associated with different emotional states in which different parts of the 'reptilian' brain are activated and release different chemical signals, those signals slightly overlap in function: we still fear to some extent because we crave, and crave because we fear, because both impulses are

---

8   Ellis (2019) p. 151.

bound together by similar representations of our environment.⁹ The delusion involved in absolutization is an over-dominance of fixed beliefs restricting the options because of the over-dominance of the representations of the left pre-frontal cortex (see next chapter), but this over-dominance can be maintained to varying degrees by a reinforcing feedback loop (see 2.a) incorporating the effects of two parts of the 'reptilian' brain: the striatum (associated with craving) or amygdala (associated with fear), resulting in either a positive or a negative emphasis.

Psychological phenomena also show the polarizing of our beliefs through association in a whole range of biases (see 5.c). For instance, our understanding of probabilities has been shown to be distorted by the magnetic pull of the extremes of absolute 'yes' or 'no'. We especially have great difficulty processing small probabilities, because we tend to treat them as nil, and large probabilities, because we tend to treat them as certainties.¹⁰ For instance, we may neglect even very slight precautions against very serious infection, because the chances are so small that we treat them as nil. When cognitive psychologists Daniel Kahneman and Amos Tversky did a study into how people actually weighted their decisions in response to probabilities, they found that 1% was in fact treated as 5.5%, and 99% probability was in fact treated as 91.2% (these are of course averaged out, so many people's responses to small probabilities may be much more extreme than that).¹¹ Polarized thinking, then, is a shortcut, or substitution, using more basic and economical parts of our brains than complex and gradualized thinking does (see 5.d). We are more likely to adopt such polarized thinking either when deeply conditioned into it or when under stress.

The potential absoluteness of negative claims as well as positive can also be reinforced by their equal capacity for infinite rationalization, a point I will discuss in more detail in 4.d. Negative claims are not more limited in their scope than positive ones because they involve denial. Any positive claim negated will in theory apply to just as many instances: for instance, a claim that 'there are an infinite number of stars' is neither easier nor harder to justify than 'there is not an infinite number of stars', because every time we might believe we have counted the final star, there is still the possibility

9   Panksepp (1998) ch. 3; Gilbert (2010) ch. 2; Nicol (2011) ch. 1.
10 iv.3.k; II.2.f.
11 Kahneman (2011) p. 315.

of more that we have not yet observed. Formally speaking, the falsification of an infinite proposition is just as difficult to support as its verification.

Nevertheless, we have a strong tendency to treat negations differently from positive claims, confusing merely *logical* negation with emotional negativity. Emotional negativity can justifiably be treated somewhat differently from emotional positivity, as it involves rejecting things we hate rather than accepting things we like, but this distinction has no necessary connection with the use of words like 'no' and 'not' to deny a claim that we might believe in. *Logical* negation is merely conventional and limited to a specific context: in a different context, or even a different way of talking about the same context, the positive and negative poles can easily be switched around. For instance, the conventional negation of 'I approve of feeding chocolate to dogs' is 'I don't approve of feeding chocolate to dogs' (or more precisely 'I disapprove of feeding chocolate to dogs'): however, one could just as easily express this in the reversed form, where the 'positive' is 'I think we should avoid feeding chocolate to dogs' and the 'negative' is 'I don't think we should avoid feeding chocolate to dogs'. In a similar way, any 'negative' can be re-phrased in 'positive' terms, and vice-versa, indicating how much the use of these terms is completely contingent and contextual. By treating the denial of something we previously believed as substantially different from the affirmation, we inflate a merely contingent negation into an absolute one.

Given the equal absoluteness of negations to absolute positive claims, the Middle Way demands *even-handedness*. We should not at any point treat negative absolutization differently from positive absolutization. The implications of such even-handedness are profound, for instance in forestalling appropriation of the Middle Way by ideologies that regularly appeal to negative absolutizations, such as those of atheism and determinism. This is an aspect of the principle of *agnosticism*, which I will be exploring more fully along with the other principles in the next book in this series.

1.d. Excluding the Options

> *Summary*
>
> Dualism excludes third options from consideration by restricting the framing of our judgement. The Buddhist Middle Way helps to avoid exclusion of options, but its traditional framing of the extremes to be avoided also continues to exclude options further. Greater optionality can resolve conflicts and enable adaptation, and can be applied spatially as well as conceptually. 'Excluding the options' is an established fallacy in critical thinking, but it involves taking dualistic framing for granted rather than a logical error.

The Buddhist account of the Middle Way simultaneously helps us understand two different aspects of absolutization that directly imply each other: the absoluteness of negations and the exclusion of options. If one sets up a dualistic pair of an absolutely asserted claim and an absolutely rejected opposite, at the same time one will necessarily exclude alternative options from consideration. When we restrict our available evidence to that which confirms our view, negation also has to remain possible as a threat to that view in order to help maintain the restriction. The fear is then that if the favoured view is not maintained, the unthinkable opposite will take over. In order to maintain this view we must simply not consider any third options, because that would interfere with the belief that the unthinkable opposite threatens the favoured absolute view.

'The Middle Way' is a term for those alternative options that were previously excluded by a dualism – not for the necessary rightness of any one particular option, but simply the need to move beyond the dualism and consider those other options. 'Considering' options does not usually consist in a calm decision to put some options from some wider list on our agenda rather than ruling them out, because such a scenario already involves 'considering' everything on the list, even if we don't go into everything in detail. Rather, 'considering' an option involves allowing ourselves to think about it at all by bringing it into our field of attention. The raising of such further options by others when we are not prepared to consider them is likely to lead to instant dismissal on grounds of impossibility, absurdity, unthinkability, or similar characterizations, without further discussion. This is, of course, what usually happens to the Middle Way as a serious option in many discussions.

The Buddha's response to Malunkyaputta, discussed in 1.a above, suggests that the options we need to consider lie beyond the dualisms that Malunkyaputta was insisting on in relation to metaphysical questions such as whether the universe is infinite. The Buddha refused to answer such a question within the framework in which it was set, and the reasons he gives are practical:

> *Why have I left that undeclared? Because it is unbeneficial, it does not belong to the fundamentals of the holy life, it does not lead to disenchantment, to dispassion, to cessation, to peace, to direct knowledge, to enlightenment, to Nibbana. That is why I have left it undeclared.*[1]

The Buddha's aims (as he also spells out subsequently), are the exact reverse of this list: he declares what is beneficial, what belongs to the fundamentals of the holy life, and so on. It's also worth noting the elements of this list that are particularly focused on limiting the motivators of mental proliferation: disenchantment (*nibbida*), dispassion (*viraga*), cessation (*nirodha*), and peace (*upasama*). All of these qualities are concerned with calming craving, hatred, and delusion as the sources of absolutization. The 'beneficial' effects of not being locked into questions that are framed in terms of dualistic opposition are not just those of meeting our immediate goals, but the longer-term ones of being calm and open enough to perceive possible alternatives.

It is crucial that we interpret the Buddha's responses psychologically rather than only philosophically here. The questions that he refuses to answer are all *examples* of ones that are framed in absolute terms. Either the universe is infinite or it is not, either the universe is eternal or it is not, and so on (we cannot have partial infinity, as any subdivision of infinity is still infinity). His objections to answering these questions are practical and psychological, because they are concerned with the *effects* of offering answers to them for an embodied, situated person. Unfortunately, however, the Buddhist tradition has often interpreted these questions philosophically, assuming that their precise content is what is relevant about them rather than the absolute form that they illustrate. However, these questions just happened to be the examples of absolute metaphysical questions that people were most inclined to pose in the Buddha's time. Today, they might be far more inclined to pose other sorts of questions: 'Does God exist or not?', 'Do we have freewill or are

1   *Majjhima Nikaya* 63.8: Ñanamoli & Bodhi (1995) p. 536.

we determined?', 'Is morality universal or relative to our circumstances?', 'Is justice more or less important than freedom?', 'Is science true or false?'. The point of refusing to answer such questions is not about the specific metaphysical issues raised by those questions, but about the restrictive effects of attempting to answer questions that are framed in a way that restricts the options.

The Buddhist philosophical treatment of such questions traditionally involves identifying specific types of metaphysical dualism that are judged to be deluded: the clusters of metaphysical belief identified with 'eternalism' (*sassatavada*) and 'nihilism' (*ucchedavada*). 'Eternalism' associates the belief in an eternal self with absolutist ethics, cosmic justice, and reincarnation of a soul, and these metaphysical beliefs are associated with asceticism. 'Nihilism' on the other hand, is taken to deny all these beliefs and thus to be practically expressed by self-indulgence. As I have argued elsewhere, however, it is not the case that all beliefs that share some of the key features of 'eternalism' and 'nihilism' can be readily categorized into one of those two camps.[2] There is also no necessary association between 'eternalist' views and self-denial, or between 'nihilist' views and self-indulgence: one could be a jolly bibulous Catholic or an austere materialist scientist. Instead, I would argue that the wider perspective on absolutization that I'm offering in this book justifies us in interpreting the Buddhist formulation of the Middle Way as identifying *only some examples of the absolute beliefs that were particularly relevant in the Buddha's context*. We need to strip back and simplify the Buddhist account of the extremes in order to find a more universal account of them. I suggest, instead, that we only talk about *positive absolutes* and *negative absolutes* in any given context of judgement: a much more flexible account of what each dualism looks like, that is specific to each situation but also identifies general features of absolutization.

The rigidities in the traditional Buddhist interpretation of the Buddha's avoidance of metaphysics are, indeed, themselves an exercise in restricting the options. If we feel obliged by traditional loyalty to categorize all absolute beliefs as 'eternalist' or 'nihilist', then we must find ways of avoiding questions that take us outside that set of categories. In my experience of investigating the matter, there is no answer to questions like 'Is Marxism eternalist or nihilist?' or

---

2   Ellis (2019) 4.d.

'Is utilitarianism eternalist or nihilist?' that does not involve some degree of *ad hoc* reasoning, moving the goalposts of the theory to fit the evidence.[3]

The restriction of options involves defensive mechanisms that prevent alternative possibilities from becoming available for consideration. These can be well supported by psychology, neuroscience, and systems theory. Such mechanisms can be generally described as 'bias', and include selective interpretation, the substitution of easier processes for harder ones, the limitation of assumptions when reasoning, and the repression of any dissonant possibilities that may arise.[4] Kahneman and Tversky have especially documented the substitution process by which neural pathways that require the use of less glucose are liable to be selected over those that require more ('fast thinking' over 'slow thinking'):[5] this is discussed in more detail below in 5.d. Neuroscientific evidence also underlines the general tendency of the left pre-frontal cortex to maintain dominant representations to the exclusion of other forms of awareness.[6] In the most basic terms of systems theory, this involves the maintenance of reinforcing feedback loops of the kind that generally maintain the existing habits of organisms. Unless there is a reason to change, our organic setting is to carry on repeating the same apparently successful judgements over and over again, rather than consider alternatives.[7] This is discussed in more detail in 2.a below.

The effects of such restriction can be readily seen in virtually every practical situation, but particularly we could mention two types of situation as examples: conflict resolution and evolution. Conflict occurs because the conflicting parties constantly restrict the options to two possibilities, each involving one of them winning and the other losing. As long as either compromise or any other kind of solution is regarded as a variety of 'losing', no agreement can be reached. Mediation techniques have to offer some means of gradually introducing third possibilities into the discussion: Marshal Rosenberg's Non-violent Communication, for instance, does this by getting the participants to talk in terms of their needs rather than in

---

3   In Ellis (2001) I did offer answers to these questions, but these are ones that I am no longer convinced by.
4   iv.3.d; V.2.
5   Kahneman (2011).
6   McGilchrist (2009).
7   A process known as autopoiesis: Maturana & Varela (1980, 1987).

absolutizing terms, and then getting both sides to start to acknowledge each others' needs.⁸

A further relevant example is that of evolutionary development. If an organism is to thrive in a new environment, it must have *options* that enable it to do so, either in the form of genetic variation (enabling bacteria to become antibiotic-resistant, for instance), or in the form of a repertoire of forms of behaviour that it is equipped with to engage it. Highly adaptable animals, such as humans or rats, have many options when the conditions change, because they can adopt new strategies to find food and avoid danger. An animal that is highly dependent on only one food source, however, like a giant panda, is much more vulnerable if that food source disappears. The issue will be whether or not it *occurs* to the panda to eat something else when its bamboo dies, as well as whether it is physically able to act on an alternative option. Restricting our options, then, can make us less adaptive to new circumstances: a point that will be developed further in 2.c below.

Optionality (the state of having available options) in an organism also relates to how it understands and moves through space. In experience there is an apparently infinite number of ways of moving through space, with every possible interval or direction of space being apparently divisible an infinite number of times. At least, that's how it looks to us when we view it from a goal-driven, representational standpoint. We are used to thinking in terms of things in space that have measurable and finite dimensions and distances from each other. However, measurement is undertaken in pursuit of a represented goal: we divide up the world in order to manipulate it in some way. Without that grid of organization imposed on the world around us, it seems 'infinite' because it is immeasurable. I will return in 3.c below to the implications of this for the embodied perspective, in which we view things in a *gestalt*, whole, open, and unmeasured way in which there seem to be an *infinite* number of options for moving through space, as far as we can tell.

Restricting the options, however, also has a geometrical implication for the way in which we view space. If there are only two options and those options relate in any way to space, then there will only be two options for moving through that space. For example, the two options might be 'either you cross the Rubicon or you

---

8   Rosenberg (2002).

don't', the Rubicon here being treated as a line rather than a river. Crossing the Rubicon is taboo, the breaking of a rule; and any other action than staying on this side of the Rubicon is assumed to be 'crossing the Rubicon'. In this way of thinking, then, the space we conceptualize is not infinite and full of apparent options: instead it is *discontinuous*. The restriction of options is thus often realized in space (and also in time, which is modelled on spatial metaphors) as *discontinuity*. Once the framework of that discontinuity is refused, it is difficult to say how many possible options open up, because we could potentially move in all sorts of ways and also describe what we are doing in all sorts of ways. We do not have to think in terms of the Rubicon, or give it this loaded discontinuous significance, at all. Not only could we conceivably go over, under, or round the Rubicon, but we could go across it and find that, contrary to the conceptual loading of our expectations, nothing much has changed.

The insight behind the Buddhist teaching of *anicca* (impermanence) appears to implicitly recognize discontinuity in time as a problem, with *anatta* (non-substantiality) making a similar point about objects (including people) in space. Our attachment fuelled by craving and/or hatred is said to create the delusion of fixity and substantiality in the world around us, to which the best response is to cultivate awareness of impermanence and insubstantiality. Unfortunately, though, these points are often interpreted metaphysically – that is, that the world 'really is' impermanent and insubstantial, rather than just that we need to overcome an unfortunate and unhelpful tendency to absolutize substance and fix time.[9] The problem is not one of having the wrong metaphysics (see 4.a), but of having a metaphysics at all, because the process of thinking metaphysically leads us to restrict the options. We restrict the options in space and time by thinking in discontinuous and essentialist terms: either there's an x (a train, a Christian, a work of art) here or there isn't, and it continues to be so in the same state (or perhaps stops instantaneously) rather than continually changing.

The Buddha's teachings in the Pali Canon do occasionally suggest a better alternative strategy to this than merely training oneself to believe that the universe is 'really' impermanent and insubstantial: that is, the use of a principle of continuity or incrementality.[10]

---

9   E.g. see Piyadassi Thera (2006) for a typical traditional Theravadin account.
10 i.1.d; II.3.

This means thinking of objects in terms of degrees of a given quality rather than in terms of discontinuous absolutes. Perhaps the best known application of this in the Pali Canon is the beach analogy:

> *Just as the ocean, bhikkhus, gradually shelves, slopes and inclines, and there is no sudden precipice, so also in this Dhamma and discipline there is a gradual training, a gradual course, a gradual progression, and there is no sudden penetration to final knowledge.*[11]

In this respect our practice needs to follow the capacities of our movement and our apparently open options as organic beings moving through space. Discontinuity (the 'sudden precipice' or 'sudden penetration to final knowledge') is the result of absolutization through the restricting of our options in time and space.[12]

'Restricting the options' is also the term used for a fallacy, alternatively known as 'false dichotomy' or 'false dilemma', in the overwhelmingly most common instance of restriction to two options. A famous instance of this is President George W. Bush's pronouncement in a speech that 'Either you are with us, or you are with the terrorists.'[13] When the options are restricted in argument, an attempt is made to claim the truth of a conclusion based on a justification that only includes two possibilities, when more are possible. This has long been recognized as an illegitimate move of argument, though not for reasons of logic (see 4.b) but (as in other 'informal fallacies') for reasons that are ultimately social.[14] Restricting the options prevents any resolution by questioning the framing of mutual opposition, and thus makes our arguments interminable and irresolvable.

The reason that people often get away unchallenged with restricting the options is partly due to general lack of training in critical thinking in the population, but also because of the belief that there are instances of 'true dichotomies', in which other options are assumed to be impossible. There are practical examples of these in the world of everyday action: for instance, either you catch a bus or you don't. Because of the kind of indivisible system that comprises a living and uninjured human body, it is not possible to have part of it on the bus and part left behind. There are other instances

---

11 *Udana* 5.5: Ireland (1990) p. 76.
12 For a more detailed discussion of incrementality in the Buddha's teachings see Ellis (2019) 3.e.
13 See http://www.fallacyfiles.org/eitheror.html (accessed 2021) for more context in critical thinking.
14 Walton (1987).

where dichotomies are socially imposed. For instance, the boundary between life and death is a vague and gradual one, but for social reasons a doctor must be able to certify someone 'dead' by applying particular criteria and making a judgement. So, in the terms of these conventions, either you are alive or you're not. However, when we look more closely we find that reframing this dichotomy *incrementally* (as a matter of degree) is more adequate, enabling us to understand the complexity of what is occurring better. So what we take to be 'true dichotomies' are not necessarily 'true' at all, but merely the result of the conventions we choose to apply. If we choose to apply different conventions, we can indeed be half-dead, or even half catch a bus (e.g. you hang onto the back). Absolutization, however, involves forgetting this point and assuming that these conventions are necessary and eternal.[15]

An ideology that adopts restriction of the options as the unavoidable norm, or perhaps even regards it as desirable, can be described as 'dualism' in one sense. Unfortunately the term 'dualism' has many different uses in different contexts, but very often the practical reason why it turns out to be problematic is the acceptance of false dichotomy or option restriction, either in one particular respect (as in mind-body dualism) or in many respects. Dualism is at work whenever, in a specific judgement, people take a binary restriction of options for granted. The overwhelming majority of philosophical and theological discussion is thus in this sense dualistic, with even metaphysical or mind-body monists in fact being dualists in this wider sense, because of their failure to question this restriction of options (rather than just plumping for one of the options as 'true') or to actively consider alternatives to it.[16] The insistence that the mind is really or ultimately material, for instance, still involves an absolute assertion based on the false dichotomy in the *meaning* of what is taken to be 'mind' versus 'body'.

The claim of a true dichotomy may also involve the intervention of logic, but is not a function of logic itself, only of its application in a given case. The basic Aristotelian 'law of logic', the excluded middle, makes it a logical requirement that *a* must either be *b* or *not b*. This simply involves the application of a set of conventions that *apply* the Aristotelian excluded middle in a particular context: for

15   II.3.c.
16   iv.4.e; VI.5.

example, we consider either that the dog (this dog, in front of us) is black or it is not. Shades of grey, within these framing assumptions, will be automatically categorized as 'black' or 'not'. It is only if alternative framing assumptions are *available* to us that we can categorize our experience of the dog's coat at a particular point on a scale of grey. It is not the 'truth' or the logic of the excluded middle that is at stake here, but how we apply it. If we absolutize, shades of grey are simply not open to consideration, but if we widen our awareness to consider different framing assumptions, they can be.

For this reason, the pursuit of alternative logics is a major red herring in the interpretation of the Buddhist case against absolutization. It doesn't matter what system of logic you use (the Aristotelian system is well established, and fine for our purposes), but whether or not you recognize that system to be conventional, and thus that any particular application of it is not *necessary*, but can be reframed. In fact, the system of logic referred to in the early Buddhist texts of the Pali Canon is the Indian fourfold logic (*catuskoti*), where in addition to the possibility of a claim or its denial being true, we also consider two other options: both or neither. Considering those further options may help us re-frame from a twofold logic that has restricted the options for us, but this is not necessarily enough. For this reason the Buddha refuses to say, for instance, not just whether the Tathagata (enlightened person) exists after death or not, but also whether he both exists and does not exist, or neither exists nor does not exist.[17] The Buddhist use of the fourfold logic just serves to remind us that fancy logics are irrelevant to the practical issue of absolutization. It is *how we use* logic and how we think about its status that is important (see 4.b).

Overall, then, the Buddha's teachings thus leave us with some key insights about absolutization and its nature, but not with a complete account. We can see it as 'mental proliferation'. We can see it in terms of particularly 'sticky' desires, but these cannot be adequately distinguished without reference to the beliefs they are associated with. We can also see the beliefs of absolutization as ones that involve the assumption of a total view, that are opposed to their opposites, and that exclude the Middle Way standing for third options. To interpret these Buddhist accounts satisfactorily, however, I have already had to bring in alternative perspectives at every

17 *Majjhima Nikaya* 63.2: Ñanamoli & Bodhi (1995) p. 533.

stage. The Buddha provides a very important, perhaps inspiring, start for understanding absolutization, but more perspectives are needed to more fully illuminate it.

2. Systems Theory

2.a. Reinforcing Feedback Loops

> *Summary*
>
> Reinforcing feedback loops, whereby organisms maintain and reproduce themselves in a self-replicating process, are a background feature of all systems. However, in the human case, the capacity for imagination adds a further capacity for balancing adaptability, that can then in turn be hijacked by more specific reinforcing feedback loops of *belief*. These reinforcing feedback loops appear as mental proliferation, and are prone to dangerous competitive escalation. This provides a crucial standpoint for understanding absolutization.

Systems theory is an increasingly adequate approach to a whole range of natural and social sciences that have developed in recent decades. It focuses on complex and dynamic systems as a re-conception of what are more usually called objects, and on interdependent conditional relationships rather than beliefs about linear causality. This in turn helps us to avoid over-simplifying our interpretation of what we experience, taking our uncertainty about it into account. Absolutization being a failure to take uncertainty into account, systems theory provides a crucial standpoint from which we can cast light on it. There are various crucial ways that systems theory can contribute to our understanding of absolutization: it shows absolutization as reinforcing feedback loops, as deluded belief in an independent system, and as fragility.

The pioneers of systems theory in biology, Humberto Maturana and Francisco Varela, developed an account of living systems that can offer an important scientific starting point for our understanding of absolutization. In systems terms, a living being is distinguished from its environment and from other living beings, not by its mere designation as an object (there are many different, often arbitrary, ways we can divide the world up into 'objects'), but by its structure or organization. This organization has the capacity to maintain and regulate itself that is particular to living beings – what Maturana and Varela call *autopoiesis*,[1] and it is the regulation of this structure that defines a living being rather than any other criterion. A living being maintains itself, for instance, by seeking food, evading danger, and repairing and reproducing itself. It does these things by various interactions with its environment that Maturana and Varela call *structural couplings* – the structure of the organism interacts with other systems beyond it in various *domains*, and both are altered by that interaction.[2] For instance, a fox eats a beetle, with the effect that the individual fox-system is nourished for a bit longer, the individual beetle-system is incorporated into the fox-system, and the surrounding eco-system moves a further way round a cycle in which activities of both foxes and beetles have a stable relationship.

Autopoiesis is in turn an example of a wider phenomenon that is also found in non-organic systems – that of closed or reinforcing feedback loops. A reinforcing feedback loop in a system maintains itself and its structure by repeating the same kinds of structural coupling over and over again: the fox maintains itself by eating more beetles (as well as rabbits and leftover pizza), and by having cubs that grow up and do the same. The individual organism is maintained at one level by reinforcing feedback loops, but is also nested within further systems, such as those of the species, the group, and the immediate environment, and these further systems can be increasingly disrupted by unchecked reinforcing feedback loops in a system within them. Disruptive non-organic reinforcing feedback loops are found, for instance, in the snowball effects of global warming, such as the loss of albedo: melting ice increases the warmth from the sun absorbed by the earth due to loss of reflectivity, leading to further warming and further ice melting. A disruptive organic reinforcing feedback loop could be an overpopulation of one species, such as too many deer in the Scottish Highlands, unchecked in the absence of predators and preventing trees from developing.

Reinforcing feedback loops of this kind can be contrasted with open or balancing ones, which *modify* the system in some way, in response to new information, to adapt to the environment (or adapt the environment to themselves): a thermostat, a driver steering along a twisty road, or a rat exploring a new food source are all doing this.[3] Balancing feedback loops reveal different systems

1   Varela, Maturana, & Uribe (1974); Maturana & Varela (1987) pp. 43 ff.
2   Ibid. pp. 95 ff.
3   Meadows (2008) pp. 27–34.

adjusting to one another so as to create a mutually more sustainable relationship – a 'balance' of a kind. For example, a thermostat is a system that responds to the temperature conditions in a house by adjusting itself, so as to maintain optimal conditions for the people in the house. The house-and-people-system maintains 'balance' with the thermostat system as long as the thermostat keeps operating and adjusting, and does not malfunction.

A further crucial contribution of systems theory to our understanding of absolutization, which will interact with these feedback loops, is its biological account of what the state of belief is like. Maturana and Varela give us a basis for understanding belief as a type of structural coupling for an organism with a nervous system:

> *The nervous system participates in cognitive phenomena in two complementary ways. These have to do with its particular mode of operation as a neuronal network with operational closing as part of a metacellular system.*
>
> *The first, and most obvious, is through expanding the realm of possible states of the organism that arises from the great diversity of sensori-motor patterns which the nervous system allows for and which is the key to its participation in the operation of the organism.*
>
> *The second is through opening new dimensions of structural coupling for the organism, by making possible in the organism the association of many different internal states with the different interactions in which the organism is involved.*[4]

The first of these modes is *meaning* (see 3.a below), whilst the second, built on the first, is what I call *belief* – although Maturana and Varela, in defiance of the recognition of uncertainty that they implicitly rely upon, insist on calling this 'knowledge'.[5] In belief, the organism makes its internal states the basis of a particular interaction with an external system. In human beings, where greater complexity allows a process of imaginative construction of events prior to action, we also need to include (in the category of internal states) represented *potential* structural couplings that only affect other internal states, along with actual structural couplings (behaviour). The former we might call *hypothetical* beliefs, and the latter *applied* beliefs. For instance, I may believe that a friend has lied to me, but never reveal it. Nevertheless, this belief continues to play its part in the internal system of my beliefs, and may influence the things I do say to, or about, that friend.

4   Maturana & Varela (1987) p. 175.
5   On the issue of 'knowledge' and its definition, see i.1.a & b; II.1.

So we do not have to reduce beliefs to behaviour as long as we recognize that it is practical change (internal or external, implicit or external) that makes a belief. In our experience, a belief is an actual or potential basis for interaction with our environment or ourselves, which could potentially be expressed as a proposition about that environment or ourselves. That may be as simple as the fox's belief that he may find food inside a dustbin, or as complex as a hypothetical belief about the effects of a different voting system on a country's politics.[6]

In Maturana and Varela's approach, beliefs stay rooted in an organism, and are subsystems within that organism. They do *not* consist in their symbolic or linguistic communications, and are *not* equivalent to what may linguistically be the 'same' beliefs in different organisms. The related idea of Richard Dawkins, then, of a symbolically-defined belief having independence as a system and replicating itself as a 'meme',[7] is a misleading alternative interpretation of the same phenomena. What we take to be 'the same' beliefs based on the same meanings in different organisms (e.g. you and I both believe that cats are carnivores) may well bear similarities, and also have shared social roles within wider cultural systems. However, to abstract these symbolic forms from the experiences of those who find them meaningful detracts from the adequacy of our understanding of them as systems, by removing the crucially particular role of the belief in the context of each individual organism. In effect, it denies the embodiment of belief. There will be more about this in the next section.

When we apply the account of reinforcing feedback loops in organisms in Maturana and Varela's work to that of belief, we get an understanding of absolutization. Absolutization in these terms is a judgement that reinforces *a belief which interacts with its environment so as to perpetuate itself,* maintaining its own structure. No modification is possible in an absolutized belief. It allows no concessions that will modify the current structure of the organism to *fit* the environment, but rather requires the use of all available resources to maintain the belief in its current form. This means that when absolutization is occurring, the direction of attention in relation to the environment will be selectively focused in ways that help to maintain the belief, as will the interpretation of what we experience

---

6   iv.1; VI.1.
7   Dawkins (1989) p. 192.

through the senses. This is what is also referred to as confirmation bias (see 5.c): we edit our experience to fit our preconceptions. For instance, my obsessive belief that my friend has lied to me may influence me to keep identifying his ambiguous gestures as signs of further deception.

The pattern of reinforcing feedback loops as absolutization in human experience, compared to balancing feedback loops, is thus illustrated in the diagram below (**figure 2**). In reinforcing feedback loops we hold beliefs (explicitly or implicitly) that form the basis of our action, and thus continue to shape the world in their terms. As we view the world in accordance with our beliefs, we select only the information that confirms it, thus constantly reinforcing the belief. A balancing feedback loop of belief differs from this only in the admittance of new information to modify our beliefs, and thus not restrict ourselves only to selecting confirmatory information.

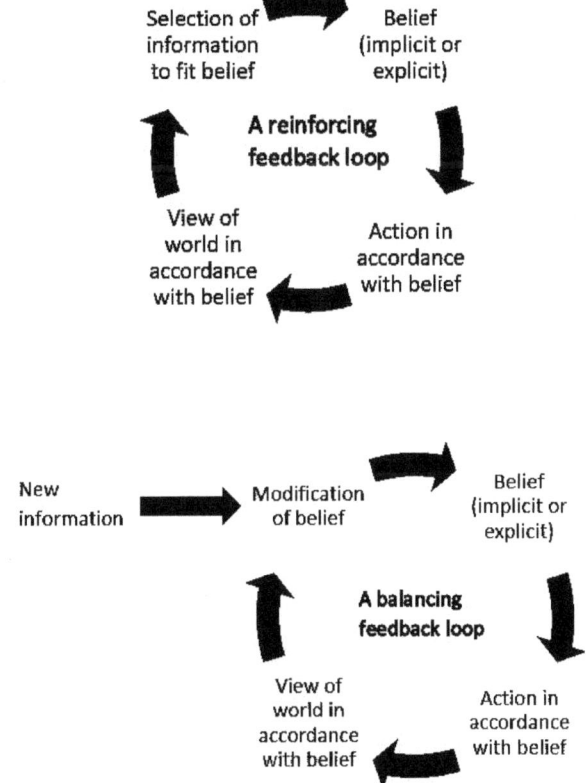

Figure 2. Reinforcing and balancing feedback loops.

Given that, on Maturana and Varela's account, reinforcing feedback is autopoiesis, you may conclude from this that absolutization is a normal and 'natural' feature of what organisms do – namely maintaining their structure through interactions with their environment. However, we need to take into account here the differences between reinforcing feedback loops of belief for more complex organisms such as human beings, whose internal states include imagination, and for those organisms that lack this capacity for rehearsal of their beliefs before they interact with the wider environment. Imagination introduces a new subsystem, or organizational domain, using *meaning* (awareness of possible states of the organism mentioned by Maturana and Varela above). This adds a further level of complexity to the organic one that produces reinforcing feedback loops at the basic level, but one that also enables absolutization and makes it uniquely damaging. Without imagination, we cannot conceptualize or represent, and those representations can neither be alterable, nor attempt to reproduce themselves unchanged.

The boundaries of the imagination are vague, but organisms that lack it entirely clearly cannot absolutize – not because they can't get stuck in maladaptive patterns, but because they lack a capacity that could potentially make them much more flexible, and that could then also be recruited to support more rigidity in the context of that flexibility. The same point applies to some of our own unconscious bodily operations, despite the vagueness of the boundaries. There are some ways that I cannot influence my digestion, or the genetic imprint in my reproductive processes, for instance, despite the capacity for imagination. We can argue about exactly where those boundaries lie (for instance, about placebo effects, where imagination seems to affect things we would normally say lie beyond its power), but there will still be some respects in which my body will carry on in its own reinforcing feedback loops regardless of either implicit or explicit beliefs.

We do not need to make any specific claims about the boundaries between imagination's presence and its absence in order to recognize that in some circumstances it can operate in some organisms, and in others it cannot. We do not have to claim, for instance, that only humans have it and that other animals do not. The boundaries are a matter for empirical investigation. Rather, we just need to recognize in systemic terms that imagination adds a new level of emergent complexity to the process of systemic coupling. This new complexity enables much energy to be saved by an organism by creating images or concepts that allow different experiences to be compared, and creating implicit or explicit generalizations to apply to a new situation. It then behaves in accordance with beliefs that have been in some way internally compared with possible alternatives, rather than simply by comparing its internal states with external ones.

This new level of complexity, by itself, offers a balancing feedback loop rather than a reinforcing one. It allows us to respond *more* effectively to new information rather than less, and thus to adapt. However, this new kind of adaptivity can also be taken over by a reinforcing feedback loop. The very conceptualizing faculty that enabled us to form new beliefs out of our imaginative processing of different experiences, can also start to give priority to perpetuating itself rather than adapting. This occurs through the processes discussed in 1.a as mental proliferation. In immediate experience, the more we dwell on particular hypothetical beliefs, the more we reinforce them, and in the longer term, a pattern of dwelling on particular hypothetical beliefs becomes associated with triggers in our experience that re-create those patterns.

Mental proliferation is also an instance of the phenomenon of *escalation* that is noted in systems theory when reinforcing feedback loops come into contact with each other. Our capacity both to adapt and to absolutize our beliefs developed in a paleolithic environment little changed by us, but the more we have persisted in our close-looped beliefs unchanged, the more we have changed our environment instead of ourselves. In this new environment, our absolutized ways of operating in previous ones are no longer adaptive, but nevertheless we persist with their escalation, in increasing competition both with the non-human environment and with each other. The effects of reinforcing feedback loops multiply exponentially, so that the more we persist with them, the greater the pressure to continue doing so, and the bigger the negative effects on our environment (including on ourselves and others). Donella Meadows gives some simple examples of this from everyday experience:

> *The escalation system… produces the increasing loudness of conversation at cocktail parties, the increasing length of limousines, and the increasing raunchiness of rock bands. Escalation could also be about peacefulness, civility, efficiency, subtlety, quality. But even escalating in a good direction can be a*

problem, because it isn't easy to stop. Each hospital trying to out-do the others in up-to-date, powerful, expensive diagnostic machines can lead to out-of-sight healthcare costs. Escalation in morality can lead to holier-than-thou sanctimoniousness. Escalation in art can lead from baroque to rococo to kitsch. Escalation in environmentally responsible lifestyles can lead to rigid and unnecessary puritanism.[8]

In any of these examples, it is the human persistence with beliefs that they think tell the whole story, neglecting any wider context, that creates the escalation. We assume as we get louder at a party that it is more important to be heard than to keep the surrounding environment quiet. We assume as we become more environmentally puritanical that the consequential value of our environmentally responsible behaviour is necessarily more important than its impact on our mental states or social relationships. If this happens even in contexts where we are sincerely trying to be reflective and responsible, it is hardly surprising if it happens in war zones.

The efficiency that we gained as imaginative organisms has thus taken a reinforcing process that previously merely maintained our identity as organisms, and made it into one that can potentially destroy ourselves and our planet. Systems theory does not merely show us a 'natural balance' between reinforcing and balancing feedback processes, but, in our specific context as humans, a dangerous runaway process that is a maladaptation of an initially helpful one.

As with more basic pre-imaginative reinforcing feedback loops in organisms, a case can be made that our more complex reinforcing feedback loops, too, have an adaptive or 'natural' function in the circumstances in which they first commonly arose: that takes us into the realm of bias, which I will return to in section 5. Clearly, absolutization can only have developed as a response to a particular set of conditions where it was in some ways favourable to us as organisms, but it is crucial to recognize how much those conditions have changed in the modern context of human life. In the modern context, we are caught up in a complex proliferation of interacting reinforcing feedback loops, all of which threaten to spiral out of control as they multiply themselves at the expense of the wider system. Climate change is only the most obvious and best known of these, but one can also mention mass extinction of other species; a cycle of increasing inequality in human societies; a co-dependent cycle

---

8   Meadows (2008) p. 125.

between economic exploitation, stress, and political extremism; and a cycle of polarization, alienation, and distrust amongst communities using disconnected sources of online information. This is not the place to discuss these cycles in detail, but they need to be constantly borne in mind in the background as the ways absolutization is shaping our world.

2.b. Assumed System Independence

> *Summary*
>
> Absolutization involves the assumption of the independence of an isolated cognitive system, whose representations can be considered apart from awareness of the psychological and neural process of their development. Systems theory offers no evidence of any such independent system being possible, and neuroscience gives evidence of how this assumed isolation operates so as to continually delude us.

The idea that absolutization consists in *the assumption that we have the whole story* also carries within it a substantial conflict between the perspective of absolutized beliefs and that of systems theory. When we examine anything as a set of relationships in a system rather than as a fixed object, those relationships are always found both within the system and beyond it. In other words, we never find independent systems, only ever interdependent systems. Yet the perspective of absolutization is one that assumes an independent system. Such an independent system can be *hypothesized*, but is not found in any system we can observe, so the belief in it clearly seems to be the result of overgrown hypothesis alone.

The principle that there can be no independent systems is so pervasively implicit in systems theory, that it is rarely stated explicitly. However, Donella Meadows includes it in her formal summary of systems principles:

> *There are no separate systems. The world is a continuum. Where to draw a boundary around a system depends on the purpose of the discussion.*[1]

The status of this principle clearly cannot be absolute. We have not yet observed any independent systems, but that doesn't mean that we can prove that they do not exist anywhere in the universe. However, the independent system that we tend to believe in when we are absolutizing does not reside in some remote part of the universe that we might speculate about in theoretical physics. Instead, it resides literally under (or at least, behind) our noses in the mindbrain. There is no evidence for the independence of our 'cognitive' system, yet we continue to believe in it.

Whenever we hold an absolutized belief, this independence is assumed, due to the circular nature of the evidence we appeal to

1   Meadows (2008) p. 190.

(see 4.c) and the way that the cognitive system itself is assumed, in the very process of absolutization, to be independent of the body and the perspectives, meanings, biases, and conflicts that occur within it. Instead of noting the wider context of the belief itself in the systems that it takes part in, we focus only on the *content* of the belief, and the justification of that content in terms of other beliefs that we already have. Another way of putting this is that we think of our beliefs only as philosophical phenomena rather than as psychological phenomena.

Perhaps one of the most dramatic demonstrations of the folly of our assumptions about the independence of the cognitive system is recent research on the unconscious effects of haptic sensations (i.e. things we are touching) on judgements. People sitting on hard chairs were more rigid in their decision-making than people sitting on soft cushions, and favoured harsher judgements towards criminals.[2] People given a hard clipboard to hold rated job candidates as more serious than those holding lighter clipboards.[3] We don't simply go through a process of 'reason' based on the 'evidence', to reach 'truth'. Rather we make motivated judgements as complex animals with layers of experience shaped by successive desires, fears, and associative meanings.

Not only their experimental subjects, but even psychologists themselves, can sometimes assume the independence of the cognitive system, when considering beliefs as psychological objects, but not simultaneously considering the psychological nature of *their own* beliefs as part of a system that interacts with what they are observing. This is the issue with unembodied empiricism (see 4.d) that focuses only on the justifications to be gained from observation, without considering its own context as a belief and making the adjustments required by theoretical uncertainty. A basic example of this would be the assumption by psychologists that cognition is sufficiently separate from 'values' to be discussed separately, when values have already shaped the psychologists' own assumptions framing an investigation.

The interdependence of systems is also the reason why systemic or embodied approaches that question the independence of human beliefs are *not* reductionist (as unembodied empiricist ones may

---

[2] Ackerman, Nocera, & Bargh (2010); Schaefer et al. (2018).
[3] Ackerman, Nocera, & Bargh (2010).

be) when they suggest that our cognitive processes should be contextualized in the experiences of the human body. A reductionist approach is an absolutizing approach, because it assumes that a particular kind of theoretical account (for instance, a 'materialist' one) is complete and final. Thus the belief that a 'physical' or 'material' explanation of human processes is final is reductively absolutizing, but one that merely takes the processes of the brain and body into account as an important aspect of a wider system is not. On the contrary, placing our 'cognitive' beliefs in an embodied context is one of the best ways of *de-absolutizing* them.

The assumed independence of the cognitive system is dependent on *representationalism,* the belief that propositions gain their meaning from their relationship (actual or hypothetical) with reality, rather than from their relationship with the body. This belief about meaning, and the standpoint of the embodied meaning thesis by which it is thrown into relief, will be discussed below in 3.a. However, the key thing to note for the moment from the systems point of view, is that our 'cognitive system' cannot possibly be treated as an exception from the general observation that systems are interdependent.

Absolutization thrives in the medium of the biases that are associated with making an exception of ourselves, being blind to our own role in things. As Daniel Kahneman notes, 'It is easier to recognize other people's mistakes than our own.'[4] Yet there are a variety of ways of reducing this blindness to our own states, such as mindfulness that increases our own current self-awareness, creating prompts to self-awareness over time, using others to reflect our states back to us, or even using technology to monitor our states and report them to us. The difficulties that are involved in recognizing our cognitive system as part of a psychological system, rather than as a completely decontextualized set of conceptual thoughts, are genuine but not insuperable. They do not give us any excuse to shrug our shoulders and dismiss our delusions as inevitable. The biggest problem is not so much the individual discipline involved in thinking otherwise, once we are motivated enough to do so, but the ways that absolutized beliefs have often become deeply enculturated into our social systems.

The delusion of the separate system can also be readily explained in neuroscientific terms, and it is here that the work of

---

4   Kahneman (2011) p. 28.

Iain McGilchrist becomes highly relevant in focusing our attention on the self-reinforcing tendencies of the over-dominant left hemisphere of the brain.

> The left hemisphere, because its thinking is decontextualised, tends towards a slavish following of the internal logic of a situation, even if this is in contravention to everything experience tells us. This can be a strength, for example in philosophy, when it gets us beyond intuition, although it could also be seen as the disease for which philosophy itself must be the cure; but it is a weakness when it permits too ready a capitulation to theory. The left hemisphere is the hemisphere of abstraction, which, as the word tells us, is the process of wresting things from their context. This, and its related capacity to categorise things once they have been abstracted, are the foundations of its intellectual power.[5]

This decontextualization is one that cuts off recognition of the functions of the right hemisphere, which connects us through open forms of attention with information from the senses,[6] awareness of our emotional states from proprioception,[7] and with the imaginative synthesis of different aspects of our experience through metaphor.[8]

The process by which the left hemisphere achieves this decontextualized dominance seems to be one in which the symmetrically parallel parts of the brain in both hemispheres are simultaneously activated by a stimulus, but the left hemisphere then *inhibits* the right via the corpus callosum.[9] The corpus callosum links the functions of the two hemispheres, but it also has an inhibitory function, so that each hemisphere can focus on its specialism without disruption from the other. A review of the evidence by van der Knaap and van der Ham concludes that there is insufficient evidence either to attribute an entirely positive function of coordination, or entirely one of inhibition, to the corpus callosum.[10] That it has both functions, however, would be consistent with our experience both that our cognitive system is actually a dependent part of the wider system of our body, and that it maintains a theoretical independence from that wider system. Each time the dominant left hemisphere inhibits the right, the cognitive functions associated with Broca's Region and located in the left pre-frontal cortex (discussed further in 3.a)

---

5   McGilchrist (2009) p. 50.
6   Ibid. pp. 37–40.
7   Ibid. pp. 59–61.
8   Ibid. pp. 115 ff.
9   Cook (1984); McGilchrist (2009) pp. 17–18.
10 Van der Knaap & van der Ham (2011).

are decontextualized. In sum, we maintain beliefs because the states of our bodies in response to stimuli give us a justification for them, but we think that we maintain those beliefs because they are 'true'.

This assumed system independence fits into the overall pattern of absolutized beliefs, as not so much a particular belief but as a pattern of *how* we believe. We assume that our feelings at this moment are the only ones that matter, even compared to the ones we are likely to feel in an hour's time. We assume that the 'evidence' we have just examined (perhaps of a conspiracy theory on the internet) points to the truth of the theory, regardless of the other evidence that may be more widely available of entirely contrary theories. We assume that the interests of our own group or nation must be far more important than anyone else's. In all these examples, then, we take one aspect of a wider system and assume that it is an isolated totality. Although systems theory provides the clearest framework in which the mistake that this kind of thinking involves is thrown into sharpest relief, there are many other ways that we could identify it.

2.c. Fragility

> *Summary*
>
> Fragility is the tendency of a system to remain stable only up to a 'tipping point', when the effects of its reinforcing feedback loops become incompatible with the environment. Absolutized beliefs drive human actions to such tipping points, after which the beliefs dramatically 'flip' to their opposites, as can be seen both in psychosis and in dramatic religious conversion. In the human system, absolutized beliefs are fragile because of a lack of antifragility or resilience – resilience which is experienced as grounded confidence and comes from testing against a breadth of experience.

In addition to the process of reinforcing feedback loops and the interdependence of systems, one other aspect of systems theory can substantially inform our understanding of absolutization. This is the way in which absolutization creates the possibility of *fragility* in a system. This in turn can be seen as an aspect of the *non-linearity* of systems in response to reinforcing feedback loops. Systems can surprise us by changing in dramatic and unpredictable ways, as a causal input of some kind ceases to have an even or proportionate effect, and may even start to have the reverse effect after a 'tipping point' has been reached.[1] For instance, adding an excessive amount of fertilizer helps your crop grow up to a point, but beyond that point, it first becomes ineffective and then poisons it. A long lecture without a break may start off being engaging and informative, with the audience learning, but as their concentration flags they may start first to become bored, then even alienated from the topic, deterred from further learning.

Absolutization particularly lends itself to these kinds of non-linearity effects, because it interferes with the absolutizing person's adaptation to new conditions. The absolutizing farmer keeps pouring on that fertilizer, and the absolutizing lecturer drones on and on, their judgements caught up in a reinforcing feedback loop that overrides any awareness of the effects of their actions. If forced to recognize them, they may eventually be unpleasantly surprised by the non-linear effects of their well-intentioned actions. Actions justified by absolutizing judgements (which continue to reinforce absolutizing beliefs) continue in the same pattern regardless of

1 Meadows (2008) p. 91.

the environment, until eventually the strength of countervailing conditions from that environment causes the reinforcing feedback loop to be suddenly overridden and reversed.

The reasons for this fragility can be appreciated both on a philosophical and at a psychological level. At the philosophical level of the content of the belief itself, the infinite scope of that belief means that it cannot be modified before a point of total change, since any reduction of infinity is still infinity (see 4.d). At a psychological level, also, the exclusion of alternatives means that all new information will be interpreted in terms either of the absolute belief or its negation, *until* the build-up of justification for the negation is so great as to flip the belief.

In some circumstances it may take a very long time – even millennia – for that build-up to occur sufficiently to trigger the flip. Absolutized beliefs can be tenacious as well as fragile (particularly in the enculturated form of metaphysical belief – see 4.a). Nevertheless, when change does occur it does so totally and discontinuously (see 3.c) rather than gradually. Fragility following tenacity can be seen, for instance, in the sudden breakdown of a long but repressive marriage, or the unexpected breakdown of what seemed like an entrenched political system in revolution.

The phenomenon of rapid flipping between an absolutized belief and its opposite is characteristic of sudden conversions, such as that of St Paul, struck by a flash of light and a revelatory voice on the road to Damascus.[2] In the case of religious conversions, the pressure from the environment is primarily a social one: the old religion is associated with beliefs that create a reinforcing feedback loop that is in ever-increasing tension with a new environment. This conflict will also be reflected internally through the repression (see 5.a) of alternative views or of any sympathy for them. This conflict can take the form of fanatical one-sidedness in consciously attacking the view one is repressing. St Paul was most strongly persecuting Christians at the time of his dramatic conversion to Christianity, just as intense homophobia can be a sign of repressed homosexuality.[3]

The dramatic breaking of fragile absolutized beliefs is a distinctive process that has been traced in parallel both in the case of dramatic religious conversion and in the case of the onset of schizophrenic

2   Acts 9.
3   Adams, Wright, & Lohr (1996).

psychosis. These two instances have been brought together in a comparative paper by Wootton and Allen.[4] Both cases begin with an 'overextension', in other words the proliferation of an absolutized belief caught in a reinforcing feedback loop through its attempts to overcome a conflict. This is followed by the intrusion of this increasing conflict into consciousness, where it may cause anxiety or depression. Some sort of transition event then provides the tipping point where the repressed belief breaks through, perhaps triggered by some external event that stresses and disturbs the bodily system (in St Paul's case, falling off his horse). This disinhibits the repressed beliefs, although to start with this may be experienced in ways that conflict with an accustomed sense of reality, for instance as hallucinations in which the repressed belief takes the form of a vision or a voice. The person then feels a sense of submission to the new imperative, with a sudden abandonment of the old absolutizations, and the new beliefs can then become normalized and perhaps socially recognized. The difference between psychosis and religious conversion here then seems to be that in the latter, the normalization can occur in socially acceptable ways and be recognized in a conversion ceremony.

The same fragility can also be observed at group level, in the form of mass movements of people not only being dramatically converted to one perspective, but equally dramatically moving back to the previous one. Reference to repression (5.a below) and group binding (5.e below) will be needed to understand this more fully, but the basic pattern of fragility is clearly reproduced. The Chinese Cultural Revolution (starting in 1966) provides some strong examples of this, in which young Red Guards were not only led to denounce the whole socio-political system they had been brought up in, but pretty soon also to denounce the denouncers. As a recent historian of the Cultural Revolution writes:

> *Different sides took turns [at] purging and being purged. This process was accompanied by alliances and mergers between various subfactions... and reversals of values.*[5]

What seems to be less commonly remarked in discussions of both dramatic religious conversion and mass political conversion is the

---

4   Wootton & Allen (1983).
5   Yang Jisheng (2021), quoted by Rosemary Righter in a review in the *Times Literary Supplement* 4 June 2021.

way that *both* the new and the old belief are absolutes. The change is thus just what I call a *flip*, a total change from one absolute to its negation, rather than an adjustment from an absolute view to a provisional one. As long as an absolute belief remains absolute, it can only yield by flipping to its negation. Of course, there are also some occasions when an absolute belief gradually ceases to be absolute, because it has been put into a larger context: the process of *integration*.[6] Integration clearly can occur in response to a variety of processes – for instance a process of maturation, the effects of suffering, of education, or of bodily-based practice. These processes will normally make new alternatives *meaningful* in a way that they were not before, because they have been made newly accessible or relevant. The absolutization thus falls away because the blockage of alternatives has ceased.

Developmental psychologist Jean Piaget tracked the process of moving from an absolute belief to its opposite and then to a more integrated position in terms of what he called 'disequilibrium'. A particular schema is maintained as a basis of belief as long as its functionality is not disturbed beyond a particular critical point. He then found three different levels of response to this disturbance. What he called 'alpha reactions' merely maintained the dominant belief. 'Beta reactions' are equivalent to flips – they modify the schema only to enable two alternatives – the original dominant belief and its opposite. 'Gamma reactions' are integrative adjustments, which allow further possible impacts on the conditions to be considered and anticipated, so that multiple alternatives are now available beyond the original framing. According to Piaget, the process of moving from alpha to beta to gamma reactions can happen at any point of human development, but marks a process of breakthrough.[7]

An illustration of the distinction between a 'flip' and an integrative adjustment is found in the story of the Buddha's early life. The Buddha starts off with a flip – leaving the Palace for the Forest in a youthful rejection of his background that is famously total (he leaves his family and wealth behind, cuts his hair, and takes off his rich clothes) and embracing the opposite. However, when he leaves behind the absolutization of the ascetics in the Forest he does so

---

6 i.6; II.5
7 Piaget (1985); Boom (2009) pp. 141–2; Kruglanski (2004) pp. 34–5.

due to a rooted bodily experience – that is, a childhood memory of reaching an absorbed meditative state.[8] At a social level, the break with the ascetics can still be represented as a dramatic split representing a tipping point. However, the Buddha's clear break with the second absolutization then enables him to begin a more effective process of individual integrative development.

The disconnection of absolute beliefs from meaning in the body (see 3.a) may also be responsible for the superficiality of the apparent confidence we place in them. These beliefs are supported by the meaning offered from a constructed abstract representation which ignores the dependence of that representation on bodily experience. There is thus a sense in which we never fully understand these absolute statements, but rather accept them because of our dependence on the group with which they are closely associated (see 5.e). Craving for the group's approval and fear of its rejection may well substitute for a sense of the meaning of absolute statements, before we even get on to its justification. Given that an inextricable part of this meaning is emotive and consists in a sense of security about the things we are believing, we can only maintain a front of apparent confidence by separating the emotive meaning from the cognitive in a way typical of implicit representationalism, and getting our emotional security from the group's acceptance rather than from deeper experience. The loss of group acceptance, then, can easily result in the sudden loss of the associated beliefs and an adoption of similar replacement beliefs, as we readily see in the way that converts match their change of beliefs with a formal change of allegiance between groups.

This fragility can be contrasted with the antifragility that we may develop by considering criticisms of, and alternatives to, our beliefs within a larger provisional context. Antifragility (a term coined helpfully by Nassim Nicholas Taleb[9]) is the quality of things that actually get stronger through difficulty, like a muscle strengthened by exercise. Provisional belief is like this, because it is not only *justified* through observation (the quality that scientists tend to focus on) but also made *meaningful*, even as a whole, in relation to our experience. Research has shown that direct experience as the basis of a belief increases both the confidence with which the belief is held

---

8   Ellis (2019) section 1.
9   Taleb (2012).

and the consistency with which it is applied.[10] Our confidence in it can then be organically increased by widening the experience that forms a basis of comparison for the justification of the belief.

The fragility of absolutized beliefs is thus a result of our *lack* of confidence in them in the normal, embodied sense that we have confidence, say, that the chair we are sitting on is not about to collapse beneath us (see 7.d below).[11] This also helps to explain the way in which we may still lack genuine confidence about (and feel underlying anxiety about) beliefs that we have adopted as 'rational' due to group pressure rather than because of a gradual extension of our embodied confidence to encompass probabilistic evidence. A statement like 'Your chances of dying in a plane crash are actually much lower than in a car crash' are unlikely to help someone with a phobia of flying unless they have related the evidence behind this statistical point thoroughly to their experience, rather than simply being told it abstractly on authority.

Whether absolute beliefs remain indefinitely entrenched, flip into their opposite, or are gradually absorbed into a larger provisional context depends entirely on the surrounding conditions and the ways we respond to these conditions. If the conditions do not change, the belief does not change, but of course our changing universe creates an increasing probability that new conditions will reveal the inadequacy of an absolute and ill-adapted belief, the more time goes on. As Taleb points out, unexpected conditions ('Black Swans') may destroy our fragile beliefs, from unexpected crashes in the stock market, to pandemics, to rapid changes in weather destroying agriculture. If the conditions do change, the first adaptation from an absolute belief is normally a flip. It is only when conditions (external or internal) make the inadequacy *both* of the first belief *and* of its opposite clear that the Middle Way starts to become an option, as we are forced to re-examine the more basic framing of our belief.

In terms of systems theory, the property of antifragility is often described as 'resilience': however, in contrast to the apparent stability created by reinforcing feedback loops, this resilience may be hard to see or understand without a definite effort to compensate

---

10 Fazio & Zanna (1978).
11 Also iv.1.e; VI.1.

for our limited view of all the intersecting systems involved. As Donella Meadows writes:

> Resilience is something that may be very hard to see, unless you exceed its limits, overwhelm or damage the balancing loops, and the system structure breaks down. Because resilience may not be obvious without a whole system view, people often sacrifice resilience for stability, or for productivity, or for some other more immediately recognisable system property.[12]

She gives the example of cows whose production of milk is boosted by the use of bovine growth hormone. If you take the whole system of a cow, the energy that goes into that productivity is taken away from the cow's long-term resilience – for instance in resistance to disease. To expand on her example, it's since evident that to avoid disease, antibiotics have also been over-used in dairy farming, with potentially catastrophic effects in terms of its large contribution to general antibiotic resistance.[13] Thus the pursuit of short-term profit (driven in turn by an economic system that incentivizes it) introduces serious fragility not only into dairy farming itself, but also into some of the wider systems of health and agriculture of which it forms a part. This fragility is not only a product of the system that has been created in the world, but also of the absolutized beliefs of the people responsible for creating and perpetuating it: the belief that profit should be maximized at all costs, the belief that the capitalist system that incentivizes that belief should be maintained at all costs, the belief that any degree of exploitation of animals and interference in their systems is justified by profit – all of these are examples of absolutized beliefs that have been perpetuated because they remained unquestioned when a larger perspective was necessary. It offers just one small example of the whole range of absolutized beliefs that have contributed to the increasingly likely collapse of our ecosystems.

To conclude this section, it should be clear from these three areas of systems theory that we can use it to advance a stage further in our understanding of absolutization from the Buddhist account. Where the Buddha identified 'mental proliferation', we can develop this into the tendency of absolutized beliefs to escalate their self-perpetuation in reinforcing feedback loops. The extremes of belief that the Buddha identified as needing to be avoided for the Middle

---

12 Meadows (2008) p. 77.
13 Williams-Nguyen et al. (2016).

Way are the ones that have these self-perpetuating features, as illustrated by the man with the arrow in his eye in the Buddha's simile. This tells us much about the structural features and effects of absolutized beliefs in relation to their environment. The assumed independence of the cognitive system from the standpoint of absolutizing belief gives us a further understanding of the delusion discussed by the Buddha. Finally, the concept of fragility provides one standpoint for understanding why absolutization can seem attractive in the short term but is unsustainable in the longer term when a wider variety of conditions come into play.

3. Embodied Meaning

3.a. Representationalism

> *Summary*
>
> The development of embodied meaning theory, which shows meaning to be based on associative neural connection in response to experience, gives a context for understanding the limitations of representationalism. Representationalism assumes that meaning consists in the relationship between propositions and the actual or potential 'reality' that they describe. Absolutization assumes representationalism because its propositional claims as a whole are entirely 'semantic' and deny the variation of meaning with experience.

In 2.a above, I quoted from Maturana and Varela, pioneering systems biologists, on the basis of meaning and belief in organic systems. Here, once again, is the section of that quotation that relates to meaning:

> *The first, and most obvious [way that the nervous system participates in cognitive phenomena] is through expanding the realm of possible states of the organism that arises from the great diversity of sensori-motor patterns which the nervous system allows for and which is the key to its participation in the operation of the organism.*[1]

This relationship between 'possible states of the organism' and 'sensori-motor patterns' is better known, when developed by the work of George Lakoff and Mark Johnson, as *embodied meaning*.[2] Embodied meaning is most basically the way in which the interactions of an organism with its environment create habitual patterns in its brain and nervous system. These patterns do not necessarily determine our actions ('structural coupling'), so they are not the same as beliefs (the second of Maturana and Varela's 'complementary ways'), but they offer the set of resources from which beliefs

---

1   Maturana & Varela (1987) p. 175.
2   Many commentators seem not to recognize this term, although it was used by Lakoff and Johnson, and to instead use the somewhat misleading term 'cognitive linguistics': but embodied meaning is neither exclusively cognitive nor exclusively linguistic.

can be formed. In the context of a human being, these patterns are *experiences* of the way that previous stimuli modify the effect of new ones, also correlating with the patterns in our brains and nervous systems.

Previous stimuli modify the effect of new ones by creating associations, so that the *meaning* of our grandparents' house, say, or the tree in the garden, is the result of our total associations with it. These are both 'cognitive' (categorizations like 'tree', 'rowan', 'the rowan tree in the garden') and 'emotive' (the house being associated with the warmth of the relationship that goes with it). When we learn the significance of symbols, exactly the same kind of associations are at work in what they mean to us (a cross 'means' Christianity, and also 'means' boredom in church). When we learn language, again, the components of language (morphemes, words, phrases, and sentences) gain their total meaning both from the associative meanings of their components and from the ways that grammar enables those components to be combined. Importantly, that associative meaning combines 'cognitive' and 'emotive' elements in total interdependence.

Lakoff and Johnson[3] offer an account of how that associative process can support the meaning even of the most complex and abstract language, beginning with the association of what they call 'basic level categories' (e.g. 'tree') and 'schemas' (e.g. 'path') and then extended into new areas of experience by metaphor. We start off with terms associated with the most salient objects in our environment and with groups of associations (schemas) around sensori-motor processes such as putting something in a container or moving towards a goal. We then divide or synthesize the categories (developing 'rowan' and 'plant' from 'tree') and extend our use of the schemas into new situations using metaphorical comparisons (the 'path' schema also gives us a process, a time progression, or a transfer of digital information). For instance, 'It's getting closer to winter' uses the path schema as a way of structuring our understanding of time, as though the progression of the seasons was a path we could move along.[4]

This account of meaning is also consistent with systems theory in seeing both meaning and belief as nested systems within the human

---

3 Johnson (2007) collects a good account of this in one book. Also see Lakoff (1987), and many other works by Lakoff and Johnson separately or together.

4 iii.1; IV.1

organism, interacting with all the surrounding systems rather than separated from them. It is an aspect of *embodiment* as a wider approach that integrates the 'internal' perspective of experience with the 'external' one of scientific observation, acknowledging all the positive ways they can inform each other, rather than creating a false dichotomy between them. Unfortunately, though, embodiment defies the trend of Western thinking, which is consistently based on absolutized assumptions instead. The embodied meaning thesis can cast a huge amount of light on absolutization, by providing us with an alternative standpoint from which we can identify that absolutization that is not simply founded on the assumptions that reproduce it.

The phenomenon that embodied meaning enables us to see is *representationalism*: the assumption that meaning consists, not in the state of an organism, but in the linguistic representations of the world held within a particular part of the human brain: the left pre-frontal cortex (particularly Broca's area and its associated areas, known as Broca's Region). Like most functions of parts of the brain, that of Broca's Region is a specialization, not an absolute exclusivity of function, but its function specifically involves unified syntactic processing and semantic understanding.[5] In other words, its normal function is to unify the meanings of propositional sentences so that we can relate the separate meanings of words to representations of states of affairs. Patients with lesions in Broca's area tend to communicate telegraphically with single disconnected words (or may attempt to avoid doing so and end up with other speech problems).[6] These patients don't lack a sense of meaning that can be connected with words and symbols, which is a function of other parts of the brain, nervous system, and body, but they do lack a sense of the kinds of meanings that can express representational *beliefs*. Representationalism takes this function and elevates it disproportionately to become the sole criterion of meaning.

Iain McGilchrist also points out the close relationship between representation and manipulation, with the latter being associated with a section of the left hemisphere closely adjacent to Broca's Region. He argues that, far from representational language developing 'in

---

5   Friederici (2002); Scott et al. (2000).
6   Kolk & Heeschen (2007).

the abstract' so that we could 'know' the world, it developed *for the purposes* of manipulation.

> Category formation provides clearer boundaries to the landscape of the world, giving a certain view of it greater solidity and permanence.... Language refines the expression of causal relationships. It hugely expands the range of reference of thought, and expands the capacity for planning and manipulation. It enables the indefinite memorialisation of more than could otherwise be retained by any human memory.... Language in summary brings precision and fixity, two very important features if we are to succeed in manipulating the world. And specifically, though we may not like to recognise this, it is good for manipulating other human beings.[7]

It is at least a plausible explanation for the development of representationalism that, taken in by the 'solidity and permanence' that our language has seemed to give the world, and deceived by others who could make use of our belief in it, we have forgotten (if we ever realized it in the first place) that our representations in language are used *for a purpose*. Instead, we started to assume its eternal capacity for representational 'truth' – not always that we possessed such 'truth', but that we were at least capable of having it.

As classically represented in analytic philosophy and traditional linguistics, representationalism takes the form of the truth-dependent definition of meaning: that is, the view that the meaning of a proposition consists in the knowledge of when it would be true. Although the classic articulation of this view in that form has been challenged in recent years by what philosophers call 'contextualism', the alternatives offered do not challenge the basic representationalist assumption that meaning comes from truth-conditionality. Rather they replace a truth-conditional semantics with a truth-conditional pragmatics, which merely seeks more complex explanations of truth-dependence.[8]

Representationalism in the sense I'm using the term also encompasses the Wittgensteinian view that the meaning of language is its (social) use,[9] since a social usage is also a state of affairs 'out there' beyond the experience of the person who finds symbols meaningful in a particular case.[10] Such a social usage could also be described

7   McGilchrist (2009) p. 114.
8   Bezuidenhout (2002).
9   The implied view of Wittgenstein (1967).
10 As Hacker (1972, p. 145) puts this, Wittgenstein's view of meaning is still 'isomorphic with the structure of reality' which is 'merely the shadow of grammar'.

in propositions, even if the language itself was not propositional. For instance, if a plumber calls 'spanner' to his mate, this is not in itself apparently a proposition, but to communicate its meaning we would have to say something like 'the plumber is communicating the wish that his mate would pass the spanner'.

Philosophical and linguistic discussions of meaning often appropriate the idea of embodiment but only apply it partially. They also tend to consider it in such a specialized context that they make no comparison of representationalism with a thoroughly embodied view when they apply assumptions about meaning to cognitive psychology, ethics, or the philosophy of science. In particular, here, I want to draw attention to the implications of representationalism in creating and supporting absolutization. Representationalism, understood in a wider context, *denies the embodiment of meaning*.

An absolute claim must be assumed to be representational, because there is no other way for an absolute claim as a whole (as opposed to its isolated components) to be meaningful. The syntactic function normally applied by Broca's Region is obviously applied to the meaning of any proposition (whether absolute or not), but when that function can be contextualized by comparison with other meaningful alternatives, we are no longer *solely* dependent on that syntactic construction of meaning. In the case of an absolute claim, however, there are no such alternatives. Its meaning must be rigorously and exclusively cognitive, excluding any emotion or other experience of the person to whom the claim is meaningful.

For instance, the proposition 'the universe is infinite' does not mean what it is taken to mean because of anything to do with the individual. The individual who speaks or understands that sentence is assumed to merely enter a passive relationship to a meaning that descends out of the potential abstract truth or falsity of the state of affairs to which it is supposed to refer – a potential truth or falsity that has been assembled solely by the syntactic construction of Broca's Region. This could be contrasted with 'the teddy bear is warm', which usually describes the bodily and emotional experiences of the person who says it. Even 'the teddy bear is warm' could also be treated absolutely, though, by excluding the subject from the supposed meaning of the term, and debating only its abstract 'truth' as a state of affairs. However, when we use this sentence to express our emotional and bodily experiences, the syntactic functions in the sentence are obliged to *interact* with all the other neural pathways in the brain and nervous system that are associated with these experiences of warmth.

The meaning of absolute propositions as a whole, then, does remain dependent on the whole body and its experiences (even 'universe' and 'infinite' have bodily associations), but the belief in absolute propositions is accompanied by an assumption that the meaning of those propositions depends only on its relationship to states of affairs, and thus on syntactic and semantic relationships. Syntactic relationships link the words in the proposition so as to be able to *represent* a state of affairs, whilst the meaning of the words in that context is assumed to be merely semantic – that is, meaningful according to the role of the word in a coherent set of potential beliefs. The 'meaning' of the words in the proposition thus becomes both definitional and conventional, so that we can look them up in a dictionary and assume that the 'meaning' of the words used is exhausted by that definition.

Not only emotive but cognitive variation in meaning is excluded by this attempt to fix meaning under a particular set of conventions. Representationalism resists 'private languages'[11] and stipulations that do not obey what are taken to be the absolute rules of meaning. Instead, those who implicitly rely on representationalism are likely to protest that new usages are not in line with what the word 'really means'. This could be described as 'popular essentialism' – the unreflective view that the meaning of a word is to be found in a dictionary, and that's that. Such popular essentialism is responsible for a good deal of conflict whenever one group begins to use a new word for a new purpose, and another resists it.

A recent case of this can be illustrated by a controversy in *The Times Literary Supplement* in which I became fruitlessly involved myself. The 'McDowell Colony', which is a foundation to support the arts based on a former farm in New Hampshire, decided to scrap the term 'colony' from its name because of the associations of the word for its users: a decision which a columnist in the *TLS*, known as 'J.C.', described as an example of 'the world gone mad'.[12] However, McDowell Board Chairman Nell Painter 'acknowledged that the word "colony" can mean a country or given location under the control of an outside power or, as would apply to MacDowell,

---

11 Famously the obsession of Wittgenstein (1967) §258. See critique in Ellis (2001) 4.e.iii.
12 *Times Literary Supplement*, 'N.B.', 24 July 2020.

a community of like-minded people. But she said both definitions carry a sense of exclusion and hierarchy, and that the first definition was far more prevalent.'[13] J.C.'s unreflective view seemed to be that of popular essentialism, namely that there was a sense of what 'colony' really means in the context in which it was being used. This is the sense that you could look up in a dictionary, and, if there were a variety of senses listed, select one of them for the 'true' sense of the word in this context. Accompanying this was obviously the assumption that what it means associatively for many of the people involved was irrelevant, and thus implicitly that the historically dominant group that got to determine the 'true' meaning of the word here were the ones that mattered. This illustrates an increasing amount of conflict between so-called 'political correctness' (which often involves a sensitivity to word association as an aspect of meaning), and the popular essentialism often assumed by those who protest against it. Such conflicts remain intractable unless people are willing to re-examine the absolutized assumptions about meaning that maintain them.

Representationalism is a deeply engrained philosophical habit which appears to infect not only the analytic philosophers and linguists who formalize it, but also many other academics who assume or apply this way of thinking about meaning: for instance, a physicist who assumes that the meaning of his paper about physics consists only in a set of propositions about the universe. It privileges 'cognitive' meaning and separates it from 'emotive' meaning, which is generally treated as second class or subsidiary. This is also a deeply self-deluded way of going about things, as it assumes that the subject can completely abstract him or herself from the object of discussion: the assumed system independence discussed in the last chapter. Not only can we have no proof of claims that are taken to be 'purely' about objects, but we cannot even discuss such claims without experiencing all our own associations as embodied beings with the symbols we are using, based on our own unique experience. Even 'the universe is infinite' does not mean the same to me as it does to you. The fact that there may be enough coincidence of meaning between our senses of the proposition for us to communicate adequately about it should not lead us to conclude that it

---

13   https://www.macdowell.org/news/macdowell-removes-colony-from-name (accessed 2020).

'means the same' to both of us – as ensuing 'misunderstandings' can reveal. It is also precisely this particularity in meaning that enables us to value and to justify some meanings over others as better fulfilling helpful functions (see 8.b) – contrary to the representationalist assumption that we need absolute linguistic meaning to justify our values.

The dependence of representationalism on semantic conventionality also reveals its association with the group that uses an absolutizing belief and the cognitive models it draws on. We adopt an absolute belief in relation to the group context, that prevents us from breaking it down or examining it in relation to other contexts, and we may feel that the group is threatened when the belief is questioned (see 5.e). We assume that the sole meaning of the proposition comes from that context, which means not only that we derive any cognitive definition of it from there, but that our sense of confidence about that proposition depends on our confidence in the group and its context. Wittgenstein tracked this type of group-dependence in language in his discussion of 'language games',[14] although he failed to link this sufficiently to psychology. For example, someone playing a Christian religious 'language game' may use the term 'grace' in a term specific to the Christian theological doctrine of atonement, and object to someone using the term 'grace' elsewhere in a less precise way that does not pre-suppose these shared group beliefs.

Our representational assumptions about the meaning of our language can exhibit the phenomena of fragility, however entrenched they may appear to be, but this usually occurs in relation to our specific assumptions about the meaning of particular language, rather than representation as a whole. Any of the examples of fragility resulting in 'flips' that I discussed in 2.c above will also show underlying flips in the assumptions made about the meaning of language. For instance, when St Paul was converted, 'Christian' very suddenly ceased to mean a contemptible minority threatening the Roman state, and instead started to mean a truthful, loving community.

The assumption of representationalism thus provides another crucial element for our understanding of absolutization, showing the implicit assumptions about meaning that make it possible, and thus how the cultural transmission of those assumptions, both

---

14 Wittgenstein (1967) passim.

implicitly and explicitly, has contributed to the phenomenon of absolutization. The perspective that allows us to become aware of representationalism, and of alternatives beyond it, is also closely aligned to systems theory. Just as the assumed independence of the cognitive (and representational) system can be seen as problematic because it defies the basic insights of systems theory, representationalism is also accompanied by a parallel denial of embodiment, which I will turn to next.

3.b. The Denial of Embodiment

> *Summary*
>
> The application of representationalism is combined with a more general denial of most of our embodied experience through the over-dominance of the left hemisphere perspective. This denial takes the form of the substitution of a disembodied shortcut for a more adequate process based on wider experience, encouraged by cultural entrenchment. This chapter briefly discusses 12 forms of this denial of embodiment.

The denial of embodiment is the implication of representationalism (3.a), as the latter posits a basis of meaning that excludes most of the body and its experience (apart from key areas of the left hemisphere associated with goals and propositional language production). It is also the immediate implication of the assumed independence of the cognitive system from other systems (2.b). All the evidence discussed in 2.b concerning assumed systemic independence when we absolutize, particularly the inhibition of right hemisphere functions by the over-dominant left hemisphere through the corpus callosum, also helps to illuminate the denial of embodiment. However, the denial of embodiment is also a more immediate alienation of *experience*. Our experience is based in the body, and its sense of meaning is inextricable from basic self-esteem, confidence, and awareness,[1] yet the cultural dominance of representationalism continually leads us to deny this basis and assume that our basis of confidence instead lies in the 'facts' and 'reasons' we have constructed in representational language.

There are a number of dimensions to the denial of embodiment in representationalism: these can also be seen as substitutions (see 5.d). Concepts are substituted for experience, the God's eye view for perspective, naturalism for embodiment, passivity for activity, deductive logic for inductive, models for schemas, signs for symbols, literalism for metaphors, values for desires, effort of will for integrated development, absolute belief for faith or confidence, and supernaturalism for archetypal experience (**figure 3**). In each case, the result is obviously not to make our thinking actually disembodied, but rather to distract our attention from the features that

---

[1] Johnson (2007) chs. 1–4.

accompany embodiment, and that provide a wider context for both meaning and the judgements that depend on meaning. I will briefly discuss each of these substitutions here, but many of them deserve the much more extended treatment they may receive in later books in this planned series.

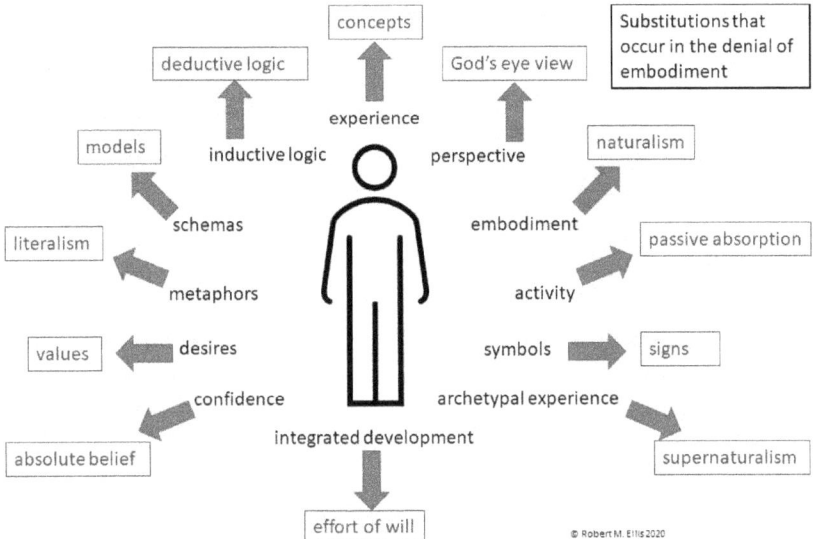

Figure 3. Substitutions that occur in the denial of embodiment.

Concepts for experience

The substitution of concepts for experience is the most basic element of the denial of embodiment. Rather than recognizing that we have had an organic experience that could be interpreted in a variety of possible ways, we identify a set of defining concepts with the experience itself, on the assumption that these concepts are necessary to that experience. Thus, for instance, when experiencing an object such as a cloud or an elephant, the popular tendency is to insist that this object *is* as described. Similarly, in religious experience, we assert that this *is* definitively an experience of God. Rather than recognizing that the words we are using have a meaning in relation to our bodies and apart from the objects, we identify the very meaning of the words with the supposed objects. Analytic philosophy adds only a further refinement on the same set of assumptions, by following Frege in distinguishing *sense* (the shared, 'objective' meaning of a word) from *reference* (the variable ways we use it).² However, since 'sense' is still truth-dependent, this merely puts the conceptual substitution at a slightly abstracted remove from the specific object in front of us, and makes it instead dependent on objects in general rather than experiences.

God's eye view for perspective

Our bodies also have a particular perspective: one point in space and time from which we observe other possible points in space and time. Our perspective is also shaped by our specific sense organs, our genetic predispositions, our past experience, and our goals in relation to what we experience. All of these features of perspective emerge from simply having a body with particular limitations. However, the denial of embodiment in the absolutizing perspective involves the substitution for this of a supposed God's eye view, what Thomas Nagel famously called the 'view from nowhere'.³ The view from nowhere supposedly describes the world as it is free from perspective, using supposedly neutral language. We are, of course, not doing this, however well-justified our beliefs are, but when absolutizing we continue to deceive ourselves that that is what we are doing.

Naturalism for embodiment

Our embodiment implies a view of the world in which we need to take ourselves into account whenever we try to describe or theorize aspects of that world. However, the denial of embodiment substitutes naturalism for this embodiment. Naturalism is the attempt to *describe* nature *as it is*, and is generally identified with the descriptions of nature that can be justified by science. Considerations of embodiment can be readily appropriated by theoretical approaches that merely pay lip-service to 'embodiment', but actually treat it as just another set of objects to be described rather than as a prompt to adopt practical and provisional approaches that take our limitations fully into account. There is nothing wrong with description, but it is the *provisionality* of description (putting it into a larger practical context) that makes description, whether scientific or otherwise, compatible with embodiment, not the mere appropriation of words like 'embodied'. If one is really trying to avoid the delusion that our

2 Frege (1966) p. 59.
3 Nagel (1986).

words are formed in dependence on a nature that they mirror, a great deal of circumspection is needed before falling back on terms like 'knowledge', 'truth', 'ontology', and 'metaphysics' (other than critically or archetypally) – terms that seem to have an unbreakable magnetic pull for philosophers, who keep returning to them even when they have supposedly given up the basis for doing so.

There are more and less sophisticated versions of naturalism, in which our descriptions get adjusted to a greater or lesser extent to take into account our limitations in describing the world, but simply making our descriptions more complex does not remove the basic denial of embodiment involved in trying to describe 'nature' as though we did not have a particular view of it. For instance, Mark Johnson, following the tradition of 'methodological' naturalism developed by Dewey, recommends a 'pluralist' approach to naturalism in which different possible levels of explanation for phenomena are recognized, avoiding the reductionist approach of assuming that there is only one 'true' level of explanation.[4] However, this does not seem consistent with the wider insights of Johnson's thought. The particularity of our view of things as individuals requires the *provisionality* of any description, which is another way of taking into account that it is not simply a description. Recognizing different levels of description for different purposes does not necessarily make those descriptions provisional, when it is an interaction with psychological criteria that are required for provisionality in practice,[5] rather than a mere shift in philosophical description.

Passive absorption for activity

Our engagement with the world as embodied organisms is *active*. That means that we constantly interact with our environment on the basis of our goals as organisms. Not only do those goals shape our view of our environment, but as we achieve them we change both our own state and that of the environment. Having taken into account our perspective at one time, we are obliged to continually take into account changes in our perspective. However, the denial of embodiment substitutes a passive model in which we absorb information from the world, and the complexity created by the continual changes in our perspective together with the effects of our goal-orientation is ignored. For Descartes, our observation

4 Johnson (2018) pp. 34–5.
5 II.2.

of the world was conceived as a kind of proscenium arch theatre through which we observed the world – the 'Cartesian theatre' in the phrase coined by Daniel Dennett.[6] Empiricist philosophers have similarly thought in terms of 'sense data' coming in, as though the 'sense data' were neutral to the experience of the person receiving and interpreting it. The model of passive absorption, once again, involves denying the implications of having a body with its particular and constantly changing standpoint.

Signs for symbols

The embodied perspective involves symbols: in other words objects that we encounter in experience that have meaning, whether these are things in the world, pictures, sounds, or words. The meaning of a symbol is not fixed, but depends on the changing interpretation of the experiencer as well as the nature of the symbolic object itself: for instance, a cross may mean anything from ecstatic experience to boredom in church. However, the denial of embodiment involves substituting signs for symbols. Signs have a clear and fixed meaning which can either form or imply propositions about the world (e.g. a red traffic light implies 'You should stop'). Cognitive meaning is thus privileged over emotive meaning, with a false dichotomy created between them. The meaning of a sign is also assumed to be the same for everyone experiencing the sign (the 'sense' in Frege's terms).

This distinction between signs and symbols is derived from Jung, who I think clearly identifies the crucial practical distinction between what we take to be a representation of a known thing and what we take to be a representation of an unknown thing. His distinction does not reflect universal practice in the use of the two terms, but some such distinction needs to be made. Jung describes the distinction thus:

> *The concept of a symbol should, in my view, be strictly differentiated from that of a mere sign. Every view which interprets the symbolic expression as an analogous or abbreviated expression of a known thing is* **semiotic**. *A conception which interprets the symbolic expression as the best possible formulation of a relatively unknown thing which cannot conceivably, therefore, be more clearly or characteristically represented, is* **symbolic**.[7]

---

6   Though Dennett (1993) seems to have been more concerned about the singularity of the 'audience' in space and time than about its passivity.

7   Jung (1946) §815.

Jung gives the example of 'the winged wheel worn by railway employees' which may look like a symbol, but normally functions only as an identifier of railway employees. When we assume that a sign identifies a thing, and that is all there is to the sign, we confine ourselves to a disembodied representationalist understanding of the sign. However, when we recognize it as symbolic, we start to recognize the diffusion of interpretation by which every part of our bodies may contribute to our rich experience of the meaning of that symbol. Of course, the winged wheel may also sometimes operate as a symbol, for instance evoking a range of railway associations.

Deductive for inductive logic

The embodied perspective implies that when we reason, we link together claims that we acknowledge as having only an inexact and approximate relationship to each other. All reasoning must thus be provisional (or, in more traditional terms, 'inductive') in nature, since no matter how exact the relationship between logical symbols may appear, it is dependent on our interpretation for its relationship to things in the world. However, the denial of embodiment involves substituting for this imprecise inductive logic a precise deductive logic. We work on the assumption that the precise relationships between concepts in our constructed models must correspond to precise relationships in some kind of reality. I will return to this point below in 4.b.

Models for schemas

Meaning in embodied experience depends on image schemas and basic categories – that is, sets of associations that occur in types of experiences that we have as dynamic, active organisms.[8] For example, the experiences of walking along a path or packing objects into a container form schematic associations with a set of symbols (such as the words 'path', 'box', or 'in') that we then draw upon in other similar situations to give those symbols meaning. However, the denial of embodiment takes particular cognitive models that have been developed in dependence on these schemas, and uses *them* as an assumed basis of reality to provide abstract meaning.[9] Mathematics provides the strongest example of this, in which the presence of a schematic model is constantly denied in favour of

---

8   Johnson (2007) pp. 135–46.
9   Lakoff (1987) pp. 121–35.

Platonic absolutism.[10] Rather than using the experience of how we learned to count as the basis of meaning for numbers, for instance, we assume that numbers are essential to the structure of the universe. In the process, we lose awareness either that the model we are using is contingent, or that it depends on a schema.

Literalism for metaphors

The extension of embodied meaning from image schemas and basic categories to a wide range of language depends on the development of metaphor and metonymy. Metaphor is thus a basic and functional aspect of meaning, as our ability to find most symbols meaningful depends on an association that begins with a parallel between two contexts.[11] The denial of embodied meaning, however, is accompanied by literalism – that is, the assumption that terms get their meaning from a direct semantic relationship to the world they are describing. Metaphor is demoted to a peripheral ornament of literary language that is assumed to be reducible to a literal comparison.

Values for desires

The legacy of the denial of embodiment in ethics is the substitution of values for desires, with the assumption that they are fundamentally different. Values (whether ethical, aesthetic, prudential, social, or political) are usually understood as rationally defined commitments that are *opposed* to desire. However, our embodiment means that values are and must be desires, otherwise we would have no motivation for fulfilling them. The substitution implies that we then either end up denying the desires forming our values, or pretending that our desires are fully recruited to our rationalized principles, rather than addressing the psychological conflicts that can be created by the attempt to oblige oneself to do things that one does not entirely want to do.

Our unmotivated 'values' thus often end up as institutionalized failures, used for social signalling purposes, rather than goals that seriously motivate our judgements. There is thus widespread confusion about morality and its purpose, with the naturalists arguing that its purpose is one of signalling rather than of actual motivation,[12] and others continuing to insist on dogmatic values setting a rational

---

10   See Lakoff & Nuñez (2000).
11   Johnson (2007) ch. 7.
12   E.g. Sperber & Baumard (2012).

challenge that we call ethical, whether they work or not. There will not be space in this book to discuss these ethical aspects of the denial of embodiment (or their embodied alternatives) in any depth, but I have discussed them elsewhere, and am planning to do so again.[13]

Absolute belief for confidence

In the embodied perspective, cognitive and emotional meaning are inseparable, and our emotional confidence in a belief that is grounded in experience is indivisible from our degree of cognitive justification for it. As long as such beliefs remain non-absolute, they can be justified and acted upon to a degree, but remain provisional and open to challenge. However, the denial of embodiment involves the replacement of this incremental confidence with a knife edge of absolute belief, according to which a belief is either totally justified or totally unjustified, regardless of its relationship to our bodily and empirical confidence. As Plato (through his mouthpiece Socrates) puts it in one of the most revealing lines of his *Republic*, 'You can't use the imperfect as a measure of anything.'[14] In Plato's account through the character of Socrates, which basically offers a manifesto for the systematic absolutization of our thinking, the body betrays and imprisons the mind with its sensual uncertainty and connection to carnal appetites.[15] For Plato's many imitators ever since, 'relative' belief is still assumed to be somehow dependent on absolute belief, rather than the other way round: a pattern we can see in many contexts, from insistence on the primacy of mathematical models in science, to the belief still widespread amongst Buddhists that spiritual development is dependent on belief in the Buddha's total enlightenment.[16] At an everyday level, it is simply the requirement for complete answers sabotaging the effectiveness of our partial answers: the perfect being the enemy of the good.

Effort of will for integrated development

From an embodied perspective, effort is energy applied by the body (with inextricable mind) to a task. The more fully the energy is used, the more effective it is likely to be in fulfilling its goals, but the usage of that energy can be divided by conflict that reduces our ability to

13   i.7; VIII.
14   Plato *Republic* 504c: (1974) p. 241.
15   Plato: *Phaedo*: (1993).
16   Ellis (2020a) pp. 162–6.

achieve goals. Integrative development, by reducing that conflict, thus enables us to gradually extend both the goals we try to fulfil and our ability to fulfil them. The denial of embodiment, however, associated with absolute views, creates conflict, and distracts from the fact that it is reducing our ability to fulfil goals by the ideology of will. Wilful effort is energy that is applied to repress contrary beliefs, tensing and stressing the body unnecessarily in the process, and perhaps temporarily achieving goals despite contrary beliefs, but not sustainably. The dynamics and the evidence for these psychological phenomena will be explored in more detail in 5.a.

Supernaturalism for archetypal experience

What I describe as archetypal experience is a particular type of meaning: one in which our recurrent contact with particular symbols *inspires* us to recognize our potential for integration, and thus to continue practising to develop it. This process of inspiration, which I have discussed in detail elsewhere,[17] is entirely compatible with an embodied perspective, because it involves getting in touch with positive associations in our brain and nervous system. However, one of the darkest achievements of the denial of embodiment is to strongly associate that embodied process of inspiration with absolute beliefs. It makes little difference whether such absolute beliefs are 'natural' or 'supernatural', but supernaturalism is the form of absolutization that has hijacked religion and often turned it into a reinforcing feedback loop of projection (see 5.b) and substitution (see 5.d). As I will discuss further in 5.f, the same symbols that are used in absolute beliefs (particularly, and obviously, God), but *with greater contextualization,* can have a beneficial archetypal function.

---

17 Ellis (2022).

3.c. Discontinuity

> *Summary*
>
> Discontinuity in space, time, and conceptual space is a feature of absolutization due to the restriction of options in space. This is maintained by the over-dominance of left hemisphere sequencing over right hemisphere sustained attention, and makes us ignore the continuity of all organic processes. Although discontinuity is needed for practical judgement, absolutization takes this discontinuity out of that practical context.

I have already mentioned another crucial feature of absolutization that we can readily recognize by considering the conditions of embodiment: that is, the way in which the restriction of options also creates *discontinuity* in space and time. In 1.d I discussed the way that the absoluteness of negation creates binary discontinuities in space and time, such as 'either you cross the Rubicon or you don't'. Without that absoluteness of negation, we would experience an open and apparently infinite set of options for movement. I also suggested that insights into this point are found in the Buddhist teachings about impermanence and insubstantiality, and in the incrementality of the beach analogy, 'with no sudden penetration to final knowledge'. Much more can be said about discontinuity, though, as a feature of absolutization that can be made clearer from an embodied perspective. The perspective that augments our immediate experience with most clarity here is that of neuroscience.

The ability to experience continuity in both space and time is dependent on sustained attention, a property of the right hemisphere of the brain, which is connected to the senses and imagination. Studies of patients with lesions in left and right hemispheres have shown the dependence of continuity of attention on the right hemisphere.[1] This continuity of sustained attention can be experienced in mindfulness, where it is rooted in bodily awareness. It needs to be contrasted with *sequencing*, which is a left hemisphere organizational ability. As Iain McGilchrist writes:

> *Sequencing, in the sense of the ordering of artificially decontextualized, unrelated, momentary events, or momentary interruptions of temporal flow – the kind of thing that is as well or better performed by the left hemisphere – is not*

1   Harrington, Haaland, & Knight (1998).

> *in fact a measure of the sense of time at all. It is precisely what takes over* when the sense of time breaks down. *Time is essentially an undivided flow: the left hemisphere's tendency to break it up into units and make machines to measure it may succeed in deceiving us that it is a sequence of static points, but such a sequence never approaches the nature of time, however close it gets.*[2]

Although I think McGilchrist is incautious in phrasing this as a claim about what time 'essentially' is, it is clear that the embodied experience of time (or of movement through space) via the right hemisphere has a markedly different quality to the representational treatment of time through the left hemisphere. The right is patient, the left impatient. The right is mindful, the left distracted by its concern with goal-motivated representations. The right is *continuous*, or incremental, whilst the left hemisphere experience is *discontinuous*.

Although it is the right hemisphere that gives us access to this continuous embodied experience of time passing, all the indications seem to be that continuity is a feature of bodily, or organic, life, and discontinuity is our conceptual overlaying onto this continuity. Continuity is a feature of organic, and indeed non-organic physical, processes: the growth of a plant, the growth of a child, the rusting of a piece of iron, the movement of a planet through space. Some processes happen more quickly than others, but fast processes are the result of systems reaching a tipping point of rapid change (death is an obvious example), not of instantaneous change.[3] Even death is a process, even if we impose a model of instantaneous change on what we observe by formalizing a 'moment of death'.

Organic processes do not seem to proceed in a series of jerks from one static position to another, but rather they *flow* continuously. In principle we could capture them in a series of frames like those of a cine film (or the analysis in Zeno's paradoxes), but to capture the full complexity of what is occurring, we would need an apparently infinite number of frames – so we cannot do this in practice. Rather, we have to accept the inability of discontinuous sequencing to track the living experience of sustained attention.

*Dis*continuity needs to be seen against this background of continuity as the organic norm. Clearly not all discontinuity is absolutization, but rather discontinuity is a feature of left hemisphere processing for representation and action. In order to be able to act,

---

2   McGilchrist (2009) p. 76.
3   II.3.b.

we have to assume a certain state of affairs that we can act in, in which not only our goals stay still, but also our means, and all other background conditions relevant to achieving those goals. Even if we are able to rapidly update our representations as we act, as a football player does when moving across a pitch with the ball whilst taking into account the movements of the other players nearby, our continuous updating is dependent on our earlier judgements rather than starting from scratch. Discontinuity is thus a practical requirement in judgement, but absolutization occurs when we take our discontinuous *representations* to be the whole story, ceasing to pay any attention to the continuity in the background. In hemispheric terms, this probably involves an *over-dominance* of the left hemisphere, whereby it inhibits the right hemisphere to an extent that prevents it from responding to new information from the right.

This need for some discontinuity is also recognized in cognitive psychology as the *need for closure*. Arie Kruglanski, in his *Psychology of Closed-Mindedness*,[4] points out that both closed- and open-mindedness are essential for our practical functioning. However, he also distinguishes usefully between 'freezing' (the necessary discontinuity for decision-making) and 'seizing' (the defence of a judgement as permanent): it is clearly the latter that is equivalent to absolutization, with discontinuity in the process of judgement being necessary but not sufficient for it. Kruglanski also points out rightly that too much open-mindedness can be problematic, because it prevents practically necessary closure. So absolutization should not be identified solely with closure in the process of judgement.

As a feature of absolutization, then, discontinuity involves a dichotomy imposed on a continuous experience *that is assumed to be a representation of reality*. It is thus not the discontinuity created by the act of making a judgement, but discontinuity in the content, that is most significant, this discontinuity in the content also correlating with prematurity in the closure of the judgement. If we manage to maintain awareness of more than two opposing options (see 1.d) before we make a practical judgement, we are able to do so provisionally, but if we exclude those alternative options – of which there are a potentially infinite number given continuity as our organic position – we absolutize. This discontinuity can take the form of an assumed absolute boundary in various metaphorically

4   Kruglanski (2004).

related representations: in space, in time, or in conceptual space. For example, we could absolutize a spatial boundary such as a national border; we could absolutize a point in time before which the Golden Age allegedly occurred; we can absolutize in conceptual space by applying a rigid metaphorical boundary – for instance by absolutizing anyone who is politically further to the right than a particular hated conservative figure.

Discontinuity is one of the most readily identifiable features of absolutization in the conceptual content of our thought, the test being *whether the concepts we are using are capable of incremental interpretation*. If we are capable of thinking of them as a matter of degree, as qualities on a spectrum in metaphorical space, then it is evident that absolutized negation is not taking place, because new options are being introduced as we reflect. These new options also provide a wider provisional context for any discontinuous practical judgements we may be making. However, if we believe that the only *possible* alternative to one belief is a dualistic opposite, and that the conceptual framing we are using for this *must* be correct, this offers a straightforward test for absolutization. This is one test I apply, for instance, in determining that metaphysical beliefs are always absolutized (see 4.a) – because they are always either true or false, not capable of conceptual interpretation as a matter of degree. For example, either God exists or God does not exist: the conceptual framing of the debate about God's existence does not allow us to apply an incremental model in which God exists to some extent. Indeed, this is the case for any claim about 'existence' whatsoever.

A simple example of the damaging effects of discontinuity is that of racism. When thinking about human skin colours, we can imagine a spectrum in conceptual space. These skin colours, or other obvious racial features, are the effects of complex factors, mainly those of genetic inheritance. However, in order to maintain a racist belief, one has to be able to apply an absolute discontinuity so that one 'knows' who is in the rejected racial out-group as opposed to the accepted racial in-group. The concepts of 'black' and 'white' are imposed on a complex range of what should often be more closely described as pinky-brown colouring. To reject complexity, in the southern US the 'one drop' rule (that one drop of black blood was enough to make you black) was frequently applied to determine the in-group and out-group. Of course, we can make provisional judgements based on approximate skin colour when appropriate (for instance, concerning the effects of exposure to sunlight and vitamin D absorption), but I will not need to elaborate for most readers, to point out the negative effects of this discontinuity applied in an unconditional way in all sorts of contexts, including slavery, discrimination, and (in India) caste rigidity.

However, the value of pointing out discontinuity as a feature of absolutization, in interdependence with all the other features, is that not only these more obvious examples, but also more subtle and long-term ones, can be more readily understood in connection with each other. Absolutized discontinuity about everyday matters (such as rejected foods, unfavoured garden areas, or decontextualized construction measurements) can have effects, but rather than knowing that they are always negative in ways that we can easily recognize, we can identify that we have not applied as full a complexity to our judgement as we might have done, increasing the likelihood of neglected conditions subsequently affecting us in unwanted ways. The more other features of absolutization we can identify along with discontinuity, the more confident we can be in this judgement.

3.d. Interpretation

> *Summary*
>
> Embodiment provides a wider context to help us distinguish whether statements that are apparently absolute in content are *psychologically* absolutizing. The presence of conditionality, practicality, or a focus on meaning all provide contextual indications of non-absolutizing. Individual words or symbols also cannot be absolute by themselves unless they represent a belief. Nevertheless, absolutization can in practice be identified quite clearly in many contexts.

How do we judge what is or is not an absolute claim? It would be very easy to adopt a superficial interpretation of absolutization and use it to start 'policing' other people's language for particular forbidden words, as has occurred in some of the more unfortunate manifestations of 'political correctness' that have caused such a reaction from the right in recent years. To guard against this, I think it is important to interpret the issue of how we identify absolute claims in the wider context offered by embodied meaning. Since absoluteness depends on psychological states in interdependent relationship with philosophical content, we cannot simply read off the presence of absolutization from that content without taking psychological states into account. Of course, there is also often room for doubt in judging others' psychological states, and potential for self-delusion in assessing our own. A principle of charity is thus often appropriate, assuming the best in ambiguous cases because that is more likely to be a practically helpful policy. Unless it is clear that absolutization is taking place, not only from the content of the propositions used but from their context, it may be preferable to assume that it is not, so as to avoid any further conflict that might be created by mistaken objections to assumed absolutization.

Aspects of the context of apparently absolute propositions that may *prevent* them from being absolute include conditionality, practicality, and meaning-focus. All of these in one or another way may provide a wider context of provisionality to propositions that might otherwise be absolute.

Conditionality is the most directly intellectual and linguistic of these three ways of avoiding absolutization whilst using some of its language. We are conditional if we discuss a given situation with a second level of language used explicitly to raise awareness of a possible alternative to the absolutized level. Whether or not we actually use the term 'if', to discuss absolutes conditionally we examine them 'as if' they were the case without taking them for granted. A conditional approach like this allows us to explore and discuss absolute beliefs, as I am here, without holding them. The mention and discussion of absolute beliefs, or even the generalization of beliefs about them, does not necessarily indicate absolutization itself, as no representational assumption, restriction of options, or infinite rationalization need be going on.

Conditionality adds an additional level of awareness to a statement, which can make it part of an exploratory learning process, as shown for instance by Ellen Langer's research. In one of Langer's experiments, students were separated into three groups and each given a lesson on the same content (urban development), but presented either absolutely, conditionally, or as 'one possible model'. They were then given a test to attempt to measure how well they were able to use the information presented. Those who received the information conditionally, with sources emphasizing how it was relevant only in a particular context and comparing it to other possible contexts, were able to make much more creative use of it than those who had received it either absolutely, or even 'as one possible model' without any direct awareness of alternatives.[1]

Practicality also provides a different kind of context to our interpretation of apparently absolute expressions – one of implicit provisionality in relation to a shared goal, which may never be articulated by those involved, but is shared in the social context in which communication takes place. Practicality creates a distinction between two different uses of the term 'necessity', practical and philosophical. If a more experienced craftsperson tells another less experienced one that 'careful measurement is absolutely required' before cutting, we do not need to take the 'absolutely' or the 'required' absolutely, because they do not involve a general representational claim – only a specific one in relation to the task.

Where this point becomes most debatable is where it is claimed that propositions that are explicitly absolute in form (even in the context of philosophy or theology) are practical in application. This, for instance, is the contradiction in the early pragmatist philosopher William James' supposedly pragmatic approach to religion.

1   Langer (2014) pp. 125-6.

> *On pragmatic principles we cannot reject any hypothesis if consequences useful to life flow from it. Universal conceptions, as things to take account of, may be as real for pragmatism as particular sensations are. They have, indeed, no meaning and no reality if they have no use. But if they have any use they have that amount of meaning…. The use of the Absolute is proved by the whole course of men's religious history.*[2]

Writing in 1907, James here shows no appreciation of the negative practical effects of absolutization that is *not* practically contextualized, nor does he give us any clear way of distinguishing the 'use' from the abuse of the Absolute. Nevertheless, he does give what at first seems an inspiring account of what I would call the archetypal function of absolutes (see 5.f) when suitably contextualized:

> *The you so glorified, to which the hymn is sung, may mean your better possibilities phenomenally taken, or the specific redemptive effects even of your failures, upon yourself or others. It may mean your loyalty to the possibilities of others whom you admire and love so that you are willing to accept your own poor life, for it is that glory's partner. You can at least appreciate, applaud, furnish the audience, of so brave a total world. Forget the low in yourself, then, think only of the high.*[3]

However, the final sentence even in this rousing passage betrays the remaining danger. Thinking only of the 'high' and forgetting the 'low' can rapidly lead us into an idealization that does not actually afford a practical context. A practical context requires both a problem and a solution, a starting point and a mode of improvement, with both needing to be held in practical tension. It is thus not sufficient simply to assert that the Absolute can be useful, nor to describe its effects in such a selective way as to forget the flip side – for instance the horrors of Islamic State with which I began my introduction. I thus find James' view of the 'use' of religion alarmingly naïve. Whilst a 'practical' context in the restrictive sense of craft is quite easy to envisage, a long-term one requires a much more rigorous critical awareness of the ongoing tension between conditions and ideals, and of how to maintain that creative tension – the Middle Way, in fact. I will be discussing the parameters of this more fully from section 7 of this book onwards.

A focus on meaning may also provide a different kind of contextuality to an apparently absolute claim, especially in the arts, and also

---

2   James (1981) p. 123.
3   Ibid. p. 125.

sometimes in religion. Most people, unfortunately still encouraged by most philosophers, do not appreciate that there is any distinction between meaning and belief (except, perhaps, in particular provisional spaces, such as novels and films) and constantly conflate belief with meaning. Phrases such as 'I understood the true reality of my life' or 'God guides me in every step' may in many cases refer primarily to the speaker's *meaningful experience* of new insight or potential – a type of experience I would describe as archetypal (see 5.f). It is primarily the poverty of existing discourse around the interpretation of such experiences, and their continuing dominance by traditions dominated by absolutism, that causes many people to continue to discuss them in absolutized terms, when there is no necessity to do so. In interpreting such language, it is crucial not to automatically leap to the conclusion that they must necessarily be absolutizing. The absolutizing is not a function of their experience itself, but of the way it has been interpreted in a cultural system that allows it to be used for purposes of dominance (see 5.e).

In this connection, it is also helpful to recall that absolutizing beliefs are ones that can only be expressed in propositions. Single words, symbols, or terms cannot by themselves be absolutizations. Even if we have a strong association between a particular word or symbol and absolute beliefs (e.g. God), it does not follow that the word or symbol by itself is absolute – indeed, it is incapable of being absolute *by itself* without an accompanying proposition attempting to represent a belief. The meaning of the single word 'God' can be interpreted in embodied terms, and the assumption that talk about God of any kind must be absolutizing fails to take into account the specific set of conditions and assumptions that are practically necessary for absolutization. The only exception to this is when a word by itself actually refers to belief in a proposition, so is actually a shorthand for referring to that belief within the terms of a particular cognitive model: thus, for instance, 'theism' can be absolute because it is (usually) a shortcut for the belief that 'God exists'.

Despite these caveats of interpretation, there are still plenty of cases where it is almost impossible not to interpret a proposition, even in its context, as absolute. These include cases where there is an explicit context of belief involved, as for instance in the reciting of a creed, or a philosophical discussion. When an absolute claim is used deductively to justify another one, linked by what are taken to be unassailable logical relationships (see 5.b), one's understanding of both claims as absolute is redoubled. When absolute claims are defended with *ad hoc* rationalization (see 5.c), are claimed to be independent of experience (see 2.b), are justified using an infallible source,[4] show themselves to be fragile in the face of challenge (see 2.c), or are used as tools of power and group conformity (see 5.e), the weight of evidence that we are dealing with an absolutization becomes ever stronger. The need for contextual interpretation should not be used to let dogmatists off the hook, whether the dogmatists are others, or ourselves.

---

4   iv.3.e; V.2.

4. Philosophy

4.a. Metaphysics

> *Summary*
>
> Metaphysics is equivalent to absolutization because it involves claims about reality inaccessible to experience, so is discontinuous and dogmatic. Sceptical argument and philosophy of science offer tools that can help make some impression on it. Heidegger's failed attempt to save it involved disguised sceptical argument. Merely philosophical arguments against it in logical positivism and postmodernism have failed, due to their lack of any systemic, embodied, or practical perspective.

Having surveyed three major approaches that can contribute much support to understanding absolutization (Buddhism, systems, and embodiment), I can now no longer put off tackling some of the central sources of resistance in Western philosophical tradition. 'Philosophy' in the broadest sense is just a discourse in which our core assumptions can be considered and challenged (and in that broader sense I'm happy to call myself a 'philosopher'). Philosophical education still to some extent inducts one into this broad discourse. However, in a narrower sense, 'Western philosophy' offers a tradition of dominant approaches that entrench absolutization and try to make it seem unavoidable. Although there is no undisputed philosophical position, there is very often an undisputed *framing* in which pairs of absolutes (as discussed in 1.c) maintain an unquestionable unholy alliance. For instance in the mind vs body 'debate' you can choose between mind-body dualism, mental monism (all is mind) or physical monism (all is body), but what you cannot do is question the conceptual distinction between mind and body or its importance. If you attempt to do so, the philosophers will immediately put you into one of the metaphysical categories and insist that that is what you must mean, because long training has apparently made it impossible for them to consider thinking outside categories formatted in terms of the distinction. This narrow and damaging tradition limits people's thinking under the guise of broadening it, and remains damaging despite the marginal ways that some philosophers have tried to question it.

This tradition is far more intellectually important than might be deduced from the proportion of people who actually study philosophy explicitly, because it largely proceeds by analysing and/or rationalizing widespread intuitions about such issues as 'truth', 'knowledge', 'meaning', or 'good'. These intuitions are shared by other academics and thus passed on by them to those they teach or otherwise influence (e.g. through writing or broadcasting). Mainstream academics in the natural and social sciences thus often reflect such mainstream philosophical stances uncritically when they discuss philosophical issues, but without considering philosophical assumptions. Indeed, most influential philosophy now takes place outside philosophy departments, for instance in the guise of social, political, or cultural theory, management theory, or high-level scientific discussion.

Apart from the philosophy of meaning and language, which I have already discussed in 3.a, the central areas of philosophy that most strongly entrench absolutization are metaphysics and logic, although all other areas of philosophy are also affected by the assumptions made in these. Indeed, the philosophy of meaning and language has been formed on metaphysical assumptions, largely because metaphysics came first in the chronological development of Western philosophy.

By 'metaphysics' I mean claims that are taken to represent a reality beyond experience. The term is thus practically synonymous with 'ontology', and the verb 'to be', used in a final sense, figures strongly in metaphysical claims. 'There is freewill', 'The world is really a place of suffering', or 'The cup is really there' could thus all be metaphysical claims. Whether they are *intended* to be metaphysical claims needs to be subject to a contextuality check. Terms like 'is' and 'really' can also be used in provisional ways framed by conditionality, practicality, or a focus on meaning (see 3.d). 'The cup is really there', for instance, could have been preceded by 'I could have sworn I put that cup on the table in the next room', and accompanied by a gesture of relief pointing at the cup in this room. Nevertheless, claims about 'existence' that are *not* thus contextualized are metaphysical. Philosophical traditions are riddled with such claims, in the Western tradition from the Pre-Socratics onwards. For instance, Parmenides claimed that reality is unchanging, whilst

Heraclitus claimed that reality is always changing, both regardless of our experience of change and stability.

In practice, the terms 'absolute' and 'metaphysical' are, I would argue, interchangeable, but problems are caused by the different ways that metaphysics has been understood. Some of these ways are not consistently absolute, or involve a confusion of absolute and non-absolute features. If one understands metaphysics consistently as attempting to represent a reality inaccessible to experience, metaphysical claims clearly have all the features of absolutization that I have already discussed. This 'reality' constantly runs before any experience we may offer, with the potential to defy it, offering infinite scope for rationalization (see 4.d below). The very concept of 'reality' is discontinuous and involves a restriction of the options (see 1.d): we cannot have a 'more real' or 'more true' claim – it is either real or it is not. Metaphysics as an absolute thus always gives birth to its opposite – claims about falsehood and unreality that lie just as much beyond experience as those about truth and reality.

If metaphysics is identified with claims about reality, we can question it using epistemology, which I would understand as the investigation of how we justify our *beliefs* (not just our 'knowledge'). The most practical and helpful aspects of epistemology for identifying and avoiding absolutization are sceptical argument and the epistemology of science. Sceptical argument makes us aware of the unavoidable uncertainty of the embodied human condition, for instance by pointing out the limitation of our senses, the dependence of our beliefs on prior assumptions, or the impossibility of disproving that we might be deluded in any specific belief we may have.[1] Provided one avoids the interpretation of scepticism in the frame of absolutization, it is merely a prompt to provisionality, a thoroughly *practical* set of arguments that has been wrongly interpreted by far too many Western philosophers as impractical. We see this practicality illustrated in the Pyrrhonist and Buddhist traditions where sceptical argument was first used. The target of these practical sceptical arguments was metaphysics, not provisional beliefs of a kind that are compatible with uncertainty.

The epistemology of science, unlike analytic epistemology (which merely engages in intuition-mongering about 'knowledge' and associated concepts), deals with practical beliefs that people already

1   i.1.a & b; II.1.

hold, and asks how well they are justified. Science has developed a whole set of procedures for improving the justification of our beliefs, through evidence, but sceptical argument makes us aware that any scientific generalization can be subsequently falsified by a 'black swan' – a new observation that goes against all those made so far. This (along with the limitations of the language it uses and the embodied limitations of scientists) makes it clear that science can only ever access provisionally justified belief, not metaphysical truth. Such key figures as Imre Lakatos[2] and Thomas Kuhn,[3] through historical investigation of how scientific method is actually used successfully, showed how greater justification is offered by the fruitfulness of paradigms that offer a variety of ways of being tested.[4] They thus offered an alternative paradigm to the suffocating obsession with 'truth' and 'knowledge' of the metaphysical philosophers: one that emerged directly out of successful practical experience and showed justification to be *a matter of degree*.

However, this model of metaphysics as dogmatic absolutization that is challenged by epistemology (or at least some aspects of it) is in turn challenged by the Heideggerian tradition that prefers to put things entirely the other way round. For Heidegger, philosophy is metaphysics, but what he means by that is intended to challenge dogma. He describes philosophy as 'universal phenomenal ontology',[5] that refines experience into a holistic understanding of 'Being', whilst it is epistemology that is seen as betraying experience by debating our 'knowledge' of specific objects. There are ways that we can be provisional in our holism and dogmatic in our particularity, but it is the dependence of metaphysics on representationalism, not its holism, that makes metaphysics unavoidably absolutizing. Whether we see 'reality' as whole or part, as subject or object, or both or neither, it lies beyond our experience and beyond the grounding of language in our bodies. It is epistemology that is at least capable of asking critical questions about supposed representations of reality, and it is thus revealing that many of Heidegger's supposedly 'ontological' critical points are disguised epistemology. For instance, he is critical of the belief that we can understand the world in terms of explicit rule-governed language, that we have a

2   Lakatos (1974).
3   Kuhn (1996).
4   See 10.a below, also Ellis (2001) 2.b.iii.
5   Heidegger (1962) p. 62.

representation of the world in our minds, that we can have a God's eye view, or that there are independent building blocks out of which we can construct our understanding of the world:[6] all of these are sceptical arguments that make us aware of uncertainty. It seems likely that Heidegger himself later came to realize that his inversion of the relationship between metaphysics and epistemology was unsuccessful, as he could not offer any account of 'Being' without falling into the traditional dogmas of metaphysics. He abandoned the projected Division 3 of Part 1 of *Being and Time* in which he intended to offer a phenomenological account of being as a whole, destroying the manuscript that he originally produced,[7] and later turned to theology instead.[8]

Two philosophical movements of the twentieth century – logical positivism and postmodernism – have had a sense of there being a problem with metaphysics, but neither of them has consistently rejected representationalism, nor incorporated the implications of embodied meaning into their perspective. The logical positivists claimed that metaphysical claims are 'literally senseless',[9] because they lack verifiability: in A.J. Ayer's terms, that means that no observation is relevant to making them more probable.[10] As I will argue in 4.c and 4.d, this is correct in its identification of the impermeability of metaphysical claims to observation, which we can identify philosophically as circular or dogmatic justification. It is also a sign of the assumed independence of such claims from the wider system, as well as the reinforcing feedback loop employed in their justification. Some members of the logical positivist Vienna Circle even started to recognize the relationship between metaphysical belief and repression, describing metaphysics as *Kampfmittel* – fuel for conflict.[11]

However, the logical positivists were mistaken in their representationalism of meaning, which they relied on when they attempted to base meaning on potential justification. This completely bypasses the embodied basis of meaning, and ignores the dependence of propositions on the cognitive models, metaphors, and schemas that make those propositions meaningful to us in experience. In

6   Summarized by Dreyfus (1991) pp. 4–7.
7   Polt (1999) pp. 36–7.
8   Solomon (1972) pp. 238–43.
9   Ayer (1971) p. 8.
10 Ibid. ch. 1.
11 Edmonds (2020) p. 140.

the process, the logical positivists were unable to understand how moral or religious symbols are meaningful, despite the very obvious experience that we all have of them actually being meaningful to us. They were apparently led by the strength of their dogmatic commitment to representationalism to even deny their own obvious experience, by imposing a fact-value distinction in which only 'factual' claims could be meaningful and other sorts of claims only appeared to be so!

The logical positivist enterprise is a sharp reminder of the dangers into which any attempt to avoid absolutization may fall if it begins only with a partial diagnosis of the problem, and is not constantly alert to the possibility of perpetuating further absolutization. Its cure is pretty much as bad as the disease. The logical positivists only identified the problem with metaphysics partially, because they adopted a merely philosophical approach to it, seeing it as an issue in the justification of propositions that could be sufficiently analysed at a linguistic level. They apparently did not consider the psychological processes that underlie these linguistic indicators, not only because of over-specialization but because of the relatively limited development of psychology in their time.

The logical positivists saw that some philosophical stances were dogmatic, because such stances had a self-perpetuating tendency to block off new experience, but in response they sought alternative foundations that ended up being equally dogmatic. It is possible that if logical positivism had not become so attached to verificationism, it might have evolved into a more adequate doctrine. Darren Bradley argues that Rudolf Carnap's early account of logical positivism does not depend on verificationism and could stand without it, being based only on the epistemic recognition that metaphysical claims cannot be *justified*.[12] However, there was an unavoidable urge for the logical positivists to find alternative absolute grounds for scientific claims to accompany their rejection of metaphysics.

The alternative foundations provided by verificationism created a dogmatic view of science, which became discontinuously justified in a way that non-scientific assertions were not, due to being (representationally) 'meaningful'. Dogmatic assumptions about meaning underwrote their equally dogmatic dismissal of the value of ethics, religion, and aesthetics. Even where scientific claims were

12 Bradley (2017).

concerned, their over-dependence on linguistic analysis left them open to all kinds of merely analytic objections. If you load your expectations of meaning onto the relationship between propositions and reality, you have to get those propositions right in order for them (apparently) even to be meaningful, and of course they never are quite right, because there will be further conditions not taken into account by those propositions.

The logical positivists illustrate that it does not help us to overcome positive metaphysics by introducing negative metaphysics. At best, this can be part of a necessary reaction whose value becomes more evident when it is seen as part of a dialectical process of disengagement. We may need to think in terms of negative metaphysics (purely in the sense of metaphysical beliefs opposed to the ones we held before) at a particular point in our development, in order to break through to a point where we are no longer justifying our beliefs through metaphysics, but this will be a temporary stage in development whose value is only evident in relation to the next stage.[13] Furthermore, it will not necessarily help us to eliminate some forms of metaphysics but not others, if we have not adopted the provisional, agnostic, and even-handed approaches that are needed to free ourselves from it more broadly. Arguably, the logical positivists did free themselves from the dogmas of rationalism and moral absolutism. However, the weight that they then put on representationalism just meant that another form of metaphysics substituted for the previous ones (see 5.d). Freeing oneself from metaphysics does not demand only assertiveness and courage, but also a patient, embodied practical process in which our new positions are also subject to the same scrutiny as the old.

The other recent philosophical movement that has recognized a problem with metaphysics is postmodernism. To go much into the complexities of postmodernism would require a book in itself, but its attempts to address the problem of metaphysics deserve at least a brief acknowledgement here. This response often has similar limitations to those of logical positivism, in the sense that solutions are one-sided rather than even-handed, linear rather than dialectical. Where logical positivists diagnosed the problem of metaphysics as due to a lack of representational verifiability, postmodernists have often seen it much more as an all-pervasive feature of 'narrative'.

---

13 See Ellis (2019) pp. 165-9.

'Narrative' exploits the human tendency to identify with the hero in a story[14] to project an unquestioned set of assumed metaphysical truths where none could otherwise be found. Jean-Francois Lyotard, for instance, identifies such deluding 'narrative' not only in religion, but also in the legitimation of scientific knowledge, and even in the use of pragmatic arguments.[15] In some ways this postmodernist critique of metaphysics resembles mine in questioning representationalism (see 3.a) and also recognizing the ways that absolutization is a tool of power (see 5.e). However, its analysis of the problem is far too solely dependent on the linguistic level, and is also subject to the 'nirvana fallacy' of criticizing a failed solution without offering any alternative.

Postmodernism in general tends to leave us with a 'flat', relativist view of the world as all linguistic surface, captured by the postmodernist theologian Don Cupitt in the image of the long-legged fly from W.B Yeats' poem of that name.[16] The long-legged fly is a pond skater that sits on the surface tension of the water without entering its depths, and in the same way the postmodernist view is that to avoid delusion one sits contentedly on the surface of language, not attempting to pierce beyond that surface (in Richard Rorty's terms, rejecting 'pre-linguistic consciousness'[17]). What I have always found odd about this image for postmodernism is that in Yeats' poem 'the mind moves upon silence' – suggesting to me a state of mind in which proliferating feedback loops have been suspended. Anyone who has experienced anything like such a state in meditation may be aware that it is not the total 'silence' of language itself that is its most significant feature, but rather the obsessive or anxious states that drive the repetitive *use* of language in our thinking. The idea that language has 'depth' of meaning is a representationalist fallacy built on the literalization of a metaphor. This metaphor is that *change in bodily state is depth*. When we experience changes that we experience in our bodies, we talk of these as 'deep' changes. Postmodernists have recognized that these experiences are not literally 'deep'. However, the avoidance of 'depth' for linguistic 'surface' is just a negative absolutization of that metaphor – one that entrenches its literalization even more than before. We still have

---

14   See Ellis (2022) 4.c.
15   Lyotard (1984); Ellis (2001) 4.h.vi.
16   Cupitt (1989).
17   Rorty (1989) p. 21.

experiences in our bodies, whether or not we are over-literalistic in the ways we ascribe words to those experiences, and those experiences are still prior to linguistic meaning rather than created by it. Postmodernists tend to regard psychological accounts of our mental states as just another kind of 'narrative', but that fails to take into account their additional value when brought into dialogue with practical, systemic, and embodied perspectives.

The 'flatness' of postmodernism is also its relativism. Its criticisms of representationalism in meaning are superficial because they involve Wittgensteinian accounts of meaning that reduce it to communicative function in social groups. This approach to meaning does not avoid representationalism, as I have argued elsewhere,[18] merely substituting the representation of a social state of affairs as the basis of meaning for a picture of the world. In dependence on such an account of meaning, our beliefs of all kinds are also seen as merely socially and linguistically dependent. There being no criterion of value that can help us to distinguish between different socially-justified beliefs, we are left with relativism (in the sense that all beliefs are of equal value). It is important to note that this relativism continues to have all the features of absolutization. The assumed system independence is that of mutually sealed-off 'language games', and the reinforcing feedback loops of justification are those often described as 'nihilism'. It is assumed that there is no justifiable value because there is no absolute value, because the only allowable criterion for value is that of absolute value, therefore there is no justifiable value. At best, then, postmodernists then fall back on 'irony', or liberal democracy,[19] or just the intellectual value of deconstructing grand narratives. Grand narratives do, indeed, need deconstructing: but we also need positive alternatives.

Merely philosophical objections to metaphysics, then, have done nothing to avoid metaphysics. Due to the absence of any practical, embodied, or systemic perspective, they have perpetuated metaphysics in forms that merely relativize the 'reality' beyond phenomena or assume its non-existence, rather than offering any kind of provisional perspective that comes to terms both with the hopeful and the limiting aspects of our embodiment. Caught up in the same

18   Ellis (2001) 4.e.ii.
19   Here my dominant example is Richard Rorty (1989). Rorty's view of meaning can be interpreted as expressivist rather than representationalist (see iii.3.e; IV.3), but the effect of perpetuating metaphysics negatively is the same.

framework as the absolute philosophers they rejected, relativist philosophers have failed to shift the grounds of argument. As a result, metaphysics in philosophy has not been dealt the death-blows it deserves. Rather it continues to flourish on university curricula both within philosophy and beyond it, not just as a critical exercise, but as one where metaphysical beliefs are seriously put forward.

Philosophical apologies for metaphysics invariably focus not on the practical, embodied situation of a person making judgements that may or may not include metaphysical beliefs, but rather entirely on the content of the metaphysical beliefs themselves, sustained by their circular relationships to other metaphysical claims in metaphysical discourse, and the impotence of other arguments with metaphysical presuppositions to dislodge them. Metaphysical attacks on metaphysics produce only paradox. One needs instead to be completely clear that *the alternative to metaphysics is provisionality*, realized in the mental and bodily states of a person who is willing to recognize uncertainty about ultimate 'truths' as the basic condition of human experience, who is using language provisionally because they are open to alternative frames, and who regards that provisionality as a matter of *practice*.

The most common argument used in such philosophical apologies is that metaphysics is in some sense inevitable, which I will discuss below in 4.e. However, the absoluteness of metaphysics is largely self-perpetuating as a matter of culture and habit. Its proponents are unlikely to be persuaded out of it by argument when they have had many years of practice in thinking that way. It is probably bodily work that can best help to create the conditions for thinking beyond metaphysics, particularly mindfulness practice, which helps us to directly experience the contingency of our assumptions, plus the intense stickiness of those we are inclined to absolutize.

4.b. The Absoluteness of Deductive Logic

> *Summary*
>
> Absolute deductive logic is believed in absolutizing thought to link together metaphysical claims in chains of certainty. Such logic was shown by Hume to be uninformative about the world. It can instead only be used critically to show inconsistency, whilst induction allows incremental justification of beliefs. Changing logical systems does not help with this, as it is the absoluteness of our interpretation of logic that is the problem. Absolutization tends to make us over-inflate logic's usefulness in claims about fallacies, rationality, or 'reasons' in the world.

Metaphysics as an aspect of absolutization is accompanied by an equally absolute set of assumptions about the necessary links between propositions. Just as metaphysics requires a representationalist set of assumptions in which meaning comes from the relationships between propositions and reality, logic requires an equally representationalist set of assumptions to link those propositions together in relationships of entailment – that is, relationships whereby if proposition A is true, proposition B must also be true. The appeal to hypothetical truth (or falsity) to bind together two propositions in an entailment relationship is exactly the same as the one required for metaphysics. We are then not dealing with an entailment relationship between *experiences of a body*, as in that case, there would be degrees of probability and commitment rather than a model based on necessary relationships between 'true' and 'false' propositions. Instead we are dealing with assumed or projected relationships that lie beyond any such experience: a linking of 'realities'.

This is the model of *deductive* logic, and philosophy traditionally goes some way towards acknowledging the difficulties by introducing another type of logic – inductive. Inductive logic, unlike deductive, allows for the derivation of merely probabilistic belief from experience: classically, we see a large number of swans that are white and conclude 'All swans are white'. The gap between deduction and induction creates the philosophical 'problem of induction', which just consists in the recognition that induction does not measure up to the supposed certainty of deduction. 'All swans are white' we are told, is uncertain because inductively derived from observations, whilst '2+2=4' is certain because deductive.

It was David Hume who recognized here that the problem is not that of induction failing to measure up to the perfection of deduction, but of deduction lacking the engagement with experience that induction offers. His 'fork' distinguishes 'abstract reasoning concerning quantity and number' from 'experimental reasoning concerning matters of fact and existence', and he urges us to consign any attempts at abstract reasoning on matters of fact 'to the flames: for it can contain nothing but sophistry and delusion'.[1] The abstract reasoning of mathematics, for all its rigorous coherence, is uninformative without assumptions concerning the world we experience (which it then merely quantifies and analyses), whereas the world of inductive reasoning, for all its imperfection, is at least informative about matters that reach beyond our prior assumptions. It is perceiving this simple point, in the teeth of centuries of dogmatic rationalism, that constitutes Hume's genius.

Deductive relationships follow the account of absolutization offered so far by forming a closed system obeying consistent rules. In order for one claim to be deduced from another, we have to assume a consistency of meaning of supposed signs between them. This ignores the embodiment of the people understanding the propositions, as discussed in section 3 above. We also have to assume the relationships between those people to be a closed system, of a kind that is inconsistent with our understanding of systems. For example, in a simple logical syllogism such as 'Felix is a cat; cats are carnivores; so Felix must be a carnivore' we have to assume that the meanings of 'Felix', 'cat', and 'carnivore' remain absolutely consistent for all time for whoever may read and consider this syllogism. However, individuals (and our understanding of them) change – we may turn out to have been wrong about Felix being a cat (he may be a cartoon character, or a composer!). The boundaries of what counts as a cat depend on shifting and contested definitional boundaries in biology, as does the definition of a carnivore (What proportion of one's diet has to be meat? What counts as meat?). Even if our formal definitions are identical, our associations with the terms, and thus their meanings, remain different: some people worship cats, and others hate them. Different individuals with different experiences

---

1 Hume (1975) §132.

may have very different understandings of the terms of this syllogism, and the commonality of their understanding depends on shared cultural assumptions. Deductive logic can only be assumed to form absolute relationships by ignoring embodiment, yet it has been assumed to do so by a great many philosophers, mathematicians, and others through the ages.

Although we cannot use absolute deductive logic to justify absolute statements, it can be used *critically* to show how a set of beliefs is inconsistent, a chain of reasoning is not logically necessary, or an absolutized belief is unjustified. That is because only one fault has to be pointed out to show how a supposed absolute entailment is *not* absolute. There are many such sceptical uses of deductive logic to show its own limitations in this book. What it cannot be justifiably used for is to support any positive assertions about the universe. For that, we need what is often called 'inductive logic'.

'Inductive logic' is merely a matter of probability based on the frequency of experiences, regardless of the varying ways we interpret those experiences: so it is not 'logic' in the same absolute sense at all. The use of the term 'logic' suggests a framework that makes induction a problem, when its imperfection and fallibility should be obvious to anyone who recognizes the uncertainty created by sceptical argument and the basis of that argument in embodiment. Instead, we really need a different term for a relationship of probabilistic justification between two embodied beliefs that have a practically-defined relationship. This relationship of justification differs from a 'logical' one because it is not between disembodied propositions, but between the organisms that believe them, which often have sufficient commonality for their beliefs to overlap. A new term to replace 'logic' would need to take into account the uncertainties not only of the relationship between belief and reality, but also of the relationship between the meanings of the words used to express those beliefs at different points. In the absence of such a term, I am obliged to talk about *justification*, on the understanding that justification is always a matter of degree. Justification refers not just to the extent of the support given to beliefs by experience, but also to the process by which we link together different beliefs with other beliefs and experiences. Far from the Platonic assumption about reasoning – that it improves by being abstracted from the body – we need to assume the opposite, that it is the self-containment of the absolutizing mind that is delusive, whether it is the essentialized object or the idealized reasoning of that absolutizing mind that is at stake.

This is not a problem with logic itself in its own terms, but with the rationalist assumption that logic is informative. Logic can reliably help us to analyse the relationships between signs in a closed conceptual system, as long as we do not start attributing features of that closed system to the world. It is thus a distraction to hope that alternative 'logics' to the dominant Aristotelian form will have any practical effect on absolutization. The fourfold logic, or *catuskoti*, used in India at the time of the Buddha, along with modern alternatives such as fuzzy logic, modal logic, and dialetheism, may all operate helpfully within certain contexts to define the relationships between signs in a closed system. However, no logical system can substitute for the absence of total representational meaning implied by embodiment. It is not the way that we conceptualize logical relationships that is the issue, but the absoluteness with which we do so.

The tendency to use 'logic' in an implicitly absolute form as a substitute for the approximate relationships of justification results in its inflation: in other words, we attribute lots of features to perfectionistic 'logic' that are properties of other, imperfect, systems. In particular, training in reasoning focuses our attention on assumptions, because it leads us to analyse the ways in which our own or others' beliefs are traceable to assumptions in argument. However, the whole difficulty with assumptions is that they are *not* justified by reasoning, rather they form the starting point for it.

Understanding our own or others' assumptions is invaluable for distinguishing absolutized ones, as well as considering the relationship between non-absolutized assumptions and the evidence that may support them. However, we then wrongly attribute this benefit to 'reasoning' or 'logic'. In a similar way, we learn from training in reasoning how to identify 'fallacies', which again is useful for identifying absolutization. Conventionally and according to Western philosophy, however, these fallacies are identified with defects in logical reasoning. Closer examination (see 4.f below) shows that 'formal' fallacies that are traceable to defects in logic are practically irrelevant to judgement, and the 'informal' fallacies that are actually relevant have nothing to do with defects in logic.

Another aspect of this inflation is a frequent appeal to the concept of *rationality*. There are many varied definitions of this concept, but they all attempt in some way or another to extend the supposed absoluteness of deductive logic to other areas of experience that possess none of that absoluteness. For example, it may be considered 'rational' to act consistently in one's self-interest,[2] notwithstanding the constant changes in what we think our self-interest is and whether we are focused on it. The 'reason' in the 'rationality' here is the consistency of our thinking, but that consistency is built upon assumptions (about 'self-interest') that cannot be examined in the same 'rational' terms. In the process, we falsely distinguish 'rationality' from 'emotion', when in experience (and in the brain and body) these phenomena are constantly interdependent. The basis of this 'rational' viewpoint is thus 'irrational', making a nonsense of the whole construction. Rationality then becomes a weakened substitute term for 'good' (a bit like 'professionalism' or 'appropriateness'), that we use in the place of an account of ethics compatible with experience. All of this illustrates not only the absolutization phenomena of inflation (discussed further in 4.f), but also those of substitution (discussed further in 5.d).

The projection of absolutized logical relationships onto the world at large can even extend to our use of language about causality. Much of the language we use about causality is identical to that used about logic: for instance, 'implication' can refer either to a logical or a causal outcome, and 'consequence' can be used of a logical implication as well as an empirical event caused by another one. Lakoff and Johnson identify a blend of metaphors used in this conceptual connection – that thinking is moving and that reason is a force.[3] Only those trained in philosophy or critical thinking, though, are likely to distinguish systematically between reasons and causes, and the use of the same terms creates widespread confusion. We thus habitually project our absolutized beliefs about necessary relationships between concepts, and assume them to be necessary relationships between things in the world. It thus seems to appear obvious to many, even with mathematical and scientific training, that determinism is a feature of the universe, even when our phenomenal understanding of causal relationships in the universe as a whole is minuscule. Leibniz's 'principle of sufficient reason' takes this delusion to its full logical conclusion, by stating that logical

2   E.g. in Blackburn (1998).
3   Lakoff & Johnson (1999) pp. 215–16.

relationships *must* imply causal ones and nothing in the universe happens 'without a reason'.[4] A similar rationalistic arrogance is displayed in the 'ontological argument' for the existence of God, which takes a purely logical argument about an infinite being to be evidence of the existence of an actual God.[5] Statistics and the refinement of empirical science have done much to improve our understanding of causal relationships aside from such deluded projections, but at every stage they have to contend with the damage done to our understanding of the world by the absolutization of logic.

---

4 Leibniz *Monadology* §32: (1890) p. 222.
5 E.g. Descartes (1968) 3rd meditation.

4.c. Foundationalism and Circularity

> *Summary*
>
> In the absence of any justification for metaphysical claims in experience, metaphysical thinking employs foundationalism (dogmatic assertion of the truth of starting points). When challenged, it then uses circular and *ad hoc* arguments to substitute for experiential justification. Circular argument proliferates and creates reinforcing feedback loops. By projection, rationalists often accuse others of the very circularity they demonstrate themselves.

Absolutization is maintained by the predominance of logic and metaphysics as assumed independent systems. This not only happens explicitly in philosophy, but is done implicitly by those who make statements about 'reality' (e.g. in science or in religion) that lack a larger practical context, or who justify some of those statements by deduction from metaphysical starting points (such as those of materialism or supernaturalism). The assumed independence of the system created by logic and metaphysics from the wider set of embodied systems in which they are nested is reflected in the lack of further justification available for absolute claims. These are assumed to either be *self-evident* (forming a 'foundation' for further beliefs), or justified by circular argument. Foundationalism and circularity are dependent on each other, since one can only attempt to justify a foundation by referring it to itself in a circular fashion, and one can only attempt to justify circularity by making the whole context of the circle foundational. Both involve ruling out the obvious alternative that we *do not and cannot know* what ultimately justifies our beliefs (if anything), a possibility that is dismissed only with the rationalized anxiety that there *must* somehow be an answer.

The classic example of foundationalism in philosophy is Descartes' *cogito*: the belief that a foundation for 'knowledge' of real existence can be created through the infallible thinking of clear and distinct ideas.[1] However, foundations do not have to be purely philosophical or rationalistic to operate as such. Hume attempted to create an empirical foundation in his theory of ideas and impressions, so that we could erect a tower of empirical knowledge from the bricks of the smallest and most basic identifiable elements of perception

---

1 Descartes (1968) 2nd meditation.

('impressions'),[2] despite the obvious difficulties in identifying any such ultimate constituents. Wherever we find absolutization, there is a similar foundationalist structure, in the sense of a metaphysical claim about an object (or subject) beyond experience, and this metaphysical claim is then used with assumed absolute logic to support other beliefs. For example, a belief about my enemy's essential badness makes me deduce that he had a bad motive when he acted in a particular instance.

Foundationalism is often supported by appeals to authority: that is, the implicit assumption that reference to a particular source (be it a text, an expert, or a governmental body) finally settles any questions about the truth of what is claimed. The theology of revelation in various religions (particularly Christianity and Islam) thus attempts to justify religious assertions through reference to a foundational proof text (scripture) or other source of absolute authority (such as the infallible pope of the Catholic Church). Confusion arises here because we do justifiably refer to authoritative or credible sources to support our claims (as I do in this book) by showing that they are *more likely* to be correct. However, credibility at all points needs to be carefully distinguished from absolute authority. We can justify a provisional judgement in a practical situation using credibility: for instance, without technical knowledge of medical procedures or technological devices, we rely on the opinions of experts. However, we can do this without absolutizing their view, by weighing what they have to say heavily in the balance with any other evidence.

Circularity is a response to some sort of demand for further justification for a foundational claim – met by a substitution for such justification that merely goes through the motions of fulfilling it. Again, Descartes provides the classic example that will probably spring first to the mind of anyone familiar with Western philosophy. This is the 'Cartesian Circle', where Descartes claims that his clear and distinct perceptions prove the existence of God, and also that God's existence as an omnipotent and benevolent being guarantees that Descartes cannot be mistaken in his clear and distinct perceptions.[3] However, this is just one example of absolute claims being supported only by other absolute claims in a closed system of logic and metaphysics.

2   Hume (1975) chs. 2 & 3.
3   Descartes (1968) 3rd–5th meditations.

This circularity continues to operate in the judgement of empirical information using metaphysics and logic, to ensure that such empirical information is appropriated into a metaphysical system rather than used to challenge it. The *ad hoc* hypothesis is a classic example of this. For instance, when Galileo observed mountains and craters on the moon using a telescope, this challenged the contemporary view, following the astronomical theories of Aristotle, that the moon must be a perfect sphere. One of Galileo's contemporaries then proposed that the gaps between the mountains and craters must be filled with a transparent substance.[4] This reflects an obvious attempt to make the evidence fit the theory, regardless of the likelihood of the hypotheses being advanced to defend the theory. *Ad hoc* hypothesizing is in turn just an application of the underlying bias that creates circularity: confirmation bias (see 5.c). In confirmation bias, to which we are all subject to different degrees, we select and interpret the information available from our senses in order to fulfil our assumptions. This creates a circular process, because the selected information also then strengthens the assumptions.

Circularity of argument reflects proliferation, which can be understood as a circularity of argument within one mind: we keep recycling the same points in order to 'prove' them to ourselves and others through familiarity. The obsessive states of craving or anxiety that drive proliferation also drive circularity, as we feel obliged to justify claims that we identify with, even though we have no further justification for them. Within a group that accepts a given absolutization, such circular justifications will seem legitimate and probably not be questioned.

Circularity of argument is also obviously reinforcing feedback loops. When employed *a priori*, circular argument directly excludes any outside influences from beyond the loop by avoiding any input from the senses. When the circularity is about an empirical matter, limited evidence becomes part of the closed loop, but it is the possibility of further disturbing evidence linked to alternative possible beliefs that is excluded. In the process of scientific research, circular *ad hoc* thinking may take the form of commitment to an unfruitful research programme – that is, to a theory that is no longer offering new forms of investigation or testing. This is illustrated by the above example from Galileo, where the old research programme was

---

4   Drake (1978) p. 168.

Aristotelian and the new one was Copernican. Without *new* ways of testing, we just recycle old ones, and we resist new theories by forcing them into the old paradigm. As Lakatos and Kuhn pointed out,[5] it is not necessarily the case that such an unfruitful theory is *false*, or even that it lacks all confirming evidence. However, continued attachment to the theory at the expense of pursuing opportunities for investigation is increasingly likely to indicate absolutization in the scientists who cling to it as the contrasts between an old paradigm and a new one open up.

Following the phenomenon of projection (see 5.b), rationalists are likely to accuse those who rely on empirical evidence of the very circularity they employ themselves in order to try to support foundationalism. A particular instance of this is the Five Ways of Thomas Aquinas: a set of arguments for God as a metaphysical prime mover, first cause, necessity preceding all contingency, absolute standard of comparison, and ultimate goal.[6] The structure of all these arguments involves the assumption that an imperfect and empirical cause, standard, or goal would 'beg the question', leading either to an infinite regression or to a circularity of justification. However, given the uncertainty of empirical information about the universe, we do not know whether this is the case or not. This Thomist argument, still a staple of Catholic theology, is effectively another way of claiming that uncertainty is intolerable, so therefore we must pretend to resolve it through a metaphysical substitution even though we cannot actually resolve it. It also trades on the basic confusion already mentioned between logical and causal links. The odd thing is that rationalists fail to notice here that rationalist thinking also creates circularity (for example, God provides revelation, and revelation reveals God) and infinite regression (Who moved the prime mover? Who created the creator?). If we rely on embodied experience, however, we get a fade into uncertainty, where instead rationalism offers circularity within constructed certainty. A fade into uncertainty at the edges of our understanding is not the same as a circularity of argument, even if circularity remains one of the ultimate possibilities in the uncertainty. People who live in rationalistic glass houses should not throw circular stones.

---

5   Lakatos (1974); Kuhn (1996).
6   Aquinas (2008) 1: Q2, A3.

The belief in any kind of foundation is unacceptable because it ignores the fade into infinity that we will experience with closer investigation, and substitutes an absolutized conceptual explanation that has been given a magical free pass from the very infinite regression it claims to end. It thus merely perpetuates absolutized ways of thinking, whilst distracting us from experience and halting our investigation of it. Circularity is another kind of substitution: this time of a closed feedback loop for an informative justification that can refer us to further experience. Circularity of various kinds is a tell-tale sign of absolutization wherever you encounter it, and an indication of the bankruptcy of absolute deductive reasoning when it lacks new information as a starting point.

4.d. Infinite Rationalization of Experience

> *Summary*
>
> The philosophical content of metaphysical beliefs can be linked to the psychological defences of absolutization by the way that infinite scope allows endless rationalization. This is exemplified in *ad hoc* argument, and can be supported by cognitive dissonance theory. Its further implication is that metaphysical beliefs are impervious to observation, and thus also to probability.

One of the key conditions of absolutization that crosses the line between philosophy and psychology is that of infinite rationalization. Absolute claims are *infinite in scope*, meaning that they attempt to represent a state of affairs that applies to an infinite number of instances in at least one respect (not necessarily in all respects). Obviously this applies to claims that explicitly discuss infinity like 'The universe is eternal', but is also far more widespread than may be recognized by those who focus only on the most explicit cases. All metaphysical claims are infinite in scope in this way: for example, 'Tom *really is* evil' offers no limits to Tom's evil judgements, character, or behaviour. Often all that is required for infinity of scope is strategic vagueness in one respect: for instance, 'I will recompense you at some point in the future' refers to a potentially infinite set of future moments when the supposed recompense may occur.

Infinity of scope thus allows infinite rationalization. A justifiable relationship to experience may be promised, but the promise is never fulfilled, and instead absolutizations are substituted. A clear instance of this to start with is *ad hoc* argument, sometimes known as 'moving the goalposts' or 'no true Scotsman'. An example of this, involving Galileo, was given in the previous chapter. In *ad hoc* argument, a judgement is made according to what appear to be clear standards at the beginning, but these then change as the argument proceeds.[1] They are able to change without limit, because of ways that a potential infinity of scope has been assumed in one of the terms. 'No true Scotsman dislikes porridge' allows a potentially infinite number of 'false Scotsman' exceptions, to evade any possible counter-examples of Scotsmen who dislike porridge.

---

1   Chalmers (1982) pp. 51-3; Popper (1959) p. 82.

Ad hoc argument is obviously an attempt to make the evidence fit the presuppositions of the theory, of a kind that allows infinite manipulability in our interpretation of what we observe, so that it does not matter how improbable or unobserved our additional assumptions are. For instance, in the example of *ad hoc* thinking mentioned in the previous chapter, of the alleged transparent substance filling gaps on the moon, we can find the vulnerability to such an *ad hoc* usage in the infinite scope of the moon being claimed to be a *perfect* sphere. Perfection is a complete state that cannot change over time, making it infinite in terms of its duration. In that claimed perfection, the flexibility is removed from our adjustment of theories about the moon to fit experience, and placed instead in our adjustment of the interpretation of experience to fit the theory.

A further example can be found in the long-standing theological debate over 'the problem of evil'. The problem of evil is supposed to be an argument for atheism that points out that if God has the characteristics ascribed to him of being omniscient, omnipotent, and omnibenevolent then he must know about evil and suffering, be able to stop it and be motivated to stop it. It is thus argued that a God with all these characteristics cannot exist. To this there is a ready theological response: unknown to us but known only to God, there may be ultimate good in what we take to be evil, whether that ultimate good consists in part of being a consistent design, or in giving us freewill.[2]

Both the atheist argument and the theistic response here offer infinite scope for rationalization, in accordance with the infinity of the 'existence' of God being argued over. The atheist argument, as a challenge to God's 'existence', actually accepts all the framing of traditional theism uncritically by first of all taking God's 'existence' to be important, secondly accepting the definition of God's essential features as a condition for this 'existence', and thirdly by seeking to disprove that 'existence' in the same way that theism has sought to prove it. The claim that God as defined in this way 'does not exist' has just as infinite a scope as the claim that he does. Any potential experience purporting to show God's existence can be dismissed in the same way that theists can dismiss any counter-evidence.

2   The 'Augustinian Theodicy': see any introduction to the Philosophy of Religion.

It also needs to be noted that even in statements that contain no explicit source of infinite scope, one can often be summoned up through interpretation. Let's take a basic empirical statement 'the cat is on the mat'. To treat this absolutely, we only have to interpret it in absolute terms either positively or negatively – the kind of interpretation that may be associated with particularly vexatious, abstract philosophical discussions. For instance, one could assume that the cat is *eternally* or *essentially* on the mat, and appeal to Platonic claims about the essential cat when challenged with observations about the capacity of the cat to get up from the mat. Alternatively, one could interpret the statement in a way that is necessarily false, e.g. that the uncertainty about the truth of whether the cat is really there implies that any statements about it are false. In these cases, one imports infinite scope into one's interpretation of the proposition, and thus makes it absolute, by interpreting it in a narrowly representational way (unfortunately often typical of philosophers), without further context.

Infinite rationalization is at one and the same time clearly a feature of the philosophical content of absolute propositions – their infinite scope in some respect – and also a feature of the psychological state in which those propositions must be judged correct, namely the defensive mechanisms by which alternative possible beliefs are psychologically repressed. Rationalization as a defensive mechanism prevents any examination of the absolute belief by diverting activity into an entirely abstract realm, where the framing ensures that conceptual decoys will be endlessly substituted for examination in relation to alternatives.

The infinite scope provides such a useful facility for the defensive mechanism, that in most cases where infinite scope is made explicit, there will be absolutization present, even though the relationship is not one of necessity. We can talk with infinite scope without absolutizing by providing a context of conditionality, practicality, or a focus on meaning, as discussed in 3.d, but without these there is no evident motive, in practice, for making a claim of infinite scope. Perhaps some such claims may be dismissed as 'innocent speculation', but such speculation is only rendered innocent by being explicit about its conditionality: 'the universe may be infinite', rather than 'the universe is infinite'. On the other hand, a sufficient intensity of absolutizing defensiveness can make us interpret almost any claim in the terms of infinite scope that are necessary for it to fulfil its defensive function. The most vexatious forms of dogmatism or of supposed 'scepticism', in which an entrenched person nit-picks their way to a superficial verbal victory, are of this kind.

That absolutized belief is impervious to the changes initiated by observation follows from its infinite rationalization. In the above examples, two observations – of the moon's mountains and craters and of suffering in the world – made no impression on absolutized beliefs because of the way that an unlimited number of conceptual substitutes could be deployed for any modification that could be made by observation. No observation on any degree of non-sphericalness in the moon is sufficient to address further *ad hoc* defences. Similarly, no possible example of evil, no matter how horrendous, and no matter how innocent its victim, will make the slightest difference to a theist who is convinced of the ultimate justice of God.

This imperviousness to observation does not mean that absolutized beliefs cannot appeal to observation, only that alternative beliefs stimulated by new observations cannot change absolutized belief without accompanying psychological changes enabling the belief to be held in a non-absolute way. If absolutized beliefs change within their own framing, they do so discontinuously (as already discussed in 2.c). New observations may create a build-up of cognitive dissonance that eventually breaks the absolutized belief as a whole, but they are unable to create gradual change or adjustment in an absolutized belief when the build-up of dissonance can be indefinitely rationalized within the conceptual framing.

Cognitive dissonance theory suggests that this rationalization is due to a minimization of stress or effort. For example, in Leon Festinger's famous study of failed prophecy in an apocalyptic religious cult, most members of the cult found it easier to believe that the aliens they believed were about to destroy the earth had changed their minds and decided to spare it, than that the whole story about the aliens and their intentions was false.[3] This follows the 'fast thinking' explanation of absolutization: we construct limitless further rationalized beliefs rather than questioning an absolutized belief in part because it's easier to do so – once you have laid down and entrenched the neural tracks for rationalization, it's easier to keep following them. A further type of explanation for this phenomenon depends on social perception of self-identity: we feel

---

3   Festinger, Riecken, & Schachter (1956).

we have too much to lose in our perceived social status if we admit an error, so prefer to maintain the status we associate with our absolute belief (see 5.e for more on this).

Whilst they remain impervious to observation, absolutized beliefs continue to feed themselves with empirical meaning that is used to support their bloated dominance, by appropriating and incorporating the fruits of experience. In this way, extensive metaphysical systems are created, like those of Catholic theology, in which all phenomena are made apparently consistent with the metaphysical framing. Thomas Aquinas provides an early example of this, when he appropriates Aristotelian thought to Catholicism, incorporating 'natural law' but with subsidiary status within the overall 'divine law'.[4] In this way any observations that might seem to challenge divine revelation are diverted and appropriated to apparently support it, but the basic belief in divine revelation can remain unaltered. This means that increasing numbers of commonly used neural pathways are given over to usage solely in accordance with the absolutized belief.

By 'observation' I mean any new sense-experience, whether this experience directly offers new information (e.g. I see my neighbour has left his house) or consists in experience of communication from others that offers new information (my neighbour tells me he is about to leave his house). Such new information does not have to be correct information (or 'knowledge'), nor can we assume it has the kind of pure independent existence assumed by that philosophical construction, 'sense data'. Instead, all the evidence points to the constant interaction of our sense experience with our preconceptions.[5] We only ever see what we're looking for, hear what we're listening to, and so on – whether we're 'looking' and 'listening' in a narrower left hemisphere sense as we focus on objects related to our goals, or being alert in a wider right hemisphere sense for potential threats and opportunities. Even our 'alert' settings involve unconscious screening processes,[6] as anyone who has managed to habituate themselves to sleeping through the hourly tolling of a church clock through the night will be aware. So 'observation' as experience that could potentially alter our beliefs already

---

4   Aquinas (2008).
5   E.g. Chabris & Simons (2010).
6   See Le Duc, Fournier, & Hebert (2016), and much other psychological research on emotional inhibition of startle responses.

takes the form of meaning prior to belief-formation, because our sense-experiences have already made an impact on us by creating potential neural pathways even when we have not developed new beliefs in response to new sense-experience. That meaning remains repressed and marginalized in our mental economy until we allow it to interact with the dominant beliefs that determine our actions.

The philosophical implications of the imperviousness to observation are profound. Perhaps the most important of these is the recognition that empirical claims can in no way be used to support metaphysical ones: for instance, no amount of scientific investigation tells us about ultimate matter, and no religious experience tells us about the 'existence' of God. It is not that empirical claims only make a small impression on metaphysical claims – they make *no impression at all*, because the meaning of absolute claims as a whole is dependent on the assumption of representationalism in a way that is wholly separated from the embodied meaning that new empirical information would relate to. In turn this makes the closed abstractions of infinite rationalization meaningful only within that limited subsidiary frame. Meanwhile the meaning of provisional claims modifiable by experience depends on their relationship to embodied experience in a way that can be more directly acknowledged. Experiential meaning has no access to this separated, parasitic, additional zone of meaning so as to synthesize with it, as long as the exclusivity of that zone is maintained.

As empirical observation has no purchase on absolute belief, neither does probability, which depends on the frequency (as well as sometimes the quality and relevance) of observations. To describe a claim as more or less probable is to attempt to weigh the information gained from previous observations with regard to the prediction of future ones. Such judgements can also be modified by further information, whether you adopt the Bayesian system of modifying the old probability with regard to the new information, or attempt to create a new probability based on the new totality of information. Absolute claims are thus just as impervious to assessments of probability as to any other products of observation – probability is simply irrelevant to them. For instance, Richard Dawkins' claim that the existence of God is 'highly improbable'[7] is based on a misunderstanding of the isolated representational meaning that people are relying on when they talk about the existence of God.

7   Dawkins (2006) ch. 4.

4.e. The Claim that Metaphysics is Inevitable

> *Summary*
>
> The claim that metaphysics is inevitable depends on the complete abstraction of metaphysical claims from the embodied context of them being held by a person. We do constantly make background assumptions, but these can't be described as beliefs until they become practically relevant in some way (though not necessarily explicit), when we can distinguish absolute from provisional ways of holding them. Absolutization is a problem because it is practically relevant, but most alleged inevitable background metaphysical beliefs are not.

If the system of metaphysics and logic seems under threat, the metaphysicians' last line of defence is the claim that metaphysics and logic are *inevitable* features of human thought, and thus that anyone criticizing them must necessarily be hypocritical in doing so.[1] The habit of metaphysicians is to think in terms of the necessity of the content of metaphysical beliefs, and then to transfer that necessity to the embodied situation of a person who holds them. We are all thus supposed to assume metaphysical beliefs whether we like it or not, with no distinction being made between metaphysical and provisional ways of holding beliefs that may in some respects look similar.

This argument denies the possibility of provisional belief or provisional reasoning as an alternative to absolutization. It ignores the psychological aspects of belief, which suggest that absolute beliefs can alternatively be put in a context of awareness where they can be compared with other possibilities, to assert that even a belief that claims to be provisional must *a priori* be built on philosophical assumptions that are absolute. This can only be asserted by completely abstracting the supposed philosophical assumptions made from the context where they are used by a living organism.

It is one thing to use a metaphysical belief to try to justify a judgement in ordinary experience – as for instance in the Catholic use of beliefs about Natural Law to tell young boys that they will go to hell if they masturbate. Here the absolute belief is clearly employed in a chain of deduction. However, it is quite another to claim that a metaphysical belief *must* be present when its usage is of no

---

1 E.g. Zięba (2008); Valore (2017).

immediate relevance to the present situation. When I walk across a room, for instance, I don't need to maintain a claim that space is not infinitely divisible as I do so, and when I mark down a future appointment I don't have to believe in the absolute linearity of time. The assumptions I make when I do these things are merely parts of my experience, contextualized by wider practical concerns (see 3.d), and it is only if they were called into question that whether or not I was absolutizing them might become relevant. Similarly, by reasoning in this book I am not necessarily assuming absolute connections between elements of deductive logic. I am merely hoping that the provisional beliefs I am linking together have enough correspondence in meaning with yours for some of that meaning to be shared. The test of whether this has happened sufficiently will be practical, depending on whether my words can make any difference to your judgements in the long term. In all cases it is the widest practical context that influences interpretation that we need to look at, rather than the supposed theoretical foundations of interpretation.

The kind of metaphysical beliefs that we are said to be unable to escape are those of background assumption or framing: beliefs about the forward progression of time, say, or the infinity of space. We are said to assume that, for instance, the world did not begin last Thursday, with all our memories prior to that being falsely implanted.[2] What is normally noteworthy about these arguments for the inevitability of metaphysics is that they are themselves metaphysical: they confront us with an entirely abstract scenario beyond experience, trading on the fact that it recedes infinitely from whatever experiential assertions we may make, then appealing to ignorance by challenging us to deny that we make such assumptions, before concluding positively that we do make them. Such arguments work well for sceptical purposes, to merely make us aware of the uncertainty of our assumptions, but they do not establish that we possess otherwise irrelevant positive beliefs. The assumptions involved are not normally ones that we could use deductively to make any difference to our practical judgement. I will plan for next Thursday in exactly the same way whether or not the world actually began last Thursday.

Of course, there are cases of assumptions that we make and do not normally reflect upon, that do potentially make a difference to us as

---

2 See https://rationalwiki.org/wiki/Last_Thursdayism (accessed 2021)

practical, embodied beings. My assumption that objects are always solid is challenged when I run into a hologram, and my assumption that Wednesday must always follow Tuesday may one day be challenged by an international agreement to introduce a decimal week. However, it is precisely the fact that these background assumptions have become practically relevant in some circumstances that makes the way I hold them also relevant. *Assuming* something involves applying it, explicitly or implicitly. If everyone else decided that Wednesday came before Tuesday rather than after it, so that the social conventions around the days of the week changed, it would be foolish of me to carry on insisting that Wednesday *must* follow Tuesday. My absolutization of that belief, as opposed to provisionality, would then become relevant. At the same time, though, it would become possible for me to be provisional about it, rather than it being inevitable that I would hold an absolute belief.

Much of the reason why absolutization is a problem depends on it both being implicitly held (without conscious reflection), and it being practically relevant at the same time. For instance, if we think of the example of the extreme fundamentalism of Islamic State (with which I began my introduction to the book), it may well be the case that many such fundamentalists cease to reflect on the justifications of their beliefs after a while. Killing and torturing opponents with the general belief that this is God's will becomes a habit, and the justification for it is left to the propagandists, not the foot-soldiers. At the same time, these beliefs remain contested and contestable in the wider world. They are practically relevant because other people, including the victims and their families, would be very prepared to question the absolute beliefs that actuate these barbarous acts. Other unquestioned background assumptions shared by Islamic State with everyone else, such as the forward linear progression of time, are not subject to the same questioning when exposed to a wider context. To establish whether or not an assumption is relevant, then, we can always ask ourselves whether it makes a practical difference to judgement in the widest context that it is likely to be considered in.

The question of which beliefs are relevant is what Werner Ulrich, in his Critical Systems Heuristics, refers to as 'boundary judgement'. As Ulrich argues, we need to resolve boundary judgements by considering alternative answers to the questions they raise, for 'only in the light of alternative reference systems can we fully appreciate the selectivity of the present one'. We also need to engage in dialogue with those practically affected. However, 'when some of the parties handle their own boundary judgments uncritically, either because they take them for granted or try to impose them on others, it may become necessary to *challenge* their claims through the emancipatory use of boundary critique'.[3] The people who try to impose their boundary judgements on others are the metaphysicians, who cannot let go of the idea that *their* boundary judgements are natural and necessary. However, in practice, boundary judgements are constantly negotiated in relation to their practical relevance for those involved.

For embodied humans, then, the beliefs that we actually make use of in practice (whether explicit or implicit) may be absolute or provisional, but they are not *inevitably* metaphysical. It is only by thinking about the metaphysical claims in a disembodied way, remote from the person holding them, that it could be asserted that such beliefs are inevitable. How much freedom a person actually has to question their absolute assumptions, of course, varies hugely with the circumstances, but we have no grounds to assume an absolute determinism. In an embodied and uncertain rather than absolutized context, we have some degree of freedom in our assumptions between totality and nullity, even if it is asymptotically very small or very large.

The claim that metaphysical assumptions are inevitable, too, when applied to the embodied context, flies in the face of our experience of changing and learning even in relation to claims that we may have previously taken completely for granted. For instance, someone brought up in a religious cult in which the guru is regarded as infallible may believe this for, say, thirty years, before the cult implodes and she is forced to confront the world beyond it. At that point she is forced to recognize that her absolute metaphysical belief in the reality of the guru's infinite knowledge is unsustainable. Whatever we may take for granted now, we cannot tell whether or not we may be forced to reconsider it in future. The content of metaphysical claims is supposedly necessary, but the holding of them is contingent.

---

3   Ulrich (2005) p. 4.

4.f. Inflation of Metaphysics and Logic

Summary

Both metaphysics and absolute deductive logic are also over-estimated through inflation, being used as shortcut substitutes for more complex experiential phenomena. 'Metaphysics' substitutes for profundity of meaning in religious experience and art, whilst 'truth' and 'knowledge' substitute for incrementally justified belief in science and education. The relativization of these terms, on the other hand, robs us of minatory ways of referring to absolutes. Deductive logic is likewise inflated, to explain fallacious thinking that lacks justification due to absolutization of assumptions.

The final aspect of absolutization in the context of philosophy that I need to consider is the *inflation* of the concepts of metaphysics and logic themselves. This takes the form of assuming that metaphysical and logical beliefs are far more important than we have any justification for seeing them as. This inflation often occurs through a process of substitution – that is, we attribute functions to metaphysics or logic that are fulfilled by other processes, because we assume they *must* be important. It is an aspect of absolutization itself that absolutized beliefs are often accorded much more practical importance than they actually have.

In relation to metaphysics, this inflation takes the form of the assumption that metaphysical claims can be directly verified through religious experience, as well as the vague mystification of the concept of metaphysics in the artistic realm. In relation to logic, in 4.b I have already mentioned the over-extension of the idea of logic in the use of the concept of rationality, and the common confusion of logical implication with causation.

In the context of religion, metaphysics has become unnecessarily associated with religious experience. This association has been so successfully entrenched in religious culture that any experience of profound inspiration, sublimity, or integration is likely to be immediately associated with a metaphysical belief: often the belief that it is an experience of God as an infinite supernatural being, or perhaps that it involves penetrating to the essential wisdom of the universe. Philosophers of religion even argue that we can *prove* the existence of God from religious experience.[1] Any attempt to separate religious

---

1 E.g. Swinburne (2004).

experience from metaphysics is also likely to be seen as reductive, even though it is quite possible to fully appreciate religious experience as such without making metaphysical claims about it. As I have argued more fully elsewhere,[2] however, religious experience involves access to temporarily integrated mental states with enhanced levels of awareness, focus, emotional positivity, insight, and inspiration. Such experiences are both highly valuable for our integrative process and highly meaningful. Their meaning can be associated with archetypal symbols that then help to provide inspiration for more integrative states in future. However, they are states of *meaning*, not of knowledge of some sort of metaphysical *reality*. The assumption that they are experiences 'of' reality is merely an unnecessary entrenched cultural association, whilst the reductive response that sees religious experience as 'just' material is equally unhelpful, because, like the absolutist interpretation, it turns complex meaningful experience into mere conceptual belief.

The vague mystification of the concept of metaphysics by non-philosophers is also an instance of its over-extension. The term 'metaphysical' in many wider artistic circles appears to mean something like 'profound'. But what does profundity (an experience of complex insights) have to do with beliefs about reality beyond experiences? Nothing whatsoever, but what seems to have occurred is just a widely prevalent *substitution* of the idea of metaphysics for the more difficult task of thinking through how we experience profundity and what it means for us. The 'metaphysical' poets of seventeenth century England, such as John Donne and Andrew Marvell, employed profound and dramatic metaphors, sometimes of enormous and disconcerting scope.[3] The mistress's body is compared to a new found land, or the year to a day. However, these metaphors connect narrower experiences to broader ones: they have nothing the least to do with metaphysics, because they have no connection with what we believe. The same can be said of 'metaphysical' painters such as Giorgio de Chirico, who produce striking images that might help us to question our current assumptions by imagining our visual experience in a wider meaningful context. Again, far from involving positive metaphysical claims, this kind of art may help us to question them. There is nothing 'metaphysical' about it,

---

2   Ellis (2018) 2.b; (2022) 4.f.
3   Gardner (2003).

but the persistence of the use of the word suggests an inflation of the concept which involves appropriation of areas of experience by absolutized belief.

It might be argued that if people wish to use the term 'metaphysical' when they mean 'profound', it is harmless, and merely pedantic to complain. Moreover, we should not attempt to essentialize the changing meanings of terms. However, my objection here is neither pedantic nor essentialist. People can use terms for whatever purposes they wish, but what should concern us is the *practical effects* of using a term in a particular way. If the practical effect of this kind of use of the term 'metaphysics' is to appropriate experience to absolutization, then it is an aspect of absolutization itself. Our response to absolutization needs to begin with clarity about its identification, which in turn requires clarity about the language we use to identify it. Without this, we do not have the basis for a practical response to it.

A similar role is played by the even more common inflation of the concepts of 'truth', 'knowledge', 'reality', and 'certainty' in philosophy, science, education, and many other contexts. These concepts are unavoidably absolute when made the subjects of positive claims (except in the contexts discussed in 3.d), as can be easily judged by the lack of incrementality in their usage. Under the discontinuous representationalist assumptions that form our use of these terms, a claim is either true or it is not: if it lacks full truth it is not true. For instance, if a dog is grey it is not true that it is black. For the same reason, under the classic definition of propositional knowledge as *justified true belief*, we cannot 'know' a claim unless it is both true and completely justified. It thus also cannot be 'certain' without these criteria being fulfilled. Given basic sceptical arguments that merely point out the implications of our embodiment (such as that our senses are limited, that we understand things on the basis of prior assumptions, etc.), it is thus clear that we do not have access to any true proposition and that we cannot have knowledge.[4] Yet both philosophy and wider discourse abound with inflations of the concepts of 'truth' and 'knowledge', whereby these absolute terms substitute for more obviously experiential ones. As discussed earlier in 2.a, even systems theorists like Maturana and Varela do this, let alone mainstream scientists and educators who talk about 'scientific knowledge' as though it was not an oxymoron.

4   i.1.a; II.1

The practically unhelpful uses of terms like 'truth' and 'knowledge' are not the ones that are clearly contextualized so as to be non-absolute (for instance, by being conditional), but the ones that prevent us from recognizing absolutization or distract us from it. We are prevented from recognizing absolutization when we no longer have any language in which to discuss it, because these terms have been relativized. This is the unfortunate turn of 'ordinary language' philosophy, which insists that the legitimate use of terms such as 'certainty' is an ordinary, relative one, and that the philosophical sense of 'certainty' as an absolute is illegitimate.[5] If we were to take this seriously (which fortunately most people don't), we would have no ways of talking about absolutization at all. This is the effect of confusing the lack of justification for absolute *beliefs* with our contrasting need to be able to use language with absolute *meaning*. The latter by no means implies the former. No term that lacks incrementality (such as 'know') can be used generally and seriously for purposes that seek to avoid absolutization, because of the point, mentioned in 4.d, that our language only needs to be absolute *in one respect* to be used absolutely. So the use of positive claims involving relativized versions of terms like 'knowledge', 'truth', or 'certainty', even for purposes that attempt to criticize metaphysics, is likely to end up in implicit negative metaphysics, making claims of 'my truth' or 'our truth' for an individual or a group that are not provisional and adaptable, but involve absolute claims for that individual or group. The term 'my truth', apart from being contradictory, is just as much of an absolutization as 'truth' in general.

We are also distracted from recognizing absolutization by conventions that make terms like 'truth' and 'knowledge' look non-absolute when they are still being used absolutely. Not only 'my truth', but terms like 'alternative facts' or 'subjective certainty' are often used to prevent us from considering alternatives and judging provisionally, despite (or rather because) of their relativity. The absoluteness of relativism was politically weaponized, for instance, by the Trump administration in the US to rhetorically disarm any objections based on wider critical awareness. The phrase 'alternative facts' was famously launched by Trump spokesperson Kellyanne Conway in the context of a dispute about the number

---

5 E.g. Wittgenstein (1967).

of people attending Trump's inauguration in January 2017.[6] The power of the phrase is presumably dependent on the way that it seems to be questioning an absolutization, even though when examined more carefully it turns out to be asserting one, and in the process undermining any process by which absolutizations in general can be questioned. A common response to this, however, is to assert that 'alternative facts' are just falsehoods, as journalist Chuck Todd did in the episode mentioned. Without any further way of applying critical awareness to the discussion, such a response may play into the hands of those who wish to manipulate relativism, by leaving the discussion as a polarized set of contradictory absolutes rather than making it provisional. The idea that 'alternative facts' are simply 'false' is itself an inflation of the recognition that they are unjustified.

A great deal of the philosophical and quasi-philosophical discourse on these matters is a confused morass of absolute terms that may appear to be 'relative', but still maintain their absolute implications in one dimension or another – as I discussed in 4.a in relation to logical positivism and postmodernism as reactions against absolute metaphysics. Relativism of this kind, far from being contextual, maintains all the other features of absolutization, and thus sets up an impregnable abstract wall around its relative assertions that prevent wider influence from modifying them (see section 8 on the need for universal aspiration). As an alternative, we need to be able to identify absolute language in *any* respect, but then interpret that language conditionally and contextually, being guardedly alert for potentially absolute claims, but also relaxed about such language when the context is not absolute.

In addition to the inflation of 'metaphysics', 'truth', etc. so as to appropriate non-absolute senses, the inflation of the concept of deductive logic is also deeply-rooted and damaging. This inflation can be found in the popular language that uses terms like 'logical' or 'reasonable' to refer to a justification that one judges adequate merely because one agrees with its premises. However, it is most developed in its negative use, in the attribution of 'logical' error to fallacious argument. The term 'fallacy' is commonly defined in terms of logical invalidity, but has popularly come to mean a claim

6   https://www.washingtonpost.com/news/the-fix/wp/2017/01/22/kellyanne-conway-says-donald-trumps-team-has-alternate-facts-which-pretty-much-says-it-all/ (accessed 2021).

that is actually false even though it is widely assumed to be true: an instance of logic being inflated so much that it turns into metaphysics. However, when we examine examples of fallacies that can be helpfully identified in practice, they are neither faults in logic nor metaphysical untruths: instead they are absolutizations that stand in the way of investigation of the kind that could help to resolve conflicting beliefs.

Established discussion of fallacies categorizes them into two types, 'formal' and 'informal'. Formal fallacies are said to break an established rule of valid entailment. For example, the formal fallacy of drawing a logically negative conclusion from logically positive premises in a syllogism could result in an argument like this one:

No Protestants are Muslims.
The majority of Irish people are not Protestants.
Therefore, the majority of Irish people are Muslims.

If we reduced the three terms in this argument ('Protestants', 'Muslims', and 'the majority of Irish people') to algebraic quantities A, B, and C, the invalidity of the argument is clear in its own terms: the system of signs used then becomes inconsistent. However, once we apply such patterns of reasoning to complex empirical systems, such 'fallacies' are only correctly identifiable because they have presumed 'knowledge' where there can be none (i.e. because of their absolutization). Religious allegiances are difficult to determine, because they usually depend on self-declaration in (for instance) censuses, without any clear definition of what is meant by any given allegiance, nor any way of determining either the representational meaning or the absolute truth of the declarations. On the available evidence it is extremely unlikely, but not absolutely impossible, that the majority of Irish people are Muslims in some sense. However, when we accept the high probability of the conclusion being incorrect despite the premises being highly likely to be correct, the connection between them is irrelevant to these judgements: instead, the 'invalidity' of the argument is just a reminder of what we don't know. Based on the argument, we don't know *whether or not* the majority of Irish people are Muslims.

These particular difficulties are just illustrations of all the sceptical problems, as well as the underlying lack of representation, that prevent absolute validity being possible in reasoning about empirical information. This can serve as an example of the ways in which formal fallacy is only assumed to make any contribution to the justification of our beliefs by a process of inflation. We feel that the precision of the fallacy being identified should tell us something precisely 'true' or 'false', but the precision is fake: actually it can only re-affirm what we generally do *not* know due to embodied uncertainty.

'Informal' fallacies are also said to break logical rules, but only in a wider context that takes into account 'content' or 'discourse'.[7] For example, in an *ad hominem* argument, a fallacious conclusion is drawn about the necessary falseness of someone's claims because of who they are, when who they are is not relevant to the truth or falsity of their claims. When we look closer, though, it turns out to be the absolutizing assumptions made in each case that make informal fallacies unacceptable: logical validity is irrelevant. Not only is every argument, informal fallacy or not, ultimately invalid once we take embodiment into account, but the unhelpful assumptions made can be analysed entirely in terms of the premises rather than the argument. Take for example this *ad hominem* argument:

> James claims that Covid 19 is no worse than influenza.
> James is not an epidemiologist.
> Therefore James' claim must be false.

The problem with this argument lies entirely with the word *must*, which marks the source of absolutization. James not being an epidemiologist may dramatically lower the chances of him being right when compared to an epidemiologist who asserts the contrary, but does not mean that he is *necessarily* wrong. Although one can understand the impatience of experts with people who make pronouncements about their specialism without much understanding of what they are talking about, the justification of such impatience is a matter of different *degrees* of credibility, not the epidemiologist being absolutely correct and James being necessarily wrong. However, one could tell that this is the problem by just looking at the conclusion and recognizing the power of sceptical argument. We could be confident before we started that neither James nor any epidemiologist would have an absolute position, and thus that anyone who assumes either will be committing a fallacy. We do not deduce this from the relationship between the terms of the argument.

7   E.g. see Gary Curtis on http://www.fallacyfiles.org/inforfal.html (accessed 2021), or Walton (2011), quoting Mackie.

I do not have space here to demonstrate this point in relation to the much wider sample of informal fallacies that would be considered to thoroughly show its generality. However, I have done so elsewhere, and am planning to do so again in a later book of this series.[8] Meanwhile, you can test out any informal fallacy for yourself simply by analysing it in terms of assumptions made rather than in terms of logical validity (I have yet to find an informal fallacy that could not be analysed in this way). You can then check that the assumptions are absolute – which, again, they always are. There is, of course, no way to show the falseness of the inflation of absolute deduction through absolute deduction: if you are not convinced, you just have to go through an inductive process of testing examples until you are.

In some respects assumptions and reasoning are not separate. Traditionally, a conclusion fails to follow validly from its premises because an unacknowledged assumption is being made. However, once one acknowledges that no conclusion in any case follows validly from its premises because of embodiment, it turns out that the fallacious assumption is disruptive to the justification of the conclusion, not necessarily because of the content of any unacknowledged addition, but because of its false certainty. Once we remove this false certainty and operate only with what we acknowledge as provisional premises, unacknowledged assumptions can potentially be incorporated into our beliefs by incrementally modifying them rather than totally disrupting them. Mistakes in our thinking themselves are not the problem: it is the *denial* of potential mistakes that is the problem. For example, once we stop thinking absolutely of whether James is or is not *necessarily* correct, we can consider the balance of evidence firstly supporting or undermining what he claims, and secondly (where that is in doubt) about his degree of personal credibility. In this way we can reach a justifiable rejection of his claims without bringing in absolutization to merely dismiss them.

In relation to fallacies, then, I must conclude the following unorthodox points:

1. All arguments by embodied beings are formally fallacious.
2. The identification of an argument as formally fallacious tells us nothing about its justification in relation to experience.

8   iv.3; V.

3. Informal fallacies do not lack justification because of their reasoning, but because of their absolute assumptions.

This provides further evidence of the inflation of logic, in addition to the points already mentioned in 4.b about the over-use of the idea of 'rationality' and the extension of assumptions about logic to causation. If we are sufficiently aware of these inflations of both metaphysics and logic, we may be able to stop absolutizations creeping in simply through the entrenched cultural inflation of absolutized terms in our language.

Considering the evidence from philosophy in this section as a whole, then, it is clear that it gives us much further information about the nature of absolutization. Absolutization is not merely a process of reinforcing feedback loops in judgement that deny embodiment and maintain the delusion of belief as a separate representational system. It is also interdependent with a whole self-reinforcing sub-system in human culture to which we can give the name of metaphysical philosophy. Metaphysical philosophy consists of self-reinforcing sets of beliefs that are assumed coherent because of the belief in absolute deductive logic, and that help to maintain the habit of absolutization in the wider culture by the deductions that are made from it in every area of life. This self-reinforcing sub-system has played a large role in maintaining absolutization in human judgement, by constantly reinforcing it in the cultural beliefs of human societies. It has defended itself against challenges by inflatedly appropriating our interpretation of experience, and by spreading the delusion that it is necessary and indispensable.

5. Psychology

5.a. Repression and Conflict

> *Summary*
>
> The insight of psychoanalysis is the recognition of conflict between different parts of our psyches that try to repress each other. This basic model, stripped of unnecessary elaborations, can also be supported by neuroscience. Conflict occurs between sets of associated desires and beliefs, emerging at different times, but each using absolutization to maintain its position over the others. This model can also be applied to socio-political conflict, which is between the desires and beliefs that are dominant within individuals at a particular time.

The final element of this survey of the nature of absolutization, in this section, comes from psychology: particularly from mainstream cognitive and social psychology, together with the mis-named 'analytic' (Jungian) approach to psychology. From broadly Jungian approaches to psychology that have influenced many aspects of psychotherapy, we can develop an account of how absolutization creates conflict, and of how this conflict is maintained by projection. From more mainstream and recent cognitive psychology, we can develop an account of the relationship between absolutization and bias, and thus of how absolutization routinely distorts our judgements. From social psychology and allied areas of the social sciences, we can also develop an account of the relationship between absolutization and group binding. Finally, I will be able to slightly ameliorate the negativity of my account of absolutization by using my post-Jungian theory of archetypes to identify some positive applications of infinite concepts.

An account of how absolutization creates and perpetuates conflict can be broadly developed from the stream in psychology that began with aspects of Freudian psychoanalysis, but was developed in different directions in Jungian analytic psychology, and has now passed fairly into the mainstream of therapeutically-oriented psychological practice, for instance in the work of Daniel Siegel.[1] This

---

1 Siegel (2011) ch. 4.

perspective posits *conflict* as the major problem of human judgement, also implying that *integration* of that conflict is the major solution. The implications of this approach, however, are rarely applied beyond the sphere of therapeutic psychology.

Freud's initial contribution is the use of the notion of psychological repression to help explain mental illness. Mental illness, if not attributable to damage or malfunction in the brain or nervous system, seems to inevitably involve *conflict* within the human psyche. We like to think of ourselves as singular selves, but do not behave consistently with that idea of ourselves over time. The depressed, for instance, in some respects at some points do not want to be depressed, but are nevertheless involuntarily taken over by depression at other points. In other more severe cases, psychosis may even involve the emergence of explicit multiple personalities.

Freud developed this basic insight from *Studies in Hysteria* in 1895,[2] but was unfortunately diverted by searching for historical causes of conflict and associating it with a rigid theory of the psyche, rather than only focusing on the practical question of how conflict can be resolved. Jung, however, then developed a much more helpful understanding of integration – namely the long-term resolution of psychic conflict as a positive aspect of human development rather than merely the avoidance of mental illness. He usually referred to this as 'individuation', but its implications are not confined to individual development.[3]

Both Freud and Jung used the model of the 'ego' and the 'unconscious' to model the basic conflict. The ego is who we think we are and identify with (at least for the moment), but other sides of ourselves surprise us 'from the unconscious'. I don't think it is necessary to always stick to this terminology to make use of their basic insights into psychic conflict. The breakthrough created by their basic modelling needs to be clearly separated from the speculative theories about the causes of such conflict that Freud particularly indulged in, from the Oedipus Complex to the Primeval Horde. We do not need to know the ultimate causes of psychological conflict in order to appreciate it as conflict. We don't even necessarily have to have a particularly developed theory of 'the unconscious' – merely to notice that our judgements are observably inconsistent over a

---

2   Freud & Breuer (2004).
3   Jung (1966) §227.

period of time.⁴ We are all inconsistent in our judgements to some degree, but those cases labelled 'mental illness' may offer particularly acute or chronic instances of it.

The psychoanalytic perspective on the disruptive effects of conflict in the psyche can also be reinforced by a systems theory perspective. Conflict within the psyche can be understood in systems terms as *suboptimization* – that is, the negative effect on a whole system when a sub-system has contrary goals to the wider system (or to another sub-system).⁵ A non-human parallel for conflicting sub-systems would be, say, an octopus, one of whose limbs is trying to grab prey but another is simultaneously trying to push it away. The suboptimization resulting from internal conflict of persons can be starkly seen in cases such as multiple personality disorder.

The psychoanalytic tradition also offers a further element that can help us to understand this conflict, not causally, but as part of a bigger pattern of phenomena – that is, the notion of *repression*. Whenever there is a conflict, two forces are each trying to eliminate the other. Freud and Jung spoke of what is repressed in the 'unconscious' as a 'complex', but also that the complex at times becomes dominant (i.e. temporarily conscious), creating the symptoms of mental illness⁶ – so it is clear from this that the repression cuts both ways, with the 'complex' also trying to repress the dominant ego and succeeding at times. It is also clear that the harm of the repression comes from its secrecy – that is, the lack of awareness joining the two opposed elements in the psyche.⁷

For two parts of a person to be opposed, they must have contradictions in both *desire* and *belief*. The beliefs, or represented states of affairs, of the two parts must be inconsistent. However, this would not matter if those two inconsistent parts were not also associated with desire, whereby each pursues represented goals against their represented background. My thesis is that such conflicting beliefs are prevented from integrating by absolutization, of which repression is a psychological feature. The struggle that Freud and Jung noted between a 'complex' and the dominant beliefs and desires is one of each trying to eliminate the other by claiming it is the whole

---

4   See Ellis (2022) 1.e for a more developed argument that we do not really need the term 'unconscious'.
5   Meadows (2008) p. 85.
6   Jung (1966) §125–6.
7   Ibid.

story, thinking of itself as an isolated system, believing that its world can be represented through language, and being caught up in reinforcing feedback loops.

The relationship between desire, belief, and absolutization can be clarified using neuroscience. Whilst desire is associated with the 'reptilian brain' or limbic system (especially the striatum),[8] the energy that desire mobilizes as part of a response to particular stimuli needs to be directed. It can only be directed in relation to an assumed representation of our environment and of our goals in relation to that environment, which is the specific responsibility of the left pre-frontal cortex.[9] Changes in that assumed representation can help to modulate the desire, whilst bodily changes in the desire will also affect our assumed representation. Whether our beliefs are absolutized (subject to over-dominance by the left pre-frontal cortex) or provisional (open to the wider awareness of the right hemisphere) creates a crucial difference in how our desires are channelled. If our beliefs are absolutized, conflict becomes entrenched, whereas if it is not, resolution of the conflict is possible.

Repression thus seems to be related to the habitual dominance of the left hemisphere over the right, with the corpus callosum that joins the hemispheres being associated with mutual repressive processes (see earlier discussion in 2.b). So at times, the right hemisphere may become dominant (or at least less repressed) as we switch into a receptive or watchful mode. However, the less threatening our environment (due to our wholesale modification of it), the less we need that right hemisphere mode, and the more common left hemisphere over-dominance can become.[10] Left hemisphere dominance is not only exerted over the right hemisphere, however, but also over alternative left hemisphere dominated beliefs that may emerge at different times, for which right hemisphere intermediation would be required for mutual awareness. This, I suggest, is the repression that Freud and Jung discussed, made conscious to us through the flips between different opposed perspectives that we saw as the effect of fragility (2.c).

The infinite rationalization of absolutization (4.d) makes it highly effective at repressing, because no new information is allowed to

---

8   Lewis (2015) pp. 56–9.
9   McGilchrist (2009) pp. 113–15.
10   This fits McGilchrist's (2009) overall thesis of the increasing over-dominance of the left hemisphere in the modern world.

modify the dominant belief. In this respect it can be compared to a warrior covered in plate armour – the protective layer of rationalization deflects any new considerations, in contrast to the vulnerable position of a provisional belief that is open to modification. Whatever the strokes of observation, recognition, or argument offered by the warring beliefs, it is most commonly the one that is least vulnerable that can withstand those strokes best. In this way, absolutization can be seen as an adaptation by elements of our psyche to assert themselves over others. It is only when the whole combat is interrupted by radical new conditions (analogous to, say, the warrior in plate armour toppling over, or the invention of cannon) that absolute beliefs may be suddenly overcome (see 2.c).

As a dominant left hemisphere belief represses another, the alternative beliefs remain meaningful, and the synaptic paths that they use remain available. However, energy is removed from them as the dominant beliefs and desires become entrenched, and their assumed representational status is reinforced. An external disruption to that dominant pattern is required to allow the possibility of the repressed beliefs re-emerging, unless we have had some practice in the process of diverting our energies into those weaker channels through well-targeted education or training.

If our desires conflict in reaching their represented goals, their energy begins to be at least partially directed towards repressing the obstacle rather than simply achieving the goal. The whole operation of the organism then becomes less efficient, since energy is now being diverted into internal conflict rather than to the fulfilment of external goals. A simple everyday example of this is procrastination: if I sit down to write, but too big a part of me wants to check social media instead, I 'waste' a lot of time pursuing this subsidiary goal, and some energy 'forcing' myself back to the main task. My overall progress in writing then becomes less efficient.

Psychoanalysis helped to demonstrate that repressed desires do not simply go away. After all, the neural pathways along which these energies are flowing are already well established, and get even better established the more we use them. For instance, the procrastinatory distraction may be temporarily repressed by what we call 'an effort of will', but once the gathered energies of that effort are dispersed, it will only take another small trigger to set the distraction off again. This phenomenon can be most clearly observed for oneself in the course of mindfulness practice, which in many ways allows us to cut out the previous observational role of the psychoanalyst and more directly analyse our own processes. However much we may resolve to stay with an object of meditation, a distraction will usually re-appear after a short while.

Of course, we cannot make absolute claims about the *in*effectiveness of repression – perhaps it does work sometimes, or sometimes it just takes so long for repressed contents to re-emerge that we lose track of them. Generally, however, the ineffectiveness of repression is an observable phenomenon that becomes clearer the longer we observe our own or others' processes. If you don't believe this, try some mindfulness practice and observe it for yourself. A repressive approach to mindfulness tends to result in alienated states,[11] of the kind that were recognized and avoided by the Buddha in the story of his early life, when he moved on from asceticism and discovered the Middle Way.[12] The ineffectiveness of repression is an aspect of the wider long-term ineffectiveness of absolutization in general.

The relationship between repression and absolutization becomes increasingly evident when we reflect on the phenomenal relationship between conflicting desires and background beliefs. When desires attempt to repress each other, they use incompatible beliefs about both their goals and the background conditions. However, that is only a problem as long as they *remain* incompatible through the rigidity of the beliefs. If the beliefs involved are provisional, in the sense that they are sufficiently associated with awareness of alternative possibilities, they can both be adjusted so that they become compatible. However, if the beliefs are absolute, there is no available mechanism for adjustment: so as long as energy keeps pouring into the maintenance of that belief, the only alternative is conflict. Think of two men squaring up who think they have been insulted by each other: as long as they keep focusing on the assumed insults, there is no option available to back down. The other features of absolutization that I have already discussed, such as the assumed independence of the belief system, the denial of embodiment, and the use of metaphysical belief, can here be seen as having a direct role in maintaining conflict, by blocking any awareness of a wider context in which that conflict could be resolved.

---

11 See Ellis (2020a) p. 47.
12 See Ellis (2019) 1.e.

Repression as a strategy maintaining conflict needs to be contrasted with *suppression*, where the latter means the prioritization of one belief in a particular situation for practical purposes, whilst maintaining awareness of both beliefs and of the possibility of reconciling them. For example, a professional encountering sexual feelings for a client in the course of his/her duties clearly should not act to make those feelings known – otherwise important social rules are broken and longer-term conflict is also created. However, not acting on one's feelings does not necessarily mean that one represses them. One may remain aware of them, and reflect on or work with them later. In the longer term, some degree of suppression is necessary for *integration* of conflicting beliefs. We need to be in a situation of relative tranquillity to be able to securely reflect on conflicting beliefs, question their framing assumptions, and reconcile them. We cannot usually in practice do this on the spot in the same situation where conflicting beliefs arise.

Repression at a psychological level in the individual can also be seen as operating at the socio-political level, and producing conflict in the same way. The only difference between them is that the beliefs and desires that conflict with each other when different individuals conflict at the socio-political level are those that happen to be dominant in those individuals at the time of the conflict (and thus gain social expression), rather than those in conflict within the individual.[13]

At the socio-political level, the dominance of absolutized beliefs takes the form of one individual, in whom those absolutized beliefs are dominant, using them to maintain dominance over another, in whom there are either provisional beliefs dominant, or other absolutized beliefs that are obliged to give way due to the social conditions. The sergeant-major exerts power over the private through absolute belief in the rules of the army, or the domestic abuser over a cowed spouse through absolute belief in his rightful power. Exactly the same pattern can be envisaged at increasing scales, as we also consider the use of absolutized belief for an individual to gain power over a group, for a group to gain power over an individual, or for a group to gain power over another group. In the third of those categories, for instance, we could take the dominance of Indian caste Hindus over Dalits, through absolute belief not only in

---

13   Also ii.1.e; II.5.

their immediate social status, but also in a long-standing supportive ideology going back to the *Law Book of Manu*. Whenever dominance is achieved in our socio-political hierarchies, individuals who are dominated by absolutized beliefs, and have learned to use them, use them as a weapon to subdue others. Actual weapons are subsidiary to this, because no person can be dominated without their beliefs being changed. Violence, or the threat of violence, is merely a way of reinforcing the power of one absolutization over another by showing our total commitment to dominating convictions – despite a risk of injury or death.

Of course, many of the beliefs that conflict within an individual will be identified with particular groups: for instance, if a desire to give up alcohol conflicts with a desire to drink it, this may appear socially as a conflict between pressure from friends at the bar versus pressure from my doctor or a spouse concerned about my health. At the level of conflict between groups, at whatever level of organization, the conflict is one between the dominant beliefs in the respective individuals who in turn dominate the groups concerned: the 'chemistry' between individual leaders can thus determine the course of international negotiations. The conflict can thus be analysed at both psychological and socio-political levels, but still shows the same features by which absolutization maintains that conflict through the rigidity of the belief for the person holding it.

The same defence mechanisms for absolutization that we saw working from a philosophical perspective – those of metaphysical belief and absolute deductive logic that are armour-plated through infinite rationalization, taken to be inevitable, and constantly inflated – can also be seen from a psychological perspective. The psychological basis of metaphysics is projection – the assumption that the things we believe must actually be the case – which I will discuss in the next chapter. Logic can also be projected, as we assume that the links between phenomena that we conceptualize are the ones in the world. Infinite rationalization has its psychological correlate in confirmation bias (see 5.c), together with a whole set of subsidiary biases that deflect new information from making any impression on us. The inflation of metaphysics and logic can also be understood in terms of substitution (discussed in 5.d), a recognized psychological process, as we substitute abstracted and merely conceptual beliefs for more difficult and uncertain experiential ones.

The further we go into the normal discussion of conflict in the socio-political context, however, the more we seem likely to lose sight of the recognition that the conflicting beliefs are held by embodied beings, who can provide a wider context in which the absolutization could be resolved. Instead, we discuss the beliefs intellectually in total abstraction from who holds them or what role they play. Even if we do that in a leisurely analytic way, the best we can usually do is then identify conflicting root beliefs. For example, we recognize that a conflict over abortion is a conflict of absolute beliefs about the value and definition of genetically human life. We then debate what is the 'true' value or the 'true' definition, usually fruitlessly – but we are still worlds away from the embodied context of a pregnant woman carrying a foetus within her, and the meaning the different options on abortion would have for both woman and foetus. Even when we identify different metaphysical beliefs with different *groups,* such as Catholics versus feminists, we usually stop short of recognizing them as psychological conflicts in which both sides are found within each of us.

To stop thinking in terms of the 'true' or 'right' beliefs 'winning', and instead in terms of resolving a conflict (the integration model), requires a major moral shift – but one that is long overdue. Despite the development of ideas descended from psychoanalysis over a century, such a shift would still be condemned by most people as a relativist one that gives up on the 'truth'. However, it is not relativist in the ways that practically matter. Relativism is damaging when it undermines the recognition that some judgements are better than others, but it can be distinguished from the *particularism* that helps us see each better judgement as taking place in a unique individual set of conditions in a particular moment.

We are so used to thinking of conflict as the conflict between individuals, that it may take a sustained effort to start thinking about it as a conflict between *beliefs* within those individuals. However, that recognition has gained increasing ground in recent times. Gandhi used it as a basis for non-violent action that was directed against opponents' beliefs rather than their bodies: as he wrote, 'The satyagrahi's object is to convert, not to coerce, the wrongdoer'.[14] Control of media and communication to manipulate beliefs has also been increasingly recognized as the main locus of political struggle, from

---

14   Gandhi (1939).

Goebbels' propaganda to manipulation of Facebook by Russian trolls. It's by switching to such a model that we can readily see why absolutization (as a judgement) is a source of conflict. When people vary so much internally in their beliefs, it is misleading and unjust to say that one person conflicts with another. Rather, one belief, judged to be correct at a particular moment, conflicts with another, also judged to be correct at that moment or another moment, in the person who holds it.

Thinking of conflicting beliefs caused by absolutization in this way, it becomes clearer that the potential resolution of any conflict depends on the disarming of absolutized beliefs. If we understand these internally, then external resolution can also be understood as the resolution between beliefs identified with by each party at that point. These beliefs may well be closely associated with the image of the person who is assumed to hold them. However, your opponent implicitly holds your belief as well as 'his' belief (just as you hold his) and your task is to encourage him to reconcile the conflict between the beliefs you each represent, as well as the similar conflicting beliefs in yourself.

5.b. Projection

> *Summary*
>
> Projection, as distinguishable from normal features of perception, occurs when we take a particular meaningful feature of an object to be its only relevant feature. We take this feature to be the 'real' or essential feature of the object and thus have a metaphysical view that excludes alternatives, with all the other dimensions of absolutization. Such projection can also be reversed into an equally deluded opposite when we assume that that feature is instead totally absent from the object.

In my most recent previous book, *Archetypes in Religion and Beyond*, a whole section is devoted to projection, including a discussion of its relationship to metaphysical belief, the denial of embodiment, left hemisphere over-dominance, bias, reinforcing feedback, power, and evil.[1] There (in the context of a book that focuses on archetypes, their function, projection, and integration) I present projection as equivalent to absolutization, consistent with its presentation here as a dimension of absolutization. My definition of projection there is

> *Projection occurs when the archetypal function operates in an individual to create a meaningful symbol, but that symbol is assumed to be the only relevant feature of a complex object with which it is associated.*[2]

For the idea of *archetypal function* (in brief, the way a symbol can operate as a long-term inspiration – not involving any metaphysical assumptions), see 5.f below. If we see a person only in terms of the archetype they represent to us (e.g. a wise person as a guru, or a lover as a perfect masculine or feminine), this is a common form of archetypal projection. Archetypal projection can be understood in a way that encompasses all projection, but the concept of projection itself is more basic than that and does not necessarily have to be understood in archetypal terms. It involves the identification of any quality that is a result of our own needs and functions in understanding an object, and assuming that it is essential to or constitutive of that object. For example, I was once hiking through a forest in Swedish Lapland, and on entering a clearing, was convinced that there was a bear on the other side of the clearing. This perception, however, was a function of my own self-preservation instincts, as

---

1   Ellis (2022) section 2.
2   Ibid. 2.a.

the object I was looking at turned out to be a dead tree covered with moss. If you are comfortable with archetypal vocabulary, you can call this a projection of the shadow, but if not, you can still understand it as a projection of fear. We can similarly project onto objects (or people) because they fulfil our goals, because they compensate for a limitation in ourselves, or because they represent an unfulfilled potential in ourselves.

Projection is a widely understood concept in psychology, but its relationship to absolutization is often obscured by its presentation as an inevitable process (in parallel to the presentation of metaphysics as inevitable). This is the effect if projection is defined in terms that are ultimately metaphysical (that is, in terms of the relationship between subject and object independently of experience),[3] rather than phenomenally in terms of experience. If we define projection simply as the belief that qualities in the subject are attributed to the object, there is no way of distinguishing projection from the inevitable aspect of embodiment that Popper referred to as 'the theory-ladenness of perception' – the fact that we cannot avoid formatting what we observe in our own terms. In this sense we always 'project', but in that sense there is also no distinction between 'projection' and ordinary perception. For the term 'projection' to be helpful to us in distinguishing experiences, it needs to identify the moral distinction between a type of belief-laden perception that cannot be potentially avoided and one that can. For practical reasons I thus define projection in terms of absolutization: that is, as the belief that the features that fulfil our desires and that we think we perceive beyond ourselves *are actually there*.

The absolutizing nature of projection involves the identification of one relevant feature which we take to be 'essential', 'real', or 'definitive' of an object (including a person). We interact with objects practically, and in order to do so we do have to assume that they have properties that will more or less directly fulfil our desires: for instance, that a sandwich will nourish us, a person can be a source of potential interaction, or a mountain can be admired as part of a landscape. Such practical interaction is not necessarily projective, as long as we are ready to recognize that these objects have other potential features that do not necessarily help to fulfil our desires as we currently experience them. The production of the sandwich

---

3 E.g. in Jung (1946) p. 582.

has ecological effects, the person may be too busy with their own concerns to talk to us, and the mountain may be scheduled for quarrying rather than only admiration. The point of projection is where we make a judgement that excludes these options (as discussed in 1.d) and insists on an account of the object that is framed by our desires – or not (setting up the duality discussed in 1.c).

Another way of distinguishing merely limited perception from projection is in terms of the awareness we bring to our desires rather than just to the object, that is, in terms of the integration of the desires that create the framing. An object that we see *only* in terms of an unexamined, uncontextualized immediate desire is a projected object: for instance, a tree is just a source of timber, and a 'friend' just someone we can get money or favours from. However, as we develop longer-term and more sustainable desires that have started to overcome the conflicts discussed in 1.a, we have more different options of ways to understand the object. This enables objects to offer inspiration for longer-term intentions that are associated with wider contextual awareness – that is, for them to have an archetypal meaning (see 5.f). The tree may be a symbol of spiritual growth, or the marker of a regular walk, rather than just timber.

A projected view of an object is thus a metaphysical view: that is, a view based on belief of what it is *truly* like as opposed to how it merely appears. To maintain such a view, we are obliged to constantly limit the options with which we interpret what we perceive. To maintain and defend a projected view of an object, we may also develop projected views of its causal relationships with other objects that reflect, not causal observations open to investigation, but assumed necessary relationships between objects (absolutized deductive logic). For example, to maintain an idealized belief that the denuded British upland landscape is 'natural', we may maintain beliefs about the 'naturalness' and necessity of grazing and eating sheep, about the land-holding system, or about the impossibility of allowing the more complex climactic vegetation to develop: all of these other supposed causal necessities will then bolster our view in any consideration of the subject. Absolutized ideologies of all kinds consist in self-reinforcing webs of such reasoning, coherent in their own terms and supported by groups (see 5.e), but infinitely rationalized rather than modified in response to challenge.

The metaphysical nature of projection also requires us to understand its opposite, which I call *reactive projection*.[4] This is the absolute denial of any truth in a projection, usually in reaction to a projection previously held and then revoked. Just as the opposite of a metaphysical belief is another metaphysical belief, the opposite of a positive projection is a negative projection, in the sense of the projection of the total absence of features that we previously believed to be totally present. Due to the danger of confusion with projections of objects that are emotionally or consequentially negative, however, I find it preferable to use the term 'reactive'. For example, a man who is in love with a woman and assumes everything about her to be good (she is beautiful, kind, intelligent, courageous, etc.) may react to being rejected by deciding that he was totally wrong in some of his previous views of her. Although he can't deny that she is still beautiful and intelligent, he now regards her as unkind and cowardly (note the selectivity here, which is consistent with absolutizations only needing to be applied in one respect to be present). This is consistent with the account of fragility I gave in 2.c: projections are fragile and thus subject to 'flips' to the opposite view once a systemic tipping point has been reached.

One of the most striking examples of projection as absolutization, recognized as problematic for millennia in some religious traditions, is idolatry. Idolatry, as the belief that an object *is* God and/or has his infinite properties, is not practically problematic because it is 'true' or 'false', but rather because of its projection of infinite qualities.[5] Rather than acting as an inspiration for our own challenging long-term development of new qualities, then, the idol can then easily be used as a shortcut to try to fix short-term desires, such as a conception or good exam results. Given that such projection can be directed just as easily on a non-located supernatural force as on a physical image, any attempt to use God to 'fix' things (such as prayers of intercession) can be seen as idolatrous in this sense, if they are not embedded in sufficient awareness of a larger context of uncertainty. This example thus illustrates how a physical object is merely a prop – it is our absolutization of a belief about it that makes a projection.

---

4   Ellis (2022) 2.b.
5   Ibid. 5.f and 5.k for discussions of this in relation to early Judaism and Islam.

Although originating in the psychoanalytic stream of psychology, the concept of projection is entirely compatible with that of bias from cognitive psychology, which I will discuss in the next chapter. Cognitive psychology can thus reinforce our understanding of projection through a synthetic process, and provide much further evidence for it. Since bias is a limiting tendency in our interpretation of experience, there is an obvious overlap (at least – I will posit an identity) with projection as an absolutized interpretation of perception. It is to this that I will turn next.

5.c. Confirmation Bias

> *Summary*
>
> 'Confirmation bias' is a broad term that covers lots of other biases, all of which refer to our tendency to interpret new information only in terms of existing beliefs. Biases involve the substitution of fast processing for slow. These are absolutizations at the point where alternatives become relevant, but we either remain deceived by the bias, or react by taking the opposite view that our biased view is completely false. Bias at this point is indistinguishable from fallacy.

Bias is a tendency to the distortion of judgement to which all humans are subject, and which has been the object of a very impressive range of work in cognitive psychology in recent decades. The progenitor of the wide range of other identified biases is confirmation bias – the tendency to select and interpret information from the world to fit our pre-existing beliefs and thus to preclude learning. This tendency has been demonstrated in psychological experiments in a wide variety of ways: for instance, when people were given number sequences and asked to identify the rules that governed them, experimenters found an overwhelming tendency for people to seek confirmation of their initial ideas about the rules, rather than considering alternative possibilities that would falsify their guesses.[1]

I will approach bias here particularly in relation to confirmation bias, but with the implication that what I will say about its relationship to absolutization applies equally to a wide range of other identifiable biases. I have made a fuller discussion of the way that other biases are all expressions of confirmation bias, and thus of absolutization, elsewhere.[2] Basically what all biases have in common is a tendency to assume the truth of an initial belief that has been formed in partial and inadequate ways. We then resist any challenges to that initial belief using what Leon Festinger called the 'belief disconfirmation paradigm': we may reject new information, reinterpret it as compatible with our previous beliefs, seek out a rationalization for rejecting it, or even misperceive objects that might challenge our view.[3]

1 Wason (1960).
2 iv.3; V.
3 Festinger (1957).

General understanding of the implications of bias research is greatly indebted to Daniel Kahneman and his synthesis of his own lifetime's research with Amos Tversky – *Thinking Fast and Slow*.[4] In this book he made clear for a wider audience the way that biases operate as shortcuts – as 'fast thinking' when 'slow thinking' would be more appropriate and effective. This 'fast thinking' is understandable, and has been developed because it saves energy and allows more effective rapid responses to familiar situations, but in the complexity of modern human life it often serves us ill. The more varied and complex the conditions we face, and the more long-term the challenges they pose, the less equipped fast thinking is to face them. For instance, an instantaneous fear response to someone with a different colour skin might have served us well in past homogeneous societies, but serves us ill in globalized ones.

Cognitive psychologists tend to contrast biased judgements with 'rational' ones – but the disadvantage of the term 'rational', as I suggested in 4.b, is that it involves an inflation of logic and the suggestion that non-absolute functions are in some sense absolute. Instead, then, I suggest that biased judgement should be contrasted with *integrated* judgement. Integrated judgement is able to overcome conflict that prevents us from applying our available energies and resources fully to address the conditions we encounter. As discussed in 5.a, that conflict is due to absolutization, as a pattern of infinite rationalization is substituted for mutual adjustment when beliefs conflict. The main missing piece of the explanatory puzzle of absolutization, then, is to show how bias is absolutization.

Cognitive psychologists have been somewhat distracted from seeing bias as absolutization, I think, by an over-concern with explanatory theories about the origin of bias at the expense of a practical framework for responding to it. Evolutionary explanations of bias sometimes turn into excuses for it, in which the ways that biases can be seen as adaptive in human pre-history can shade into the judgement that we should not be too worried about it today. However, in my view over-concern with *explaining* bias is too often a distraction from recognizing its full negative impact today. Whatever the causes of bias in human nature or nurture, it is obviously bias that has produced, for instance, the extremes of Islamic State, then more recently the election of (and continuing support for) Donald

---

4   Kahneman (2011).

Trump, with its accompanying serious threat to US democracy, and the huge setback this represented for addressing very urgent world problems such as climate change. What these two phenomena have in common is the inability of those responsible for them to respond to new information. As I write, in January 2021, there is news of Trump supporters storming the US Capitol, because they simply will not listen to explanations of the overwhelming evidence that the election that defeated Trump was legitimate. Whether or not the tendencies of human judgement were well-adapted to a past phase of human development, the urgent issue is the gaping extent to which it is *not* adapted to our current situation.

Bias can be clearly seen as absolutization if we focus, not on the causes of bias or the excuses for it, but rather on the judgements we make when we are biased. A bias in the abstract may play various roles, but for an individual *to be deceived by a bias* is equivalent to absolutization. A bias becomes relevant in the same way that I argued in 4.e that metaphysics becomes relevant, namely when the possibility of it being questioned potentially comes into experience, but it is resisted through an implicit or explicit process of substitution. A bias is a relevant bias when it makes a difference. For example, let's suppose that a person afraid of flying boards a plane, and resists their companion's contextualization of their fear in terms of the low probability of a plane crash. At that point, rather than entering into the 'slow thinking' that would be required to begin to contextualize the fear, the person continues with the 'fast thinking' of her proliferating loops of association between planes and danger. If the person had never encountered any information about the low probability of crashing, the bias would just be part of the unreflective context of that situation, but when that information is resisted (for whatever reasons), it becomes an absolutization. What makes a difference is the practical relevance of the alternative and its rejection.

Just as in every other way of understanding absolutization, we also need to be aware of the opposing reaction as an alternative possibility. A person can absolutize, not only by remaining deluded by a bias in circumstances where it becomes relevant, but also by overreacting into a negative absolutization when rejecting the bias. Thus if the person afraid of flying 'flipped' into a complete disavowal of any danger at all in flight, commenting loudly that the safety announcements were a complete waste of time because we know planes are safe, this would involve a contrary absolutization. The alternative to absolutization, as always, is not the opposing absolutization, but provisionality. There is then scope for acknowledging one's fear of flying whilst acknowledging the statistics and trying to relax unreflective fears, rather than reinforcing those fears through absolute belief.

The process of maintaining a bias seems to be one of *substitution*, which I will be discussing further in the next chapter. This often means the substitution of a slow process by a faster one. However, even if it all happens slowly, it means the substitution of an incremental process by an absolute one, substituting a process of weighing up and adjustment between different options with one of unreflective selection from two options.

That deception by confirmation bias (or by the reaction against it) is also absolutization, can be reinforced in terms of all the other features of absolutization discussed so far. Confirmation bias is proliferation, because the same deep-etched neural pathways are ever more deeply entrenched by the recycling of the same assumptions, with increasing amounts of energy devoted to maintaining them as potential obstacles appear. Confirmation bias is craving (or hatred) because the limited beliefs we continue to assume are those we identify with – whether those involve positive goals we want to achieve or things we want to reject. It is maintained by absolutizing its negations and restricting its options, so that alternatives become unthinkable. It consists in reinforcing feedback loops in which new influences are excluded and in which the belief system is assumed to be independent. It is fragile, because it merely puts off the day when a concatenation of conditions will force a traumatic recognition of what has been excluded. It is representationalist, because it assumes that the claims made about the beliefs that are constantly reinforced are capable of a precise relationship with reality. It ignores embodiment, which would force us to recognize the limitation of these assumptions. It is metaphysical, because of the assumed reality of beliefs that resist alternatives, and which are linked together using assumed absolute deductive logic. It is repressive because of its exclusion of alternative views, and projective because of its assumption that certain characteristics of an object are its essence or totality.

The distinction between bias and fallacy also needs to be deconstructed. As discussed in 4.f, fallacies are often considered to be faults in logical validity, a claim that represents an absolutizing inflation of deductive logic rather than an adequate account of the phenomena of fallacy. The unhelpful aspect of fallacies is best explained by absolutization, because of the way that informal fallacies perpetuate conflict by undermining shared social rules that help provide the dialectical basis of shared investigation to resolve disagreement.[5] In this respect, then, they are not distinguishable from biases, which also maintain conflict because they deceive us into thinking we have a total view by excluding alternatives. Whilst the emphasis in discussion of biases is psychological, that in discussion of fallacies is that of a role in argument – but this is a distinction without a difference, created by specialists trained into the habit of looking at the same phenomena only from one perspective. In practice, popular discussions of bias and fallacy blur into one another – which is hardly surprising, given their phenomenal identity.

Perhaps one of the easiest places to see confirmation bias and its effects is in the history of science, which has increasingly highlighted it as the central problem of scientific method. As already discussed in 4.c, Thomas Kuhn and Imre Lakatos both discussed the difficulties for scientists working within a failing or unfruitful paradigm that is then challenged by a new alternative. There is no point at which the old paradigm is definitively identifiable as false, just as the conspiracy theorist never receives any unambiguous indication of the falsity of a conspiracy theory. Nevertheless, new paradigms do get adopted, and the unfruitfulness of old ones gradually gets recognized, all of which helps to demonstrate that confirmation bias is not inevitable, just as metaphysics is not inevitable. The rigour with which modern scientific method sets out to avoid confirmation bias, for example through the use of double-blind testing to eliminate the effects of human expectations on the results of drug trials, is rarely extended beyond the formal sphere of professional science, but does point us to some of the crucial features of provisionality as an alternative to absolutization.

5   Walton (1987) pp. 19–20.

5.d. Substitution

> *Summary*
>
> Substitution is typical of absolutization, consisting of the use of an easier process instead of a harder one. In cognitive psychology this is often taken to involve substituting a simpler deductive process for a more complex one. However, once complex deductive processes have been made easier through practice, they start to substitute for more complex inductive or experiential investigations. Even those trained in science may switch to deduction when outside their area of comfort.

The concept of *substitution* can particularly help us to understand the motive behind absolutization, because substitution is *easier*. A complex process of 'slow thinking' uses more energy than a quick process of 'fast thinking', so we employ the latter when the former is needed.[1] Using more energy means consuming more glucose, forcing our way through less frequently used synaptic channels, taking attention away from other things we might be doing, and perhaps even threatening our social position: so it is hardly surprising that we substitute. We take shortcuts: but shortcuts can sometimes create much bigger long-term problems than the slightly greater uses of time and energy they were intended to circumvent. The economies turn out to be false.

The phenomena of absolutization can be described in terms of substitution in a number of different respects. In relation to bias, cognitive psychologists have identified *attribute substitution*. In moral thinking, shortcuts involve the substitution of authorities or prototypes for the examination of complex conditions. Metaphysics itself can be seen as a substitution for empirical understanding. Deductive logic is a substitution for more complex induction. Excluding options involves substituting a simpler version of a system for a more complex one, and reinforcing feedback loops substitute a simpler loop for a more complex balancing one. The substitution is often wrongly simplified into one of emotions in the place of 'rationality', but it can also be reasoning that is substituted for emotional complexity. The abuse of Ockham's Razor as an argument for simplicity is one sign of absolutization becoming institutionalized.

1   Kahneman (2011) ch. 2.

Attribute substitution, as identified by Daniel Kahneman and Frederick Shane,[2] involves the substitution of an easier question for a harder one. When subjects were posed a question that required a lot of effort to answer, they would implicitly answer an easier question instead: thus, an association can be substituted for a probability, or an easier mathematical problem for a harder one. When students were first primed by being asked how many dates they had recently, and then asked how happy they were, they answered the difficult question of how happy they were in terms of the simpler one of how many dates they had had.[3] This particular study is telling, in that it shows the reduction of a complex *emotional* question (that might need to be answered by consulting a range of emotional experience, as well as by establishing criteria for 'happiness') to one that can be more easily measured and then reasoned about. It is not 'rationality' that feels hard, but simply complexity, of whatever type.

Cass Sunstein's application of the concept of substitution to moral issues[4] also reveals more of its relationship to absolutization. For instance, one way that people save energy when confronted with a complex moral issue is to appeal to an authority to give them a ready-made resolution of it. This is an aspect of foundationalism as a feature of metaphysical thinking, already noted in 4.c. In this respect, an authority is crucially distinct from a merely highly credible source, who might induce further reflection on the *complexity* of a moral issue, but the treatment of an authority as *absolute* is what enables it to become a substitute rather than a stimulus. Sunstein also notes that prototypical or stereotypical cases can substitute for the complex consideration that is required to take into account the details of specific cases. As prototypes provide an aspect of the meaning of what we are talking about, they are unavoidable bridges to appreciation of the more complex meaning of a category that covers lots of cases,[5] so to avoid this kind of absolutization we first have to appreciate this more complex meaning, then ensure that the prototypical meaning does not dominate our *beliefs* by providing the only option for the meaning of a category of options. For example, if our prototypical idea of sex is heterosexual sex, we have to first broaden our understanding of the *meaning* of sex and sexuality

---

2   Kahneman (2011) pp. 97-104.
3   Ibid.
4   Sunstein (2005).
5   See Ellis (2022) 1.i.

to avoid anti-homosexual bias. In the process, we will need to avoid forming our beliefs about sexuality on the basis of a substitution of that immediate association for a more complex process of reflection.

This identification of substitution in cognitive psychology is thus also an identification of an aspect of absolutization. The substitution can only occur because of other aspects of absolutization such as reinforcing feedback loops, exclusion of options, and assumed independence of the substitute system from other systems. Above all, substitution is clearly a feature of metaphysics (although academic taboos seem to stop cognitive psychologists from considering any such link). In metaphysics, abstract general beliefs are *substituted* for provisional beliefs justified by uncertain experience. Although in some ways, abstract ideas are harder for us to grasp than concrete ones, because we have to implicitly work back through a tree of cognitive models and metaphorical extensions to find an experience of embodied meaning to link with a new abstract idea, once we have become familiar with the abstract idea, this process becomes abbreviated, the metaphors 'die', and left hemisphere representations are substituted for them. As soon as we are dealing with dead representational meanings rather than live experiential ones, absolute or metaphysical ways of thinking become *easier* substitutions. This can be experienced directly in the distinction between creative writing and cliché. Clichés are dead representations that we find it much easier to use than fresh metaphors minted from our imaginations: that's why poets need critical feedback! In the same way, expressions of belief in an absolute representational form are less demanding to understand and create than those that are provisional, and thus frequently need to be hedged to take into account our embodied limitations.

To be able to avoid a substitution, we need to be able to engage with a more challenging set of conditions using complex meaning. We have to develop that complexity of meaning first through the capacity for abstraction, and then also by recognizing the limitations of that abstraction. As we start to develop the capacity for abstraction, metaphysical generalizations may provide a point of comparison that can help to make us aware of the alternatives to merely relative absolutizations. Thus, for instance, the dogmas of the Catholic church can challenge the social dogmas of a tribe: if the tribe exposes infants, then Catholic dogmas on preserving human life would challenge that and provide an initial point of critical leverage. However, after having made the effort to think more abstractly (for instance, of human life as a whole rather than only the welfare of one tribe), a further development of complexity is needed to see that these metaphysical beliefs are themselves based on limited assumptions. At each stage of transition in our psychological development, substitution provides the misleading comfort of an easy option, using only thinking skills that have now been made efficient through long practice. The hard option at each stage is the forging of new synaptic paths into the uncertain.[6]

For similar reasons, the use of what is assumed to be absolute deductive logic is a substitution for inductive reasoning – but again, when seen developmentally it may have a transitional value. Those struggling to develop mathematical skills may understandably feel unconvinced by the idea that purely abstract deductive reasoning is an easier substitution for inductive reasoning: however, not all deductive reasoning is complex, and once again what is easier depends on what you are practised at. Sweeping generalizations based on association are deductive (for instance, that I was burgled by a black man, so all black men are criminals). Whether we remain locked in prejudice due to such reasoning depends on our openness to right hemisphere information, not just on our capacity for complex thinking. However, development in deductive reasoning may give us a further capacity to compare such prejudiced beliefs with an absolute level of critical demand. This involves the 'Socratic questioning' employed by the character of Socrates in Plato's dialogues, to reveal such prejudices by asking for a 'true' or 'essential' characterization.[7] What truly makes a burglar? What is essential to a black man? Of course, as soon as we start to ask such questions, the prejudice is put in a larger context. At this level, absolute deductive thinking has a merely critical function that saves us from the quick prejudiced substitution.

However, when we pursue this critical function to the next level and begin to ask whether deductive reasoning is positively 'valid', it is the deductive reasoning that begins to appear as a substitution for the greater complexity of induction. To think inductively about burglars, we would need to start gathering statistics about how this

---

6   The psychological stages here reflect those of Kegan (1982), which will be discussed further in the planned third volume of this series.

7   Every Platonic dialogue contains examples of this. An especially good example is Meno 72ff. (Plato 1956 pp. 117ff.).

type of criminality relates to other social categorizations. We might discover patterns in those statistics: perhaps some groups (whether those of race, or income, or gender, or education level) are more prone to being burglars than others. At that point we have ceased to ask what a burglar 'essentially' is in the manner of Socrates, and realized that any answer to this question will be an over-simplification of the complexity of the phenomena. Any statements we make about the relationship between burglary and race will be then be incremental – a matter of degree – and provisional. Of course, there will still be some use for the critical perspective offered by comparing absolute beliefs reached by deduction with the provisional beliefs reached by induction – for instance, to check out the assumptions made in the gathering of the statistics. However, at this stage, the use of deduction to reach positive conclusions is a substitution – an act of laziness probably indicative of stress, conflict, or developmental regression.

How far the Socratic stage is vital and impossible to skip is a matter for further empirical research in psychology, but its importance may be underlined by the tendency of the scientifically trained (who have formally become experts in inductive thinking) not to take it provisionally, but rather to idealize the results reached by science and assume they are 'facts'. This suggests that they may be substituting through the use of metaphysical and deductive thinking at points of difficulty when scientific thinking gets tough – particularly when moving out of a controlled scientific environment and engaging with wider issues like ethics, religion, or the sociopolitical role of science. This leads me to suspect that most scientific training contains too little basic philosophy and critical thinking. Philosophy, of course, no more forms an independent system than science does, but premature specialization can lead both philosophers and scientists to omit some of the complexity of the whole system by ignoring some of its interrelationships with other systems.

Substitution seems to account for the way in which scientists may 'switch' into a mode of religious belief for what they may claim are, in Stephen J. Gould's phrase, 'non-overlapping magisteria'[8] (otherwise known as independent systems). Science, it is claimed, cannot deal with religious issues of human meaning, so instead, scientifically-minded theologians and theologically-minded scientists let go of

8   Gould (1999).

the provisional thinking they learned in science at the very moment when it might be most fruitful. Projected beliefs about God continue to be substituted for careful investigation of what God means in human experience – presumably because they are easier. Distracting scholarly debates about the historicity of religious texts continue to be substituted for investigation of what those texts may insightfully tell us about our experience – presumably because this is easier. Debates about what 'really' is or is not art continue to be substituted for investigation of what art means to us and why – presumably because this is easier. Claims about the essential characteristics of political leaders, ideologies, thinkers, or parties continue to be substituted for the crucial issues of what public policies would be best justified, and why the best justified positions are insufficiently supported, even when public policy may determine the very long-term survival of human civilization – presumably because it is easier.

How exactly we substitute an easier task for a harder one is thus highly dependent on our specific situation, and needs to be understood psychologically, but that doesn't prevent substitution from being a crucially helpful way of understanding absolutization. Our moral intuitions about it have long been expressed in popular ideas such as that the road to hell is smooth whilst the road to heaven is hard. To avoid substitution at any point, an effort is required to face up to complexity and interdependence – even though what 'effort' means is itself complex and may also involve bodily relaxation. More than anything, we avoid it by continuing to learn, not continuing to rely on modes that have *become* easy even if they were difficult in the past.

5.e. Group Binding

> *Summary*
>
> Absolutization is a shortcut for binding groups and exerting power, by creating unquestionable shared belief on which group identity is dependent. Four recognized biases provide evidence for group binding: the ingroup-outgroup bias, groupthink, social proof, and false consensus. A reaction against group binding may produce negative absolutization for a counter-group or for individualism. This is not an inevitable feature of group relationships, which can instead be based on our experience of solidarity, and even the use of power can be made conditional.

The socio-political implications of absolutization are another crucial element of our understanding of it: so crucial that some people (such as Marxists) have tended to understand absolutization only from a political point of view. In 5.a I discussed how absolutization creates repression, and how an infinitely rationalizable absolutized judgement seems invulnerable when compared to a provisional one. I also discussed the ways that this repressive function operates at a socio-political level, as well as psychologically within an individual, and how the meanings associated with each side in an inner conflict are often social ones (different views being associated with the groups that hold them). It is this capacity for absolutization to be used to repress challenging judgements by others that makes absolutization a *tool of power*. Power is exerted by a process of substitution at a social level: rather than individuals developing a provisional and conditional sense of solidarity through experience, an easier method of absolute group binding is substituted.

'Group binding' can consist in the repression of challenge in any size of group, from a couple through to a nation or an international organization. Groups may be formally constituted as partnerships, societies, or organizations, or they may be much more informal networks of social association. The subordination to absolutized belief that is involved may be a subordination to a leader or leaders, or it may be a more general subordination to a shared idea of the group as a whole. As a method for uniting a group, it may often be long-term, a way of creating open-ended commitment. However, it may also be a shorter-term method for uniting people only in certain limited respects for a particular purpose. A mob swept up in group consciousness that storms their country's parliament, for instance, may then disperse rather than forming a coherent long-term alliance.

The psychological research that can underpin this is that on group biases – research that took place some decades ago and is now well-established theoretically, but the implications of which have still been applied far too little. Group biases are of four identifiable kinds: ingroup-outgroup bias, groupthink, social proof, and false consensus. All of these can be understood as identifying different impacts of absolutization as group binding power.

Ingroup-outgroup bias is probably the most important of these biases to begin with, as the crucial point that gives groups their power over individuals is the ability to bestow or withdraw group acceptance. As groups become absolutized, their boundaries become rigid and discontinuous, so that individuals either accept group beliefs to maintain their membership, or risk losing it, along with the negative effects on their security and welfare that this may entail. Taylor and Doria's research into ingroup-outgroup bias[1] revealed how widespread this absolutization of group boundaries can often be, and that it does not depend so much on long-term sources of solidarity through familiarity as on a simple act of identification with one group to the exclusion of others. Taylor and Doria made groups arbitrary, eliminating any elements of kinship or long-term self-interest, but nevertheless still found a strong tendency for people to judge members of their own group more favourably than those in other groups. This shows all the marks of absolutization, because it involves an instant identificatory judgement that overrides other considerations, substituting group criteria for those based on wider experience.

Groupthink is the bias identified in studies by Irving Janis,[2] by which groups give priority in their decision-making to the maintenance of harmony or authority in the group. In other words, the effect of group membership on people is often to prioritize their status in the group over the use of experience to help inform group decision-making. Similar results were found by Solomon Asch[3] in his identification of the bias of *social proof*, which focuses on the ways that groups distort other judgements apart from group decision-making. Asch

1   Taylor & Doria (1981).
2   Janis (1982).
3   Asch (1956).

found that individuals could be overwhelmed by peer pressure into contradicting even the obvious evidence of their own senses. If enough people assure us that black is really white, and we feel strongly enough that our security depends on group membership, we will come to believe that black is indeed white. Both Janis' and Asch's work shows the workings of self-censorship: in other words, repression of those parts of an individual that might challenge the group by those parts that identify with it, and thus also how group judgements become dominated by dogma.

The fourth type of group bias is *false consensus*, the tendency to assume that the beliefs within your group should be the norm beyond it. In studies by Lee Ross and others,[4] people were regularly found to overestimate the ubiquity of their own group's beliefs, which come to seem obvious. That anyone outside the group should hold different beliefs thus comes to seem shocking and unacceptable. There are clear recent examples of this as an aspect of the 'echo chamber effect' in social media: here, not only do the social media algorithms tend to collect like-minded people into groups and isolate them from challenge, but when those thus isolated do come into contact with opposing groups, greater conflict is likely to follow. This again reflects aspects of absolutization that have already been discussed: projection of one's beliefs onto 'reality', the assumption of system independence, proliferation at a social level (as the same views are repeated), limitation of options, repression, and fragility.

None of these studies show that absolutized group binding is inevitable, only that it is commonplace. They do not undermine the other insights we might have about the role of groups in judgement, such as that they can be helpful as well as unhelpful. Groups, after all, allow us to multiply the range of experience that we can draw on, so that we should be able to improve the effectiveness of our own judgement by learning from others. It is often assumed that many heads must be better than one, not least through the institutions of meetings, seminars, research teams, counselling, and collaboration. However, the effectiveness of all such group institutions depends on the provisionality of judgement of those working within them, maintained despite the interfering stress that may be triggered by the power of the group over the individual and the reinforcing feedback loops of obsession or anxiety this may create.

4   Ross, Greene, & House (1977).

Without absolutization, groups are both a vital source of emotional support, and a context for sharing understanding and experience. With absolutization, however, these advantages of groups can be thrown entirely into reverse: the group becomes a disadvantage and creates *worse* judgements than isolated individuals do.

The claim that absolutized group binding is inevitable often seems to lie behind sweeping philosophical claims about 'human nature' which reduce a complex human experience to a morally one-sided 'essential'. If absolutization was the only way that humans were able to relate in groups, this would imply an entirely power-based way of relating to each other, a 'war of all against all' as Thomas Hobbes called it.[5] Such an impoverished view of ourselves is an over-simplification of the complexity of human motives, and avoids our responsibility for encouraging cooperative motives as an alternative to merely competitive ones, just as a view of ourselves as 'essentially' cooperative prevents us from recognizing and addressing the impact of absolutization. It is hardly surprising if metaphysical ideology has been used to support group binding as a tool of power, since each reinforces the absolutization in the other. The claim that power-based ways of relating to each other are inevitable also parallels the claim that metaphysics is inevitable.

The reaction against group absolutization just creates more absolutization, as we have seen in other aspects of the phenomenon. We may react against the group binding of one group by embracing another group that is perceived as counter-cultural or rebellious, but may use exactly the same absolutized methods to ensure conformity in opposition to the first group. The need for both these opposing groups to maintain absolutized framing in which they are in opposition to each other can also create the *unholy alliance* effect, where they may unite in opposition to anyone who challenges that shared framing.[6] If we don't embrace a counter-group, we may embrace absolutized individualism, in which we assume that our view is the whole story because we are *not* part of the group, the group being necessarily wrong.[7] Of course, we may also self-deceptively think of ourselves as individualists whilst also participating in an absolutized group-ideology: one of individualism. Performative self-contradictions are a common effect of absolutized fragility.

5   Hobbes (1909) p. 96 (ch. 13).
6   II.4.f. Also Ellis (2020b) 1.i.
7   See Ellis (2020a) 2.e.

Psychology 159

That absolutization is the basis of power through repression has huge implications for the discussion of power in political philosophy. One of the central problems of political thought is that of how power can be justifiably used, particularly in the institution of government, but also by implication in any group setting, even in the family. If we recognize power as absolutization used to bind a group, as well as distinguishing this from provisional ways of relating in groups, then this provides us with a ready way of distinguishing the acceptable from the unacceptable use of power.

In accordance with the contextual interpretation discussed in 3.d, we need to judge power according to its wider purpose. If the use of power is *conditional*, or used for a practical purpose, then it can be justified in ways that the absolute use of power cannot. It is the power mode subordinated to the love mode. The use of governmental and judicial power to prevent conflict and disorder in society thus clearly has a basic justification as long as it remains clearly conditional, and constitutional governance in an established democracy can provide it with that conditionality by subjecting it to regular tests of wider consent.[8] For the same reasons, a parent's use of power over a child can be clearly justified as long as it is limited to maintaining the child's own long-term welfare.

Similar points apply to the role of authority over groups. An authority that is absolute and unconditional, having no wider context, is merely subjecting members of the group to absolutized power. However, we also use the term 'authority' in provisional and conditional ways, where a person may have a particular influence in a situation (whether formalized or not), but is not the only influence, and may be challenged. A teacher, for instance, has such authority in a classroom, but only conditional on the school, the syllabus, and the wider educational system. Similarly, an expert may be consulted because of their understanding and experience of a topic, without it needing to be assumed that such an expert possesses the 'truth': rather she contributes to wider understanding in the context of a relationship. Provisional authority in a relationship may involve *suppression* (for instance, a chair telling someone in a meeting to be silent to allow others to speak), but this should not be confused with the *repression* of absolutization, as long as awareness of the wider context is maintained. In cognitive terms, too, the

8   ii.6.a; VIII.5.

credibility of the expert may lead us to prioritize listening to them, but it does not justify the assumption of their (absolute) 'knowledge' of the subject.

The group binding effect of absolutization has had a profound effect on human history, particularly if we think of its usage in military discipline, authoritarian rule, religious 'belief', political ideology, and the maintenance of class distinctions. It is particularly at this socio-political level that we can more clearly see the enormous negative effects of absolutization in creating and perpetuating unnecessary dogma, repression, and conflict. Much more will be said in later books in this series both about the history of absolutization's effects, and about its implications for political philosophy. However, enough has been said for now to clarify its interrelationship to the other dimensions of absolutization.

5.f. Archetypal Function

> *Summary*
>
> The concepts of infinite openness that are often used in absolutizing beliefs can also have a beneficial archetypal function. This function depends on the *provisionality* of the context in which such concepts are used, and works by creating associations between archetypal symbols and experiences that involve moving beyond a limited identification (such as aesthetic, moral, or religious experiences). This function means that religious traditions should not be reductively associated with absolutization, but rather credited as having mixed effects in need of critical differentiation.

The final dimension of absolutization is a positive one: though not strictly a dimension of absolutization, but rather of associated ideas that have been contextualized so as to remain provisional. It highlights the contrasting values that *infinity of scope* may have. Whilst on the one hand, infinity of scope used in the service of a reinforcing loop of belief *closes* that belief, on the other, when used in the service of a balancing loop, infinity of scope can prompt *openness* of belief. Thus, although absolutized beliefs are uniquely suited to maintaining closure in all the ways detailed so far, *infinitely open meanings* without those absolutized beliefs dominant over them can have the reverse effect.

By 'infinitely open meanings' here, I mean any symbol that we associate with development beyond our current set of identifications. Such symbols are 'infinite' in the sense of lacking familiar boundaries. These symbols rely on metaphors that are widely used in myth and religion: those of a heroic individual, of a path, of a remote goal, of the other such as the opposite sex (possessing characteristics mysteriously different from our own), or of unknown suffering including death. As I have argued in more detail in *Archetypes in Religion and Beyond*,[1] these kinds of symbols can have the *archetypal function* of providing inspiration over time, and thus helping us to become more integrated. Drawing on, but revising, Jung's account of archetypes, and focusing on what archetypes *do* rather than what they *are*, I have suggested that there are four basic archetypal functions: the hero, the anima/animus (i.e. attractive other), the shadow, and the God archetype. These work respectively with

1   Ellis (2022).

our efforts, our relationships, our fears, and our overall potentiality to offer deep associative reminders of the possibility of developing beyond what we are now.

Such inspiring symbols can have a helpful effect on us because of their associative links to experiences of moving beyond previous limits, whether these are experiences of achievement in which we redefined our capacities, of relationship in which we entered a new zone of potential through another, of responding to threat, or of religious experience. 'Religious experience' here is understood as experience of openness, for instance a *dhyana* state of mindful absorption, an experience of sublime meaningfulness, or a vision of an imagined form that expresses previously repressed aspects of our experience. When we recollect these symbols, we partially re-experience these deep associations. It is through these kinds of experiences that archetypal symbols can have potentially transformative effects on us.

Examples of this could be taken from any religious tradition, as well as artistic and political traditions. In the context of Christianity, for instance, the concept, stories, and images of Christ are all *associated* for Christians with a variety of 'opening' experiences that lead us beyond current identifications in greater or lesser extents. This could include, for instance, a dramatic vision resulting in conversion, an encounter with an inspiring Christian person who encouraged us towards new possibilities, the opening of love in a relationship, a regular sense of openness in prayer, the symbolic response to images of the Virgin Mary, or the aesthetic response to the smell of incense in churches.

However, an infinitely open meaning of this kind can be quickly associated with absolutization through formulation as a proposition making an unconditional claim of unlimited scope. For example, a religious experience can immediately be associated with proof of God's 'existence', or of a revelatory message of metaphysical 'truth' from God, by long-entrenched cultural habit. This long-entrenched cultural habit, I argue, is due to the long-standing use of absolutization as a tool of power, not from any *necessary* association between infinitely open experience and unconditional propositions with infinite scope. Our development of new integration through experience is a matter of developing and maintaining human potential, but by associating this with the absolute claims of specific religious traditions, those traditions have often appropriated the power of such experiences.

The close relationship, but also the practical gulf, between the archetypal function of infinitely open meaning and the absolutizing function of propositions with infinite scope is one that can account for the complexity of religious traditions and their apparently contradictory effects. Religion can be either enormously destructive or enormously creative, depending on whether it has maintained an immediate association with open religious experience as an inspiration for practice, or whether, instead, it has merely appropriated such experience to support dogma. This is the distinction between what I have called *practical religion* and *dogmatic religion*.[2] These two different aspects of religion may exist side-by-side in two individuals sitting side-by-side in the same church, or in the same individual at different times.

I am not intending to elaborate strongly on this theme in the context of this book, as I have gone into so much more detail about it elsewhere. This should be sufficient, however, to point out that the interdependent problems of absolutization can in no way be reduced to problems of 'religion' – which is a complex phenomenon far too often unhelpfully reduced to absolutized beliefs alone. The new atheist thinkers who have attacked 'religion' in recent decades do no justice to its complexity as a system, even though their attacks on *absolutization* in religion have often been well justified. Absolutization can indeed account both for the reasons why 'believers' are impervious to reasoned argument against their beliefs, and for the negative moral effects of religion in creating bigotry and conflict.[3] These effects need to be set against the positive functions of practical religion in inspiring people to move beyond absolutizations through the ages. Absolutization is neither necessary nor sufficient for religion, and can also flourish both in anti-religious and 'secular' traditions of thought and practice, as well as in other types of tradition that also combine belief and practice, such as traditions of political ideology.

---

2   Ibid. 1.g.
3   See Harris (2007) for a fairly effective summary of many of these.

6. The Unity of Absolutizing Phenomena

6.a. The Blind Synthesist

> *Summary*
>
> Objections to the very idea of synthesizing the different dimensions of absolutization from different disciplines may often come from a bias of over-specialization. My alternative is not to claim a total view, but to recognize my own partial view whilst synthesizing a variety of other views that are each partial – not primarily in terms of their content, but in terms of their framing.

I have now concluded the first half of this book, giving an account of the 23 interconnected dimensions of absolutization. However, before I go on to the question of our response to absolutization, I think it's important to pause and take an overview of the whole argument.

Many elements of the argument, if taken by themselves without a systemic connection to the others, are not particularly new. For example, the ways that Buddhist tradition analyses the conditions for craving and hatred will be familiar to Buddhists, the idea of working with biases is the basis of cognitive behavioural therapy, and the problematic nature of metaphysics has been under discussion in a variety of philosophical movements. It is the positing of a *unity* between these different absolutizing phenomena that is much more likely to be controversial. For example, there are lots of Buddhists and scholars of Buddhism who persist in taking Buddhist thought to offer another kind of metaphysics, who will probably deny that proliferation, craving, and the Middle Way imply an avoidance of metaphysics. There will be some critical Western philosophers who agree that metaphysics is dogma but refuse to think in implicit terms about belief, so will not recognize the important connection I am making between metaphysical belief and absolutizing psychological states. There will also be psychologists who refuse to accept that psychological states have any particular relationship to the philosophical content of what we believe. People with these kinds of attitudes will have an influence far beyond the academic communities they move in.

All of which reminds me immediately of the Buddha's parable of the blind men and the elephant, in which different people encountered one animal from different points of view, but because of their embodied state were unable to 'see' the whole, so thought they were experiencing different things.[1] In the case of academic specializations, the 'blindness' is equivalent to an extended training in applying certain disciplinary assumptions, which then become so entrenched that it makes it more difficult to adopt any alternatives. This creates a kind of bias for which there is a French term, *deformátion professionelle*.[2] The most obvious kinds of *deformátion professionelle* are physical: the deformed shoulders of the clerk who has been stooping over a desk for a lifetime, or the muscular but obese bodies of sumo wrestlers. However such deformations are also an unfortunate side-effect of academic specialization, and come from the same general cause: the consistent channelling of energy down some routes and not others, which may then constrain our imaginations and perhaps also even our posture.

As with any other bias (see 5.c), one can absolutize by being deceived by its limitations, but also over-react by assuming that it completely negates the justification of one's position (and in the process implicitly adopt another absolutizing position). Specialization clearly has many advantages for examining particular details of a given system closely. However, it is deleterious when one's prime business is to examine the whole functioning of a system in its relationship to other systems. To some extent this has been realized by those who have undertaken interdisciplinary work in academia, but all too often such work simply adopts the assumptions of one discipline (such as the social sciences) and extends them to another, rather than examining the assumptions of each discipline or tradition in the light of the insights offered by the other.

On the other hand, those who over-react to specialization may adopt an absolutizing monist viewpoint, in which certain metaphysical assumptions are applied as the supposed key to all disciplines: the result may be a philosophical movement that is only taken seriously in certain circles (such as Hegelianism or Marxism),

---

[1] See Ellis (2019) pp. 121–5 for fuller discussion of the parable.
[2] Merton (1957) pp. 195–206.

or alternatively one that is never taken seriously at all in any wider context. At worst, it may deserve dismissive labels such as 'new age mish-mash'.

To avoid just being yet another blind man arguing about the nature of the elephant, then, one needs to move very carefully – which is what I have tried to do. One needs a method that enables one to feel more than just one small part of the elephant, but also to avoid incredible claims that one has somehow seen the whole elephant for oneself. In one sense (the one relativists would focus on), we are all blind people who can none of us ever do better than feeling the elephant from our own point of view, and that is our embodied state. I am obviously no exception to that. However, there is still a distinction between shrilly insisting that one's own feel of the elephant is the correct one, and attempting to assemble a more comprehensive view of the elephant by putting together the different accounts of it offered by different blind people. Within shared empirical frameworks, such a way of proceeding is familiar in science, but the comparison of different framing viewpoints much less so.

Having tried to do this, though, I am still faced with the likelihood that some of the blind people will continue to insist, if not that they have the sole correct view of the elephant, then that the elephant they have felt is a different elephant. There is, of course, no proof of the unity of absolutizing phenomena. However, I contend that there are strong arguments for provisionally accepting that unity: in other words, that in talking about the 23 dimensions of absolutization I have examined, I have been *largely* talking about the same phenomena from different points of view. That argument can go beyond merely pointing out the likelihood of limiting biases in those who oppose it (which is, of course, far from conclusive).

There are three prongs to that argument: first, that the precise relationship I am suggesting between the different dimensions of absolutization takes many of the likely objections into account; second, that a *concatenation* of synthetic argument, piling up evidence from different standpoints, is much more justifiable than a dogmatic use of synthesis; and third, that there are overwhelming *practical* arguments for assuming a synthesis. I will be going further into these three arguments in the remainder of this section. The final one, that the arguments are practical, also provides a transition to the remainder of this book, which examines the core requirements for any practical response to absolutization.

6.b. Clarifying the Relationships

> *Summary*
>
> The dimensions of absolutization are not deductively equivalent *a priori*, but are closely related elements of the same system that become evident in particular conditions. From the diachronic standpoint needed to relate these different conditions of emergence over time from different standpoints, though, the unity of the dimensions is just as evident as that of most theoretical constructs in science.

Firstly, then, it is worth reiterating the precise relationships that I posit between the 23 dimensions of absolutization. Some of these been mentioned already, but to summarize them in one place and to add further clarifications may help to avoid any misinterpretation of them.

As the use of supposedly absolute deductive logic is so habitual in our discourse, one point to note initially is that the 23 dimensions could not possibly *deductively* imply each other. If we are to take embodied meaning seriously, we need to recognize that each concept that has been used is embedded within frameworks of metaphor and cognitive modelling, which then helps to create meaning *in the bodily experience* of each person using it. So I am not suggesting any *a priori* equivalence between, say, projection and metaphysics. Rather, there is a close systemic relationship between them that we can identify and confidently affirm on the basis of provisional judgement from experience. There is a weight of evidence for that relationship that can be appreciated from a variety of different experiential standpoints.

Nevertheless, the relationship between the different dimensions is one of implicit equivalence (apart from 11 and 23, which are qualifications or limitations of absolutization). 'Implicit equivalence' suggests that all these dimensions of absolutization are likely to be going on in some sense whenever there is absolutization, but not that we will be aware of them all explicitly at the same time. It is thus perhaps helpful to compare the different kinds of conditions in which the different dimensions become explicit. We could call these 'conditions of emergence' for a given dimension of absolutization, and such conditions are listed for each dimension in **table 1**.

Table 1. The conditions of emergence of the 23 dimensions of absolutization.

Dimension	Conditions of emergence (in addition to absolutization itself)
1. Mental proliferation	Default mode (not concentrating)
2. Interdependence of craving, hatred, and delusion	Craving in response to a goal, hatred to an obstacle. Delusion consists in the maladjustment of beliefs that are an aspect of these responses.
3. Absoluteness of negations	Appearance of any challenge to the absolutization
4. Excluding the options	Appearance of any other potential option
5. Reinforcing feedback loops	Default mode (as 1) or defensive interaction
6. Assumed system independence	Possibility of system interdependence (e.g. suggestion of cognitive dependence on the body)
7. Fragility	Tipping point destabilizing system
8. Representationalism	Use of propositional language to express beliefs, especially when the assumed meaning of that language is challenged
9. Denial of embodiment	Being in states of left hemisphere over-dominance creating substitution, which we may particularly become aware of after transition to other states
10. Discontinuity	When we use representational assumptions in language to describe objects, particularly when subsequent awareness offers options of greater continuity
11. Contextual interpretation	When absolutization is in question due to conditionality etc.
12. Metaphysics	Use of generalized propositional language to describe 'reality'
13. Absoluteness of deductive logic	When connections of necessity are assumed between propositions
14. Foundationalism and circularity	In broadly epistemological (justificatory) argument
15. Infinite rationalizations of experience	Defending absolutized beliefs against challenges
16. Claim that metaphysics is inevitable	In response to criticisms of metaphysics
17. Inflation of metaphysics and logic	When phenomena might be explained in absolutized or non-absolutized terms
18. Repression and conflict	Whenever two incompatible beliefs become relevant
19. Projection	When beliefs are formed about objects
20. Confirmation bias	When considering evidence that might support a belief
21. Substitution	Whenever both harder and easier processes are available to us
22. Group binding	In social relationships
23. Archetypal function of contextualized absolutes	When awareness is needed over time to help fulfil longer-term needs

For any one of the dimensions, we could justifiably suggest that it will be present as an indication of absolutization given its conditions of emergence. Since the conditions of emergence occur at different times, an appreciation of absolutization does require us to adopt a *diachronic* standpoint – that is, one that recognizes that we will not have the whole picture at any one given moment, but that we will need to assemble a more complete and adequate picture of any given phenomenon by connecting our experiences over time. As we do this, some features unavoidably fade into the background whilst others come into the foreground: that is a feature of embodied experience.

I will not discuss all the conditions for emergence, as this would take too much space. The table should be self-explanatory, but let's take a couple of examples.

Mental proliferation may be said to be an implicit feature of all absolutization, because we would expect that wherever particular shortcut synaptic routes have been over-used, there will be continuing pressure to use them that will channel further energy down those routes. However, due to the context of our embodied situation, this will not occur all the time. We tend to experience proliferation at those points where we are no longer occupied with a task that readily engages our concentration to achieve immediate goals, but rather our mental faculties are 'idling'. For instance, when writing these words I am mainly concentrating on the process of formulating and typing them, sometimes accompanied by wider awareness of my body that continues to contextualize that activity. At intervals, though, my concentration may lapse, and my attention then returns to less demanding but habitual objects: for instance, thinking about a slight anxiety about a task I need to do later and whether I will forget it, or (a common temptation for those working at a computer today) an urge to check social media. Whenever my attention lapses in this way, in neural terms the *default mode network* of the brain is taking over.[1] This 'idling' is typically characterized by proliferation (or 'rumination', as it is often also called in psychiatry), as shown by the links between default mode network activity and depressive rumination.[2] If not contextualized, my awareness will increasingly dwell on the distraction. Proliferation, in that context, *is* absolutization, but given that it is not a constant context, I will not always experience absolutization as proliferation.

1 Fox et al. (2005).
2 Hamilton (2015).

For another example, let's take metaphysics. Metaphysics may be said to be implicitly occurring whenever there is absolutization, because beliefs about final 'reality' are being assumed. However, metaphysics as an explicit phenomenon is a particular way of talking. It may occur at two different levels of explicitness. The most common is where people are making claims (for themselves or to others) about unconditional 'realities', often marked by language like 'really', 'just', 'essentially', or 'actually': from 'Republicans are just bastards' to 'a dog is man's eternal friend'. Such language will not be explicitly recognized as 'metaphysical' by most of its users. A small minority, however, will use the term 'metaphysical', or some near-synonym, in an explicit way. The conditions of emergence for metaphysics thus involve particular contexts of communication, but that does not prevent metaphysics from being a general feature of absolutization.

For those dissatisfied with such an account of the relationships between the dimensions of absolutization because it is not all instantaneously explicit, it must be pointed out that this is not just an unreasonable demand, but one that could never be adequately met in describing any phenomenon. For example, when scientifically describing a particular element, such as, say, hydrogen, we will not be able to describe attributes that are always evident: rather they will remain implicit most of the time and become explicit in particular circumstances, when an experiment reveals them. We cannot just peer at a hydrogen atom through an electron microscope and instantaneously then see how it will interact with other elements. Scientists, like anyone else, depend on experience over time to construct theories, that are then reinforced by other people's experience over time. It is a misleading construction to assume that something we can construct a clear and explicit *concept* of is for that reason equally clear and explicit instantaneously in experience, for we only experience it in a wider systemic context subject to our epistemic limitations.

My first argument for the unity of the phenomena of absolutization, then, is that they appear to be united on the basis of implicit equivalence. They are 'united', not in the sense of an absolute belief in a linear equivalence, but in terms of a justifiable general belief consistent with a variety of observations from various points of view at various times. In this respect the thesis of unity meets the same level of justification as most other theoretical beliefs.

6.c. The Use of Synthesis

> *Summary*
>
> Synthesis combines understanding in different schematic and metaphorical frameworks, which is a necessary condition for creative thinking. The justification of a synthetic view, however arrived at, involves a process of combining meaning and dialectically sifting belief. Such justification becomes greater the more it can be used to explain a variety of phenomena. The approach to combining perspectives in this book is concatenative, meaning that the addition of more synthesized perspectives adds to the level of justification.

At this point, it must be admitted that the approach I have adopted differs from that of a scientist observing similar phenomena over a period of time using a consistent method. Instead, in a multidisciplinary approach, the methods themselves, and the assumptions that inform them, differ, as well as the times and conditions when these methods were applied. I have combined the perspectives of Buddhism (which is a spiritual practice), with systems and embodied meaning (which involve challenging theoretical approaches to science), with philosophy (traditionally conducted by reflection only), and with psychology (a more traditional empirical science, also influenced by therapeutic practice). Empirical justification is just a matter of accruing a sufficient range of observations, but with similar framing applied to all the observations. However, my argument for the unity of absolutization phenomena across disciplines depends not just on this but on *synthesizing* different kinds of framing. Much clarification is then needed on what 'synthesis' means and implies.

At the most basic level, 'synthesis' just means bringing together different experiences, so occurs even when we describe a single experience that combines different senses, such as a sighting of a deer that I first heard and then saw. However, as we work up a hierarchy of complexity in human meaning, synthesis can also be practised in ways that increasingly combine different frames of meaning, rather than just different experiences interpreted in the same frame. Nevertheless, this synthesis continues to be contained within a specific embodied human understanding. We are able to synthesize because we relate different metaphorical and schematic structures within the same overall framework of human experience.

Synthesizing, then, is not distinct from 'understanding' in this embodied sense: we understand a novel abstraction when we are able to connect it to our embodied tree of meaning. For instance, if I fail to understand the concept of *zeugma* as defined by Merriam-Webster ('the use of a word to modify or govern two or more words usually in such a manner that it applies to each in a different sense'), I am much more likely to 'get it' when offered an example, such as 'She went home in a flood of tears and a sedan chair'. The sensation of 'getting it', here, making a synaptic connection, probably depends on recognizing that 'in' is being used in the example in both a direct sense (in a sedan chair) and the extended metaphorical sense in which we are contained by an emotional state. The synthesis occurs as we connect this tension in the meaning with the abstract idea of *zeugma*.

The synthesis between disciplinary frameworks that I think we need to employ, to understand both absolutization and how to respond to it, is no different from this embodied experience of stretching our understanding from one framework to another. It will thus differ depending on which frameworks you begin with. It should not be confused with another sense in which 'synthesis' has been used, namely a Kantian rationalistic framework of top-down deduction that is supposed to describe the necessary conditions for experience. Kant claimed that there could be a 'synthetic *a priori*' of reasoning about the required conditions for experience that united concepts with experience, and that this synthetic *a priori* could provide a unifying universal framework of 'transcendental deduction' that could help explain the universality of geometry, mathematics, science, and even ethics.[1] However, Kant's assumption of representationalism creates a major flaw in his reasonings. He completely fails to take into account the differences in the meaning of the terms used in such rationalistic deduction for the different people engaging in it. He thus cannot prove that there is only one such transcendental deduction:[2] if it is a way of discussing the coherence we apply to frameworks of interpretation, these may differ not just by culture, but also by individual or even by the changing psychological states of individuals.

---

1   Kant (1929).
2   A point also made by Körner (1967).

A supposed 'synthesis' that is reached by assuming that the writer's standpoint is the same as everyone else's, even if it is supported by laborious reasoning, is not a genuine synthesis of meaning as we experience it. In a genuine synthesis, both a combination of understanding and a dialectic of belief are required. In terms of both meaning and belief, both sides then need to be mutually responsive. A similar point can be made where synthetic insight is supposed to be based on intuition, or on religious experience interpreted as revelation. An individual here may have had an experience of sudden *gestalt* synthesis in which a previous conflict is rapidly overcome, and lots of meanings are then connected and illuminated in that person's experience: however, it is absolutizing projection to then assume that this indicates an access to transcendental 'truth' for everyone. Clearly it would be inconsistent to appeal to any such intuitive synthesis to justify any account of the unity of absolutization phenomena. Whilst there is nothing wrong with reaching theoretical insights through intuition, they cannot be *justified* through intuition.

Nevertheless, the justification of any new or interesting theory depends on synthesis: that is, on people learning new ways of interpreting their experience using different framing assumptions, and continuing to relate these to the previous ones they held. The synthesis here takes place, not in a state of affairs represented by philosophical language, but in the meanings and beliefs of the people involved. In this case, that means both in the person writing or speaking about new synthetic theory, and in the person reading and understanding it. Where opposing beliefs are encountered that are understood in a sufficiently compatible way, that will also require a dialectical process of recognizing framing assumptions and resolving the conflict by sceptically examining those assumptions. Not uncommonly, this will also involve stretching or developing the established meanings of terminology, to allow new and less customary conceptual combinations to be used – usually in the teeth of opposition from specialists who assume that their own use of terminology has an essential justification. Such synthesis is not absolutizing as long as it does not assume that it offers an *a priori* universal explanation. Rather, *it becomes increasingly justifiable the more evidence and experience it helps to explain.*

Synthetic theory increases that justification by a broadly dialectical process of bringing different framing perspectives into critical contact with each other, and selecting those features with better explanatory potential in the range of practical, embodied contexts in which the theory is applied. This process can be short-circuited and substituted by one that merely applies the framing assumptions of one context to another and appropriates the latter (for instance, early colonial oriental studies, or Hindu monism). So, it is not the number of perspectives referred to, but those critically incorporated into a developing wider perspective, that determine the value of the synthesis.

My thesis is thus that an increasing degree of unity is demonstrated in our understanding of absolutization, the more variety of perspectives we can dialectically incorporate into it. My synthesis of Buddhism, systems, embodied meaning, philosophy, and psychology is not a matter of appropriating them all to the perspectives offered by one or two of them, but of critically working through the assumptions made in each of these areas. Buddhist insights are entirely practical, but Buddhism has also acquired a number of absolutizing, distorting tendencies in the course of its transmission (as I have explored in *The Buddha's Middle Way*). Systems theory offers liberation from our objectifying and substantializing obsessions, but these tendencies can then be re-introduced by the back door as academics interpret systems in ways that omit their own responsibility for interpreting them. Embodied meaning, again, offers a potentially revolutionary approach to philosophy and linguistics, but one that has often been appropriated by naturalistic thinkers who interpret it with a restricted context of disembodied assumptions. Philosophy is a discipline that has transmitted invaluable skills, ethical concerns, and sceptical arguments, but is at present largely lost to various dogmatic assumptions that have been reinforced by economic constraints in the academy. Psychology offers massive insights into our mental processes, but is subject to the constraints of formal scientific method, with its ineffectual theoretical attempts to exclude normative value. The weaknesses of any of these approaches can be more readily appreciated by critical comparison with the others.

This could be described as a *concatenative* approach to synthesis: by adding more critically synthesized perspectives, one creates a fuller view than could be offered by any one such perspective. In the process, both author and reader will be breaking down barriers between different synaptic channels so as to integrate them. This, of course, also depends on the embodied situations of both author and reader, and is also subject to the limitations of each, but it is vital that we do not substitute a fake absolutized process for this limited and fallible process. Rationalized top-down 'synthesis', analysis that is restricted to one set of conventions, or empirical synthesis that leaves framing unquestioned all have a much more restricted value in helping us to understand absolutization. Concatenative synthesis, on the other hand, has a practical value, as I shall go on to argue.

6.d. The Practical Arguments

> *Summary*
>
> The dimensions of absolutization also need to be understood in relation to each other for practical purposes, meaning to help us progress towards long-term provisional goals that involve reducing absolutization. The need to address neglected dimensions of absolutization will be an aspect of my discussion of the four criteria for the Middle Way in the rest of this book. In particular, the failure to adequately address practical judgement in the world in large sections of academia can be associated with the entrenched influence of representationalism, separated from the other dimensions of absolutization.

My final argument for the unity of absolutization phenomena is a practical one. By 'practical', I mean offering a theoretical perspective that could be applied by an embodied person to help achieve long-term goals. Practicality is vital for effectively addressing absolutization. Section 7 will go into more detail on the nature of practicality and offer three criteria for it: embodiment, responsibility, and effectiveness.

Practical justification depends on people actually being able to achieve or modify their goals, so cannot be conclusively demonstrated in theoretical writing. Yes, I am aware of the paradox that some people see when I write about practicality in a theoretical fashion, but I don't see any paradox, because practicality is a wider attitude, not just the brisk conduct of business in a particular context. The particular kind of practicality I am trying to promote here is one that takes more conditions into account, and thus has to be discussed in general terms. General, but provisional theory is just more widely focused practicality, as opposed to absolutized theory which has the effect of narrowing practical attitudes.

One can indicate how a theoretical perspective may be practically helpful, but more importantly, particularly how an absolutizing theory may be *unhelpful*. I want to argue that *an understanding of absolutization as a unified phenomenon* can help us to identify what is *unhelpful* in our experience in practice better than any one of the theoretical perspectives I am drawing on taken in isolation. For instance, if we draw on embodiment as well as Buddhism, this increases the long-term and general adequacy of our practical approach when compared to concentrating only on Buddhism.

This will be mainly done in the reminder of this book through my discussion of the *Four Criteria for the Middle Way*. These are specific criteria, all of which I think any effective response to absolutization will need to meet. I will be explaining how each of these criteria is needed to meet the spread of characteristics that we find associated in absolutization. Different common approaches to the phenomena of absolutization (whether Buddhist, philosophical, psychological, etc.) have different particular strengths in relation to some of the criteria, but lack an adequate response to some of the others: yet all of the criteria are practically required.

Table 2. Four criteria for the Middle Way.

Criterion for the Middle Way	Sub-criteria	Approaches that tend to fulfil this criterion	Approaches that often lack the criterion	Dimensions of absolutization not recognized in these approaches
Practicality	• Embodiment • Responsibility • Effectiveness	Buddhism, psychotherapy (though in limited context), consistently pragmatic philosophy	Academic disciplines that are not practice-led: including philosophy, psychology, systems theory, and 'embodied' cognitive science	Denial of embodiment, representationalism
Universal aspiration	• Normativity • Systematicity • Across groups • Across space • Over time	Systems theory, Buddhism, normative ethical philosophy	Relativist philosophy, social psychology	Absoluteness of negation, restricting the options, (negative) metaphysics
Judgement focus	• Positive focus on judgement • Avoiding distractions	Embodied meaning (especially with neuroscience of brain lateralization)	Metaphysical philosophy (including in Buddhism)	Representationalism, projection, substitution, confirmation bias
Error focus	• Avoiding absolute positives • Refining shadow avoidance • Emotionally positive context	Cognitive psychology of biases, Popperian philosophy of science	Buddhism; many academic, religious and political approaches	Confirmation bias, foundationalism and circularity, archetypal use of absolutes

By the time you have read my arguments for the four criteria, then, you will also have simultaneously seen how a focus on some of the dimensions of absolutization but neglect of the others is practically insufficient. **Table 2** summarizes the four criteria, together with approaches that often fulfil or fail to fulfil them and neglected dimensions of absolutization in those approaches that fail to fulfil them.

Practicality is the most important of the four criteria – indeed the others could all be seen as aspects of it. Universality of aspiration is practical because the more widely effective a practical solution is across space and time, the more practical it is. Judgement focus is practical, because focusing on *how* we judge rather than *what* we judge means that we address distortions in our judgement more effectively. Error focus is practical, because it is easier to identify distorting errors in our judgement than it is to identify correct beliefs, so the probabilities of effective judgement improve when we focus on error.

Not including all of these four criteria in one's approach, then, carries a cost. As I shall argue, this cost can be traced to the failure to connect key aspects of absolutization as a problem to the rest. I shall briefly outline this cost here, with the supporting details coming from the ensuing sections.

Very often, academically-led thinking has been much better at formalized judgement in a scientific or bureaucratic context than it has at helping ordinary people make better practical judgements in their wider lives. There is a huge gap, for instance, between academic psychology and 'popular psychology' or 'self help'. Academic philosophy has also likewise distanced itself from ordinary judgement through an over-specialized focus on very specific analysis within an isolated professional tradition. Academic scholars of religion often do not see it as part of their task at all to engage practically with ordinary judgement in relation to religion, but rather only to investigate texts and sociological evidence. Where too great a gap opens up between academic concerns and ordinary life, the stability of the whole social system can be subject to increasing polarization and conflict with the more reflective members of the population no longer recognizing a responsibility towards the development of more complex thinking in the population as a whole. That leaves a vacuum which is an opportunity for exploitative popular media, popular gurus with simplistic prescriptions, and populist politicians. Not identifying and responding to absolutization as a whole limits the effectiveness with which we address socio-political conflict as a whole.

A failure to address representationalism and the denial of embodiment in academia lies at the heart of the assumptions that perpetuate this failure. Whilst people get their basis of understanding from a wide variety of sources of varying levels of helpfulness, academics typically focus their attention entirely on attempts to describe what they believe to ultimately be the case or not, using language that is still expected to be able to represent truth or falsehood out there. That this assumption is contradicted by linguistic and psychological evidence of how we process meaning does not seem to have widely registered: or if it has, this is merely taken to be more grist to the 'factual' mill, with no implications being recognized for the very focus of human intellectual activity. Yet, if the basis of meaning lies in the body and there is no absolute representation, it is practical adaptation to this position that should become central, not only in constantly recognizing the limitations of any description of the world, but in recognizing the total interdependence of our values and of our sense of responsibility with those attempts to describe. In section 7 I will explore embodiment, responsibility, and effectiveness as different aspects of the practicality that I think academics are often neglecting, to the cost of society as a whole.

One increasingly dominant strand of academic thinking has also tended to be relativist, presenting conflicts between groups as inevitable rather than accepting a responsibility to try to address them. This can be directly related to the prevalence of the fact-value distinction in much academic thought, which discourages *normative* thought (about what we actually *should* do), except in the relatively isolated domain of normative ethical philosophy. Often, anything normative is assumed to be 'subjective' or dogmatic, and comments on ethics are descriptively-oriented. The cost of not including a broader normative dimension in one's thinking is an inability to effectively address the practical conflicts in any situation where the values of different groups clash. This, I will argue in section 8, is particularly due to a failure to recognize the absoluteness of negation and attendant restriction of options. When our response to absolutization is merely counter-absolutization, and we fail to recognize that we are merely perpetuating the same pattern by restricting the discussion to a set of dichotomous premises, the practical effect is that we remain quite unnecessarily stuck in conflicts that could be resolved by a more critical and creative approach. Such an approach, I will argue, requires an *aspiration* towards universality, the use of it as a meaningful goal, without any claim to have reached it.

On the other hand, the Buddhist approach, which is typically both practical and universally normative, often fails to focus on judgement, but instead gets distracted by metaphysical ways of expressing beliefs – even when these are supposed to be practical. This is a criticism that can be extended to many other ways of thinking that still accept metaphysics as the best way to understand things. The price of such distraction is often the uncritical acceptance of metaphysical perspectives that are associated with the power of dominant leaders or groups, followed by bafflement and conflict when these are applied in unacceptable ways. The wave of sexual abuse revelations in both Christianity and Buddhism in recent years is an instructive example in this regard. As a further development of practicality, then, we need to be able to make use of a psychologically-informed approach on the *how* of judgement rather than on *what* we judge. A relentless focus on claims about the world, rather than on the process by which we justify them, involves a neglect, again, of an understanding of representationalism, and a lack of understanding of the implications of our language not merely representing reality. It also underestimates the grip of confirmation bias and projection over our theories about the world in itself. Section 9 will explore this point further.

A lack of error focus also leaves us open to uncritical belief in positive values that we have projected onto as sources of 'truth', perhaps because we have assumed that this is the only alternative to a nihilistic lack of meaning. Many outrages are committed in the name of such absolute positive values, to which we have become prematurely committed. This underestimates the massive power of confirmation bias and the ways that a positive ideal can rapidly become a focus of defensive *ad hoc* argument. As an alternative to this it is important to note that we can be inspired by archetypal ideals that we associate with, for instance, God or enlightenment, whilst in practice focusing mainly on avoiding mistakes in what we believe. This is the focus of section 10.

As we will see, then, identifying absolutization only with some of its dimensions – for instance just as the metaphysics you happen to disagree with rather than all of it, or just a failure of embodiment in personal practice without wider application, or just as an anti-scientific perspective regardless of personal judgement – impacts on our practical response to that absolutization. Without an understanding of absolutization that synthesizes these different elements, then, the effectiveness of our practical response is likely to be impaired.

7. Criteria for a Response: Practicality

7.a. What is Practicality?

> *Summary*
>
> Practicality is a strength of Buddhist tradition and involves interconnected techniques, acknowledging embodiment and developing responsibility and effectiveness. Theory at a high level of generality can also be practical as long as it avoids absolutizing shortcuts. Restrictions in scope need to be provisional if they are not to detract from practicality, but academic specialization is often not seen provisionally. 'Pragmatic' philosophy has also lacked practicality because of its representationalism, not distinguishing the meaning of 'truth' from belief in it.

Personally I first learned about *practice* as a priority through relatively early exposure to Buddhism, which is still the prime place I find where it is taken seriously. Practice is primarily about what one does with one's life as an individual, but also as an individual acting in a wider society. It starts with the full acknowledgement of our current conditions and state, then involves regular activity to change those conditions and that state in the long term. To do that, we need to know what kinds of activities will gradually help us to change things, and also how to stay motivated when conflicting motives try to hijack our progress.

Practicality is thus a particular strength of the Buddhist approach, and depends on a full recognition of the systemic interdependence of craving, hatred, and delusion (see 1.b) found in Buddhism. In its wider context as a tradition of practice, Buddhism tries to relate our beliefs (or 'views') fully to their moral implications and make them part of a system of practice. We can see this reflected in the spread of traditional formulations of the practical Buddhist path, as the Eightfold or Threefold Path. The Threefold Path, as perhaps the simplest distillation, combines ethics (that is, working with our judgements and behaviour), meditation (working with our mental states), and wisdom (working with our beliefs).[1] Whatever limita-

1   See Ellis (2019) section 5.

tions one might see in the further details of the Buddhist path, this overall approach offers us a starting model for a practical response to absolutization. We need to be able to work in a variety of complementary ways, both to address absolutization directly and to help undermine the conditions that give rise to it.

Practicality is the first criterion that is needed in any effective response to absolutization. In this section of the book I will be offering an analysis of what it involves under three overall headings: embodiment, responsibility, and effectiveness. A response to absolutization is not adequate if it is not *embodied*, because it does not take into account our starting conditions sufficiently, and without that we are likely to fall into idealizing, substituting absolutized beliefs about what we should do for an effective response to where we really are. A response to absolutization is also not adequate if it does not help us take *responsibility* for our actions, so that we remain motivated, feel our actions have an impact, and are able to gradually stretch our ambitions. Finally, a response to absolutization is not adequate unless it is *effective*, in the sense of focusing our energy decisively to meet the conditions, whilst avoiding shortcuts that distract us and divide our energies. These three points will be expanded in the following three chapters.

It may seem easier to apply these criteria to what are already framed as practices (for instance, discussions of meditation technique) than it is to our wider-ranging theoretical beliefs. In the longer term, however, it matters just as much whether our theoretical beliefs are *practical*. It is common to contrast practice with theory, and the limitations of language in representing experience mean that there is indeed always a gap between theory and practice. However, in some cases that gap is much bigger than in others. My argument is that absolutization increases that gap, until the only connection between theory and practice is that the theory rationalizes associated practice. The absence of absolutization, on the other hand, allows a more detailed justification that engages with experience. A more fully practical non-absolutized perspective is also a more adequate theoretical perspective.

That some theory is practical whilst remaining relatively abstract is due to its level of generality rather than absolutization. What, for lack of a better term, we can only call 'practical theory', deals with practical issues at a higher level of generality, by providing suggestions that can helpfully change our response to them. For example, a specific set of instructions, say of how to assemble a piece of flat pack furniture, seems obviously 'practical'. However, a book on 'how to interpret flat pack furniture instructions' might also be practically helpful if you are struggling with them. A book on the skill of interpretation might then help us to apply similar skills to other kinds of sources, and a book of practical philosophy (as Middle Way Philosophy aspires to be) then helps to explain the value of that skill in relation to other skills, potentially motivating our development of that skill, so that it can be applied to interpreting a wide range of sources. There is no point in that gradual ascent of generality where the approach ceases to be practical – and indeed, as it becomes more general, one could also argue that it becomes *more* practical, because it helps us to address *more* possible situations. The impracticality would begin at the point where we substitute a shortcut for the actual effort of developing the wider skill needed for the practical application: for instance, we start looking for secret codes from the Illuminati in flat-pack furniture instructions.

In order to respond to absolutization, then, practicality is required: not in the sense of a limited judgement of how to act that still draws absolute boundaries around that judgement, but one that is effective in the long term because the only boundaries it relies on are provisional ones. Thus, in a longer-term, more integrated sense of practicality, an effective but decontextualized focus on a task is not practical. A carpenter who focuses very effectively on his wood-working business whilst his family and nation fall apart is not sufficiently 'practical', just as the 'pragmatic' politician who gets re-elected through a popular pork-barrel project in his locality, but neglects the environment of the wider country, is not sufficiently 'pragmatic'.

Academia in general rarely shows much understanding of practice as a perspective, and its default position is to attempt to produce descriptive theoretical positions in which standards of helpfulness are not seen as a relevant criterion (because they are unfairly assumed to be partial or 'subjective'). There is, of course, unavoidably a practical context even for academic description, but it is a narrow and proliferating one: that is, a goal of satisfying one's colleagues by coming up with an account sufficiently backed by evidence and sufficiently connected to previous theory. But a theory can satisfy academic colleagues without being more generally helpful, perhaps because causal or classificatory explanations have become ends in themselves (and probably with an absolutized position detectable somewhere, such as physicalism or determinism). For example, evolutionary explanations of biases are a major source of non-practical diversion from understanding bias itself and how to respond to it, resembling the Buddha's story of the arrow discussed in 1.a. This impracticality can be understood as due to a lack of *judgement focus*, which will be discussed in more detail in section 9.

Some forms of academic work are practical in relation to a particular professional context, such as psychotherapy or education, but then quite unnecessarily limit their discussion to the formal limits of that context. As an illustration, a reviewer from a psychotherapeutic background of one of my recent multidisciplinary books, who was generally very appreciative of it, nevertheless described it as offering helpful 'clinical approaches': a contextual limitation that completely confused me, as I had never even mentioned the 'clinical' practice of psychotherapy in the whole book! He was able to recognize the value of a practical approach, but automatically put it into his accustomed specialized professional terms without any consideration of the wider practice on which I was actually focusing throughout. Even professionals are not just professionals, having additional practical judgements to make as individuals beyond their professional lives, and it also seems that even professional judgements are likely to be improved though more consideration of a wider context.

In the broadest and most genuine sense, then, theory needs to be practical by maintaining a sense of the provisionality of any restrictions in its focus, so that it is always willing to situate itself in a wider context, even when its practical focus also requires some specialization. That provisionality applies particularly to its goals, which need to be intermediate and progressive ones rather than fixed or absolute ones. For example, a discussion of biases, to adequately address the whole interconnected nature of absolutization in a practical way, needs to aim not just to describe an identifiable bias, the evidence for it, or its causes, but to make the synthetic connections that will help people to identify and avoid biases. This will not only be in an assumed therapeutic context, but also in a context of personal practice and/or of social applications such as in education. If psychologists completely ignore the philosophy of biases, or the phenomenology of what it is like to experience a bias and

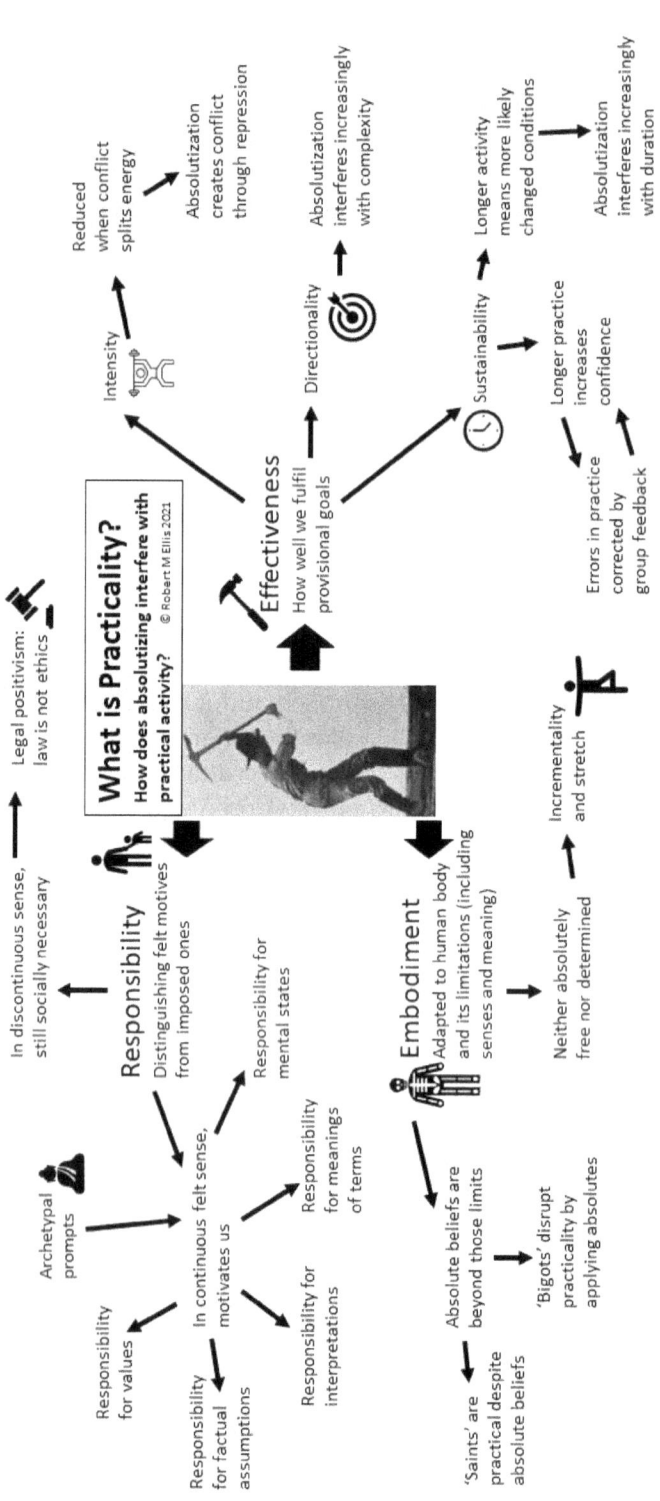

Figure 4. What is practicality?

become aware of it (for instance in mindfulness practice), their work will remain unnecessarily limited in its helpfulness. Biases need to be considered not just on the individual psychological level or on the social level, but both in relation to each other. New goals should emerge through dialogue and develop as the work itself develops, rather than being dictated by a narrow specialist group.

Practicality or pragmatism in philosophy has also been limited by its assumptions. One of the chief of these is continuing representationalist beliefs about meaning, which inhibit any distinction between meaning and belief and thus create the assumption that it is 'practical' to reduce the meanings of infinite concepts to relative ones. For William James, for instance, 'truth' is seen as a belief that 'fits', or fails to cause frustration: he compares it to a bank note that is accepted as currency.[2] There is thus effectively no distinction between 'truth' and 'belief' for James and many other pragmatists who follow a similar line. This has the virtue of trying to avoid absolutized beliefs about truth, but in the process swings directly to the opposite absolute of relativism.

To maintain a provisional belief in which third alternatives to the absolute versus relative dichotomy are considered, we instead need to maintain a sense of the fallibility of our current beliefs in contrast to an absolute truth that we do not possess. This requires us to maintain 'truth' in its absolute *meaning*, in full recognition that meaning is distinct from belief. That meaning of truth can then be used archetypally (see 5.f). James' pragmatism, then, remains incomplete and partial as an effective response to absolutization, precisely because it does not take all the aspects of absolutization into account. Later pragmatists, such as Richard Rorty,[3] tend to go even further in the same relativist direction because of an inadequately synthetic view of the absolutization they are seeking to avoid.

The diagram here (**figure 4**) helps to introduce the next three chapters by illustrating the three components of practicality that I will be surveying.

---

2   James (1981) pp. 95-7.
3   iii.3.e; IV.1; Rorty (1989).

7.b. Embodiment

> *Summary*
>
> To make our beliefs practical, our theories as well as our more immediate practical beliefs need to be scaled to human embodiment. This means adapting to our limited perspective by avoiding metaphysics – even though 'saints' may manage to maintain embodied beliefs in spite of the presence of metaphysical beliefs. It also means adapting to our limited capacities by avoiding both freewill (total responsibility) and determinism (zero responsibility) assumptions.

That embodiment is a key element of practicality should be obvious if we ask who practicality is for. The people for whom any approach, theory, or strategy needs to be practical are humans, and humans are bodies (not *just* bodies, but bodies). Our technology, for instance, is adapted to the scale and ability of our bodies: if you take the design of a car, the seats, pedals, steering wheel, and other controls are all geared to the convenience of the human body. However, in contrast all too often our theories seem to be rather like cars bizarrely designed for giants of infinite height and endless numbers of limbs. No response to absolutization is likely to work unless it is practically adapted to the human body, and the denial of human embodiment has a wide variety of effects, as already discussed in 3.b. However, the aspects of embodiment that are particularly relevant to our response are those that are adapted to our limited perspective, instead of assuming an infinite perspective, and to our limited capacities, rather than assuming we can somehow do anything.

Our limited perspective has been pointed out in sceptical argument through the ages. For instance, we perceive any given object from our own location in space, and only perceive what our senses can detect within their frequencies. Looking, for instance, at a chest of drawers, I have no idea what is behind it, what is inside the drawers (or within the wood structure), or what it may appear like in ultra-violet or infra-red light. My ability to identify features of an object also depends on my prior categorizations and on my attention: so things can change, even in an object I am 'looking at', and I may not notice.[1]

1   i.1.a; II.1.

It is precisely for these reasons that absolutized beliefs about what an object is 'really like' (that is, metaphysics) cannot be justified. Far from describing an object, our language serves particular purposes for us, as embodied creatures, in relation to that object. It is thus obvious that any effective *response* to absolutization cannot be metaphysical without potentially undermining the very awareness of embodiment that is needed for that response. Yet many responses to absolutization remain impractical because they are based on metaphysical assumptions.

This point applies to a great many philosophical approaches, and also to scientific approaches that maintain unacknowledged metaphysical assumptions. It implies that, irksome though it may seem to many philosophers, metaphysical claims (whether positive or negative) are not compatible with any practically effective response to the phenomena of absolutization.

This is not a question of entirely purifying oneself of metaphysical assumptions, which are liable to crop up inadvertently despite our best efforts, but rather of maintaining a consistent intention to avoid them. Since we do not avoid them by negating them (see 1.c), this requires us to maintain awareness of absolutization *on both sides* and consciously stay in the ambiguous zone between absolutes. This finding of the Middle Way is not a one-off enterprise in which one finds foundations for one's philosophy, but rather a process that may need to be repeated every single time we make a judgement. That is very demanding, and sometimes we will fail – metaphysics will return because it is absolutization, and absolutization will occur. However, our embodiment not only presents us with the challenge of continually facing up to it, but also (due to the renewal of judgement at every moment in organic experience) gives us endless new opportunities to do so. However many times you may have absolutized before, you can still potentially base your judgement on experience next time round.

On the other hand, as long as you maintain a theoretical commitment to metaphysics, this will obviously make it considerably more likely that you will use metaphysical beliefs to rationalize metaphysical judgements. It does not mean that all your judgements will be based on it (however much you may assume that it does, due to the inflation of metaphysics discussed in 4.f). Nor, on the other hand, does it mean that your judgement will not be substantially affected. There are two kinds of cases of the impact of metaphysics in an embodied situation that reveal its complexities: we could characterize them as 'saints' and 'bigots'.

The 'saints' sincerely hold metaphysical beliefs, but are able to make a large portion of their judgements on the basis of experience, probably with the inspiration of archetypes. For example, they may preach absolute beliefs based on appeal to scripture in accordance with their religious tradition, but also respond to new challenges with signs of uncommon receptivity, such as impulsive generosity, deep religious experience, and a compassionate solidarity with all they meet. These responses are not in any way deduced from their absolute beliefs, although their archetypal associations with infinite symbols may help them to keep returning to them. They are not saints *because* of their metaphysical beliefs, as is often supposed, but *in spite* of them. 'Saints' are not only found in religions, but also for instance in political groups or in the arts.

The 'bigots' on the other hand may sincerely hold the same absolute beliefs as the saints, but will more frequently deduce their immediate judgements from them. Features of absolutization will thus much more frequently become apparent, such as substitution and fragility. Nevertheless, far from every judgement will be deduced from the absolutization. Rather, the embodied state involves us constantly being confronted with new conditions that we need to respond to practically, in which we resort only to more immediate practical beliefs. A believing Catholic does not need to resort to the absolutizations of the creed to work out how to repair a damaged piece of equipment, or even how to help a distressed neighbour (only human solidarity is needed for the latter). The difference between the bigot and the saint, then, is not what they say they believe in the formal context of ritual, but how much they are inspired by the impact of archetypes to question their habitual judgements and make a larger proportion of them experiential.

To acknowledge our limited perspective as an aspect of practicality, then, does not imply denial of the potential positive impact of archetypes, nor denial that in practice metaphysics is not always damaging to the same extent. We can differentiate the effects of metaphysics from those of archetypes not on an *ad hoc* accusatory basis, but according to our overall experience of a person (including ourselves) who seems to be showing the features of absolutization at a particular point. For example, it's not just the propositions they're uttering that might lead us to conclude that even a 'saint' is absolutizing when they say the creed (though perhaps not at other times). It's also whether their judgements where doctrine might be applied (e.g. regarding group membership, acceptable opinions, or moral decision-making) are proliferating, fragile, projective, and substitutionary.

The second aspect of embodiment that is particularly relevant to our response to absolutization is that of our limited capacities in that response. This is another instance where it would be very easy to respond to absolutization in the sincere belief that one is avoiding it, and yet retain it in one's basic assumptions. In this case the absolutization of our beliefs about our capacities takes the form either of freewill or determinism: either we assume that our capacities are in some sense infinite, or that they are in some sense non-existent. Whether or not they are accompanied by explicit beliefs in freewill, freewill assumptions kick in, for instance, when we take praise or blame to be the whole story in regard to our own or someone else's actions. The biases identified in cognitive psychology of *illusion of control*,[2] *self-serving bias*,[3] and *fundamental* or *ultimate attribution error*[4] show how these assumptions very commonly involve attributing freewill to ourselves when we do something good and to others when they do something bad. We think we deserve praise for our efforts and that others are to blame for their transgressions. On the other hand, an implicit determinism appears when it comes to our own transgressions and other people's achievements. We tend to assume that the conditions that 'made' us act in a particular way were responsible for our faults and others' virtues.[5]

When we are in the grip of these biases, our thinking is absolute in the sense that only freewill and determinism are considered to be available options. The third option, of incremental achievement, is excluded. Yet our experience, prior to absolutizing formulation, is not of freewill nor of determinism, but rather of being impacted by conditions and responding to those conditions. Those conditions are always a matter of degree, and our capacity to respond to them independently and decisively is always a matter of degree. This is an effect of embodiment, because both our starting conditions and

---

2 Allan & Jenkins (1980); iv.3.f; V.7.
3 Jones & Nisbett (1971); iv.3.f; V.7.
4 Jones & Harris (1967); Pettigrew (1979); iv.3.f; V.7.
5 iv.3.f & iv.4.c; V.7 & VI.3 (on both the biases and the agnostic stance).

our capacity for relatively autonomous responses arise from that embodiment.

Our starting conditions are those of being able or unable to act in particular physical ways, formed not just by our strength and dexterity but also by the presence or absence of neural links that might make one possible judgement or another meaningful. Our autonomy in responding is formed by the complexity of our awareness, and the way this incorporates a capacity to imagine different possibilities before we select them. Our capacity to *stretch*, going slightly beyond what we might previously have managed, is not the result of selection from the potentially infinite array of choices that is absolutized freewill, but of recognizing both our limited capacities and our capacity for increasingly complex autonomous responses at the same time.

Such is the grip of enculturated metaphysical thinking, however, that many will immediately respond to such reflections about incremental achievement in terms that make metaphysical binaries inevitable. If you ask only whether our capacity to stretch is 'free' or 'determined', you are confining yourself back in the framework offered by absolutization. To shake free of it, it is necessary to embrace the ambiguities of embodied experience as prior to those absolutizations and not necessarily formatted by them. It means that we need to stop worrying about whether freewill or determinism are 'true' or not, and focus instead on a practical framework that will maximize our understanding of a given situation and help us to avoid formatting it in terms of absolutizing biases.

Whether we adopt the practicality of embodiment thus has further implications for the next two elements of practicality that I will be exploring – responsibility and effectiveness. If we accept that embodiment and ground ourselves in it, using mindfulness as a basis of confidence rather than abstract propositional beliefs, we can embrace responsibility without an absolute belief in freewill, and maximize our effectiveness without appealing to the dogmas of determinism. Our practical action will continue to be part of a discourse by which our judgements remain provisional and adjustable, neither entirely 'controlled' nor entirely 'beyond our control'. Instead, where experience reveals possible ways of directing our course, we can take them without worrying whether we are 'really' directing our course; and where experience shows conditions that we just have to accept and work with, we can also do this rather than worrying about whether we could 'really' change them or not in some entirely abstracted sense.

To come to terms with our limited perspective and limited capacities, practices integrating our experience with the body are central. Any effective response to absolutization thus needs to have an orientation towards such practices: for instance mindfulness practice, body scanning, yoga, tai chi. Any form of bodily relaxation, exercise, or recreation may help to some extent, but it is mindfulness that works most directly with embodiment. However, it is not the specific practice so much as the general orientation towards embodiment that is important, to give us a positive alternative basis for awareness that is not dependent on deduction from absolutized beliefs. Approaches that deny or dismiss any such alternative basis cannot be accepted as adequate responses to absolutization.

7.c. Responsibility

> *Summary*
>
> Responsibility can have both a 'felt' sense and a sense we are socially held to, but the former is needed (separated from law) as an aspect of our practical response to absolutization. Felt responsibility integrates and motivates, though it may need prompting by reminders. It applies not only to values, but to our interpretations of facts, the definitions of terms and our mental states. In all these ways we can avoid absolutizing dualities by developing felt responsibility.

'Responsibility' is a term used in two different kinds of senses. The first is discontinuous and involves *holding* people responsible, and thus justifies praise and blame, with the additional possibility of reward or punishment. In the discontinuous sense, you are either held responsible for a judgement or not – whether morally, socially, or legally, and whether yourself or another is thus held. The second, however, is *continuous* or incremental, and is also *felt* or directly experienced.

We say that we *feel* responsible for having broken a promise, or for looking after our children, or for saving the planet. This felt responsibility is an important aspect of practicality, because it gives a context to our action that motivates us to act, whether it is social training or archetypal inspiration that reminds us of that motivation. It is an aspect of embodied experience, arising from our imaginative capacity to consider possible actions that are meaningful to us through neural association. If we can imagine ourselves acting in a way that we can also feel to be within our capacities, and this awareness interacts with a source of inspiration that reminds us of the moral experiences we have had in the past, we begin to feel responsible.

This has an entirely contingent relationship with being *held* responsible: as we'll be aware, there are many 'irresponsible' people who are held responsible but do not feel responsible. There are also unhealthily guilty people who hold themselves responsible (often due to pressure from others) for things they do not feel responsible for with sufficient integration.

This distinction is complicated by the need to hold people responsible as a social and legal function. Here it is contextual interpretation (see 3.d) that can enable us to distinguish between absolutized judgements of responsibility and ones that are provisional but practically necessary. The practical necessity arises from some people being irresponsible – i.e. not feeling responsible when they need to respond to new conditions, which requires the intervention of law and social expectation to prevent damaging disruption to human society. Legal and social judgements that involve holding people responsible are thus not absolutizations if they are conditionally or practically framed – in other words, if we condemn criminals and miscreants *so that* society can function, rather than because they ultimately deserve our condemnation in some intrinsic fashion. One aspect of the inflation of metaphysics, however, is an insistence on judging ethical issues in absolutized legal terms. Responsibility as an aspect of our response to absolutization thus crucially must include a distinction between law and ethics, made so that we can hold people responsible without absolutizing.

The position that law is distinguishable from, and independent of, ethics is normally known as legal positivism, as opposed to legal naturalism that claims law's dependence on ethics. Legal positivism is normally associated with utilitarian justifications of law that only create moral justification for it indirectly by arguing for its beneficial consequences.[1] However, one can be legally positivist in this sense without being a utilitarian (or indeed a positivist). That the legal system needs to be justified by its consequences does not entail that utilitarianism is the only basis of *ethical* decision-making. Instead, we can see ethical decision-making as embodied and systemic, concerned with the stretches that can be developed in our felt experience of responsibility. This 'stretching' addresses conditions better in a variety of possible ways – whether those consist in developing our personal attributes, putting more consistency into our decision-making, or producing predictably better consequences. The law cannot be based on such a morality, because it does not offer absolute moral principles that can be extended into law, and could not justify doing so. Instead, then, the law needs to operate on a framework of social benefit without any appeal to absolutized premises. This seems to imply that any effective response to absolutization should include a legal positivist basis.[2]

It is felt responsibility, however, that is the crucial element of practicality in any effective response to absolutization. Without felt

1   Articulated, for example, by Hart (1968).
2   IX.4.

responsibility as the basis of moral action, 'ethics' is merely an imposition of society that we absolutely 'should' do this or that. Without a connection to our experience of feeling responsible, the possibility of inner discourse between 'ethical' requirements and other motivations is cut off, and we end up with the alienation and conflict of the forced: the factory worker who labours each day for a pittance only because all the alternatives are worse, but who lives only for the end of shift whistle; or the woman trapped into a marriage and motherhood she hates for the sake of respectability or livelihood, the overriding values of which have been instilled into her. Such 'ethics' is a vector for absolutization and an institutionalized failure, since it is only unsustainably maintained by socially sanctioned repression.[3]

Instead of alienating and producing conflict, felt responsibility can integrate, because instead of the absolutized ethical beliefs of holding responsible, it is compatible with provisional beliefs about helpful ways of judging. It also motivates these by bringing them into contact with associative inspirations and imaginative awareness. We may well need associative *reminders* to stretch ourselves ethically, but, as explained in 5.f, these can be archetypal rather than needing to consist in absolutizing propositions: for instance, we might recall a mentor and their attitude to a particular kind of issue. Thus prompted, we can maintain provisional beliefs about how to act that are revised in new situations, each time contextualized by a new set of imagined possibilities. Instead of there only being two options – obey the absolute ethic and thus be 'responsible', or disobey it – we then have a range of options that enables us to take into account more complexity in the conditions around us. Felt responsibility is thus responsibility to find a way rather than responsibility to act in a specific, pre-formulated way. If our archetypal prompts are working effectively, and our overall mental state is not too much weakened by external stresses, we can then *sustain* and *develop* increasingly complex and increasingly adequate moral responses. As we do this, we can gradually grow out of our need to rely on absolutizations as a shortcut.

If responsibility is understood as an experience of embodied individuals, rather than merely a requirement to obey particular social rules, then the scope of responsibility also becomes much wider. It extends not just to what are normally understood as duties of

3   i.7.b; VIII.2.

social morality, but to all judgements that may be stretched so as to become more complex and adequate. In particular, it applies equally to what have traditionally been falsely distinguished as 'facts' and 'values'. If we no longer maintain representationalism, there is no basis for distinguishing 'facts' on the assumption that our propositional beliefs about them can represent states of affairs out there. Instead, facts, like values, are the result of judgements that can be made in more or less complex and adequate ways for practical ends. More adequate factual judgements are helpful to us, not because they line up with some metaphysical reality to which we have no access, but because they provisionally represent the context for effective actions. We are just as responsible for these practical judgements as for other kinds – for making them as epistemically adequate as possible by taking as much of the evidence available to us into account as possible.

A central aspect of practicality is thus our degree of responsibility for the judgements we make about background assumptions. To judge the facts and values we apply in dependence on the way they will be applied is not the traditional absolutized expectation. Under the influence of rationalism with its inflation of metaphysics and logic, we have tended to assume that the facts and values themselves must have determinate forms *prior* to our practical application of them. Given the interdependency of facts, values, and applications in a wider system, though, this cannot be assumed. Nor can the contrary be assumed – that our goals and their fulfilment entirely *precede* the facts and values: that is the fallacy of wishful thinking. Instead, we need to appreciate that a limited range of facts and values is presented to us by a practical situation (even if we have worked to extend that range), but that we also have a role in interpreting and selecting from that range. In many cases, it is not obvious just from phenomenal experience how we should judge things, so we have an opportunity to exercise pragmatic judgement.

In urging our responsibility for such judgements, Sartre and Kierkegaard used the example of 'the anguish of Abraham'.[4] When apparently told by God to sacrifice his son, the existentialist philosophers argue, Abraham was not without responsibility for the decision to do such a heinous thing. Presented with the unavoidably ambiguous 'sign' from God that that was what he should do,

---

4 Kierkegaard (1985); Sartre (1980) pp. 31–2.

Abraham still had to decide whether or not this was indeed God's will. Does a dream or a vision really come from God? Is an angel actually God's messenger? In the end, the responsibility was his, both to go ahead with the sacrifice and then to stop it and substitute a sheep. Since phenomena cannot show us infinity, the relationship of an infinite God with phenomena will always be ambiguous. We have no 'proof', even if the temptation is to assume that we do. The judgement, then, is *practical*, not metaphysical. A thoroughly practical response is to recognize that it is practical.

I argue that there is a similar issue in the modern interpretation of what is good in a religious tradition. In Christianity, for instance, there is rich but highly ambiguous scriptural information about Jesus' teachings. Which of the recorded teachings are 'genuine'? Of these 'genuine' teachings, which of many possible interpretations is correct? How do we know in any case that Jesus did have correct teachings, since they are not correct by definition because he taught them? If you're a Christian and choose to 'follow Christ', on the basis of a particular interpretation of what Christ said, and of its correctness, then the responsibility for this is yours. No amount of complex justification from scripture can remove your basic responsibility. It is a practical decision that should be made on practical criteria.[5]

Even in science, similar dilemmas apply to factual judgements and make us responsible for them. That evidence is never entirely unambiguous is clear from the extreme conclusions that conspiracy theorists can draw from evidence. For example, an anti-vaxxer who is convinced that vaccinations are part of a conspiracy to kill everyone will interpret a demonstration of safe vaccination as a fake: the needle can't have really had the vaccination in it, or the person would be dead. There is never a 'compulsion' to interpret evidence in a particular way, as claimed by rationalizing philosophers.[6] Rather there is a set of associative habits that we have built up in response to our experience that encourage us to interpret evidence in particular ways that have proved helpful – one that breaks down when absolutized beliefs kick in to prioritize the maintenance of group identity. Scientists, however, will interpret evidence in line with the best available theoretical explanation of that evidence, in accordance with the practical value of that explanation in science

---

5   Ellis (2018) 2.e.
6   E.g. Baggini (2016) pp. 127–9, and my response, Ellis (2017).

(and also in wider society when that science is applied). In doing so, they exercise their responsibility in response to scientific values, prompted either by their community, or perhaps by scientific archetypes of truth or rationality.

For similar reasons, our responsibility also extends to the meanings of the terms we use. Representationalism encourages essentialism about terms, as a proposition could only represent reality if the meanings of its component words or terms are fixed. However, if we recognize the terms we use to instead be part of a linguistic system of meaning in our experience, their meaning depends on the role they play in that system. Following embodied meaning, too, the meaning of more abstract terms depends on metaphorical structures that can be changed by association with new metaphors or disassociation with old ones. In addition, complex or abstract terms are used in slightly different ways that require analysis if we are to take responsibility for how we are using them. If we do not take this responsibility, we can remain imprisoned in absolute assumptions that are constantly reinforced by the meanings of the terms that are being insisted upon.

As an example of taking responsibility in our interpretation of terms, if someone insists that the meaning of the term 'Christianity' must be an absolute belief in the existence of an infinite, supernatural God who sent Christ as the saviour of humankind, we are no longer at liberty to interpret the Christian tradition in terms compatible with human experience without repudiating the tradition itself. An absolutizing duality is thus forced, and third alternatives ruled out. If, however, we interpret 'Christianity' as a complex tradition, including both absolute beliefs and also archetypal symbols, practices, social groups, etc., we are in a position to gradually adapt our interpretation of it towards greater adequacy. The underlying shift in metaphor there may be from a religion as a picture – i.e. a representation of 'reality' in people's minds – to religion as a tree, branching out different phenomenal forms over time. But we could only make that metaphorical shift if we accept the responsibility for doing so, recognizing that in definition, as anywhere else, we have a range of imagined possibilities and the inspiration of motives to select from those options in the most helpful ways. I will be returning to this issue in 9.a.

In addition to our responsibility for judgements of facts and values and of meanings, there is an even more basic responsibility that is seldom acknowledged – that for our mental states. Whether we understand mental states in 'cognitive' or 'emotional' terms, the development of mindfulness and psychotherapy make it increasingly clear that these are not a 'given'. Instead, our actions in caring for or neglecting our mental and bodily states over a period of time can make a substantial difference to those mental states. As in any other case of responsibility, this is not a matter of freewill, in which we have total control regardless of conditions, but it is also not a case of determinism in which we have no control. Rather, we can influence our mental state through bodily practices such as diet or exercise, by recognizing and meeting our emotional needs (for instance, to connect with others), and by practices that may directly impact the quality of our mental states, such as mindfulness. As in our other judgements, we are thus in a position, not to start from scratch, but to *stretch* our mental states from ones that are more likely to create absolutization (usually in response to stress) to ones that enable experiential and provisional judgement. To be able to examine more than two options, we need sufficient contextual awareness, and such awareness is a product, not just of intellectual understanding and reflection (though that can greatly help) but also of our degree of emotional equanimity and our degree of bodily awareness.

A response to absolutization that fulfils practicality must thus be a *responsible* one that enables genuine felt responsibility to be developed. That responsibility provides a motivating concern and potential for stretch beyond our habitual judgements, by examining alternatives. It enables us to take responsibility for our basic assumptions (in both fact and value terms), for the meanings of the terms we use, and for the mental states in which we make our judgements. This is ethical practice in the broadest sense, and can be seen as a development of the idea of the path as an integrated ethical totality that we find in Buddhism, but it is hardly compatible with the idealized or reduced concept of 'ethics' more typical of the Western tradition (more will be said about this in 8.b below). If we take responsibility for the judgements that precede our actions, this also enables us to feel responsible for our actions and their impact as being the result of judgements that we actively made. This impact, and its role as an aspect of practicality, is the topic of the next chapter.

7.d. Effectiveness

> *Summary*
>
> Absolutization may temporarily boost the intensity of our goal-directed action, but even that intensity is reduced by conflict. The more complex our activity, the more direction rather than intensity becomes important, and the more absolutization interferes with that directionality, especially over time. In response, we need to develop genuine *confidence*, which arises from organic *practice* in embodied judgements in a varied environment, not from absolutized belief.

Effectiveness in practice depends on how fully an action is completed to meet its goals. I take it for granted that, as previously stated, these goals are provisional, but nevertheless our embodied situation is one where we need to act on our provisional beliefs and try to reach our provisional goals. That is what organisms do – indeed a large part of what it means to be a living organism. However much we may need to try to engage with complexity in our judgements at large, the relationship of action to goals is simple and linear. It occurs at the moment when we have to stop taking further complexity into account in order to act – at the point of 'closure' as described in cognitive psychology.[1] Nevertheless, I shall argue that it is affected by absolutization, and that our response to absolutization needs to be *effective* as an aspect of its practicality.

It may be easiest to start by considering the effectiveness of one goal-oriented movement at one moment. A more effective blow of a pickaxe delivers more force to the material to be broken up, and thus makes it more likely that the material will be broken in the desired way. Such force requires both strength in wielding the pickaxe and speed as it hits the material. This is straightforward Newtonian physics: force is equivalent to mass multiplied by acceleration (Newton's second law of motion). More force, if it is sufficient to overcome resistance, will result in more motion.

If we then considered the effectiveness of repeated blows of the pickaxe over five minutes, we would be looking at how well that force was sustained. Of course, in practice, the skill with which the pickaxe is wielded is also very important, because this determines where the blows land and thus how efficiently they fulfil the desired

[1] Kruglanski (2004) pp. 7–20.

objective. To consider the effectiveness of the work, then, we need to consider not only the force or intensity of the motion, but also its direction and duration. Absolutization may temporarily increase the intensity of our engagement and thus give us the impression that we are being more effective, but the more we take into account direction and duration, the less adequate an absolutized pursuit of goals becomes, and responses to absolutization thus need to allow us to be effective in carefully directed and sustainable ways.

Let me first try to account for the apparent increase in effectiveness that absolutization may give us. This results from the *intensity* that is made possible by removing 'doubts' or awareness of alternatives. The man with the pickaxe 'knows' that he is digging for victory and that his cause is right. In that context, then, no energy is diverted into hesitation about whether he is applying his efforts in the right place, or whether he will be able to keep it up for very long. The neural channels of meaning and belief are clearly activated and dominant, with no alternative channels open for the moment. The repetition of flow through these channels under the influence of a reinforcing feedback loop of beliefs and motives also makes the efficiency of that flow increasingly greater – up to a point. Up to a point, too, direction and duration can also be addressed within the framework of absolute belief. The worker will probably be supported by a group who share his absolute beliefs and are bound by them, with each person being energized by the others. Allegiance to authority within the binding group allows leaders to determine the direction so that it remains coherent, and, within the terms created by fragility, also remains durable. The team stays together, bound by its ideology and thus effectively pursuing its goals, until its absolutized beliefs snap.

I have chosen a simple task to begin with; to fulfil clear goals, however, even the intensity of application to this task is undermined by absolutization, when we start to consider the conflicts that it creates. Conflicts divert energy into two different opposed desires that are trying to overcome each other, and, as discussed in 5.a, can be understood at both the psychological and the socio-political level. A person who is diverting energy to the repression of doubts about their task unavoidably has less energy to apply to their task, just as two people who are arguing about their task are unlikely to be able to make good progress on it. Absolutization, which seemed such an easy way to create effectiveness at first, then makes it impossible to resolve the conflict, which is framed in terms of irreconcilable absolute beliefs. At the group level, a common response to this is further repression: for example, the work leader will clamp down on the two workers who are arguing and tell them to get on with the work on his direction, often with threats. Of course, this further repression creates more conflict and is subject to exactly the same limitations. A reinforcing feedback loop then develops, with each new intervention to enforce the absolute framework creating more conflict, that then has to be further repressed. More and more energy can thus be diverted as a system based on absolutization tries to patch itself, and in the process its effectiveness dwindles.

If this is the case with a relatively simple task, the introduction of greater complexity makes absolutization even more deleterious to effectiveness, because the direction of energy becomes ever more important. That complexity might take the form of increasing specialization of roles in a shared enterprise, or in the use of technological devices in which human muscular effort is replaced by mechanical processes. These processes then become far more efficient, but also require more complex direction: people have to design, make, programme, and maintain the machines, or organize the specialist teams of people. The more important the direction of the force becomes as opposed to the human energy put into it, the less effective absolutization becomes, because people have to be sufficiently open to understanding the complexity of the system they are managing to direct it effectively. Hence the development of education and science have had a crucial interdependence with the development of technology, putting an increasing emphasis on provisionality in learning and research. The man with the pickaxe only needed to learn how to wield a pickaxe, but the computer programmer needs very complex training that is constantly updated, making it impossible for her to be successful just by maintaining absolutization in that field of activity.

The more complex and interdependent the systems in which we work become, the more absolutization interferes with our directionality, but that does not prevent us from compartmentalizing our experience and continuing to absolutize in one area whilst avoiding doing so in another. The computer programmer may also be a religious fundamentalist. Totalitarian regimes may impose an absolutized political environment on their people, and yet maintain complex technology. The imposition of such boundaries on our experience, however, also has to be absolutized: in my experience as a visitor there, people in China generally do not discuss politics, and also do not question the barrier to discussing politics.

The limitations of an absolutized framework become all the clearer when we start to consider the effects of duration. The longer an activity continues, the more likely the conditions around it are to change, and thus the more likely that an absolutized framework of action will become ineffective because it will start to be misdirected in the new conditions. This, of course, is a basic insight of evolutionary theory: species die out because their abilities and behaviour are inadequate in a new environment. At a more basic level, though, we do not have to think in terms of elimination but merely in terms of effectiveness over time. If the man with the pickaxe believes that the pickaxe is the only right tool to break up the ground, and then meets a rock that is so hard it cannot be broken with a pickaxe, he will not die out, but he will be unable to complete his task. The impact of the development of new and unexpected conditions (statistically sometimes known as 'fat tails') has been much explored by Nassim Nicholas Taleb, who effectively criticizes absolutized beliefs only in terms of their ineffectiveness over time.[2]

All of this indicates that responses to absolutization need to consistently support and promote effectiveness, not just in a narrow or short-term fashion, but in a fashion that draws attention to the challenges created by complexity and sustainability over time. This requires us to continue stretching our sense of responsibility beyond parochial limitations, which is the major driver behind the second main criterion I will be discussing in the next section – that of universal aspiration. However, even within relatively narrow practical limits there are still aspects of effectiveness that depend, not on the wide extent of our consideration, but on a more immediate embodied quality of integration. This can be particularly identified in the quality of *confidence* in both our judgements and our actions.

Confidence is the basic ease and efficiency with which we can accomplish tasks that lead us down accustomed neural and muscular channels in interaction with a familiar and relatively predictable environment. I can be confident when I sit on my chair that it will not collapse beneath my weight, and that when I cross a narrow plank across a stream my balance will not fail me and I will not fall

2   Taleb (2010, 2012).

in the stream. This can extend to trust in others based on familiarity: I do not expect my friend to meet me with blows, but with a smile and a handshake. Similarly, we may extend our trust to sources of information in science or the media, or have *faith* in the power of religious symbols to inspire us over time. Such confidence is a basic condition of our effectiveness in practice. The man with the pickaxe could not break up the ground with it if he had no confidence in his muscular ability to control its course regardless of its weight, or in his judgement about where to direct it.

The belief that absolutization gives us confidence is a common delusive trap, but absolutization instead produces absolute belief in substitution for confidence, together with metaphysical inflation that makes us attribute our embodied confidence to the absolute belief. Instead, confidence is built up through a provisional process in which we make adjustments to our judgement and action in a balancing feedback loop. The better we maintain that capacity to adjust, the better justified our confidence. Absolute belief, in contrast, leaves us with fragile over-confidence, unable to adjust our direction and yet increasingly dependent on our identification with it.

Confidence develops with time and practice, and indirectly in our experientially-justified trust in the experiential justification of others. Basically, the longer we practise doing something, the more confident we become in doing it, and the more we observe others' practice, the more we can trust them. This offers the basis of a fallible type of justification that serves us much better than supposed absolute justification ever could, because it is intimately connected to our embodied experience and sense of felt responsibility. Such confidence is justified *because* it is provisional rather than despite, as our ability to consider new options and change our beliefs is what continues to make it reliable, and gives us a measure of resistance to absolutization.

It is a matter of confidence that we are able to act decisively when a situation demands it – not a matter of absolutized certainty. For example, a man who leaps into a canal to rescue a drowning child does so because of confidence in his capacity to swim and a sense of felt responsibility for others. He has reached the position of being able to act quickly and confidently because of a process of receptivity over time, not because of absolute beliefs maintained over the same time. His fast thinking, like that of a pianist playing *prestissimo*, is a result of practice at a slower speed, and could not have been achieved through constant fast thinking. The apparent absolutization of his thinking at that point thus has a non-absolutizing context.

Yet the deceptions of this need for decisiveness considered out of context have continually been used to undermine the perspective of uncertainty used by those who want to question absolutization. Critics of the sceptical argument that points out uncertainty have alleged that scepticism is impractical – when it is those who assume absolutization is necessary, on the contrary, who are impractical.[3] The accusation that sceptical awareness makes one impractical is one of the biggest calumnies in philosophical history – but one that absolutizing philosophers have managed to make stick. On the contrary, it is *lack* of sceptical awareness of uncertainty that makes one impractical, because one is then stuck in a more limited range of options to respond to any given situation.

Overall, then, effectiveness depends on the development of confidence in practical judgement being fully integrated with our sceptical awareness of uncertainty. Like embodiment and responsibility, confident effectiveness can be cultivated. In some ways it follows from embodiment, so can be supported by mindfulness and associated practices. Our confidence in doing a particular kind of thing is also generated by practice in doing it (or similar things), so practice in creative activity also boosts confidence. The arts and crafts thus have an important role to play, more effective than less creative kinds of activity because they involve constant creative judgement and balancing feedback on the results of that judgement. This feedback comes from what might be called communities of practice, which develop standards that help to encourage others to develop their activity in particular ways:[4] for example, a group of embroiderers encourages a new embroiderer to develop confidence in skills of embroidery – perhaps initially in quite a circumscribed way using models or patterns, but increasingly as a mode of more open self-expression.

Communities of practice in the arts are also a reminder of the more general ways that confidence is dependent on social reinforcement. Children often develop confidence through positive reinforcement of particular patterns of thinking and behaviour from

---

3   i.1.b; II.1.
4   See MacIntyre (1981) pp. 187 ff.

adults, and adults retain some of this need. Those with problems of confidence in particular respects may also be aided by psychotherapy, which uses the leverage of another's perspective to help dissolve specific absolutizing blockages that can disrupt our lives. More broadly, beyond the limited sphere that therapy can operate in, the role of community and friendship in developing confidence is crucial. This in turn requires the development of groups that can form links of human solidarity without the dependence on uncontextualized power that marks groups founded on absolutization. Friendship and community, once again, are practices that can be cultivated, and it is hard to envisage an effective response to absolutization that denies this basis of human confidence.

To conclude this section, then, I have established practicality as a requirement for any response to absolutization. Practicality is expressed through *practice*, by which I mean the deliberate use of certain types of activity to counteract absolutization in the long term by changing the conditions that produce it. Such practice needs to be embodied, starting with our limitations in mind and basing our awareness on the body, rather than using absolutized beliefs as a point of departure. It also needs to be responsible, stretching our engagement with the conditions around us in a way that incorporates and integrates our motives – neither creating absolutized beliefs about what we 'ought' to do, nor wholly rejecting the stretching effect of conceptualized goals that go beyond our current experience. In embracing such long-range practicality that takes uncertainty seriously, we do not reduce our effectiveness in current tasks, which can still be completed more easily because conflicts have been overcome. An effective response to absolutization thus requires an orientation towards practice that is generally lacking in many of the existing academic responses to its aspects.

8. Criteria for a Response: Universal Aspiration

8.a. Top-down and Bottom-up Universality

> *Summary*
>
> Top-down universality, which creates absolutization, involves generalization from part to whole, followed by deduction from beliefs about the whole. Bottom-up universality, on the other hand, makes use of meaningful concepts for universality to inspire a search for a more complete view. The latter is needed to move practical beliefs beyond parochialism.

After practicality, my second criterion for any adequate response to absolutization is universal aspiration. This needs highlighting as a criterion in itself, but can also be seen as an aspect of practicality, because practicality is limited by being localized. Any response to absolutization will become more adequate the more conditions it takes into account. Yet at the same time, appealing to 'universality' carries an obvious danger of absolutization, and some thinkers may immediately assume that any approach that claims to be universal must involve the dogmatic imposition of one relative perspective. That is why I have called the criterion 'universal *aspiration*' rather than only universality, and why I need to start the discussion of it with a distinction between top-down and bottom-up versions of universality. In my view, universality is a valuable dimension of any response to absolutization, but not if it is imposed rather than developed.

Top-down universality, of the kind I want to avoid, begins with absolutized beliefs that are claimed to be universal, also known as generalizations. These may involve any kind of statement, facts, or values, with any kind of scope, from the whole universe to a tiny object. They are distinguished by generalizing about the whole of whatever is being discussed, when there cannot possibly be any grounds for doing so given the limitations of our experience. The claims made are thus metaphysical, going beyond experience to 'reality', and involve a fallacy of composition, assuming the nature of a whole is represented by a part. Such absolutized generalizations can be distinguished from provisional ones by their lack of conditionality or practicality, often signalled by the use of words like 'always', 'never', 'completely', or 'entirely': 'You can never trust a Conservative', 'Tech companies are always trying to deceive people', or 'This car is totally unreliable'. However, as discussed in 3.d, it is always the context that makes a judgement absolute, not just the words of a sentence that expresses it. When an absolutization is also a generalization of parts into a whole, it is a dogmatic universal.

Beginning with a dogmatic universal, top-down universality applies it by assumed absolute deduction to a specific judgement. If all Conservatives are necessarily untrustworthy, one particular given Conservative must be necessarily untrustworthy. This deduction will be applied regardless of the specific features of this particular Conservative. Again, it would be possible to take a provisional generalization and apply it provisionally, by recognizing the interrelationship between that application and other conditions, and thus maintaining awareness of alternatives. However, top-down universality follows the features of absolutization in cutting off such alternative possibilities.

Bottom-up universality, on the other hand, adopts a provisional generalization in the light of the meaningful possibility of universality. We do not necessarily need to abandon all use of words like 'completely' or 'always', provided we maintain our provisionality (and perhaps signal it) in other ways. Nor do we have to abandon all use of concepts like 'truth', 'falsehood', 'knowledge', or 'reality' in relation to specific objects, whole classes of objects, or the whole universe. What becomes crucial, however, is that these concepts *inspire* in the role of archetypes rather than becoming the subjects of top-down deduction to arrive at beliefs about the complete truth. In order to be able to move beyond the duality of choice between an absolute truth and an absolute falsehood with which absolutization confronts us, indeed, we may well need a reminder of the possibility of doing otherwise that takes the form of a symbol associated with wider experience, prompting awareness of associations and identifications beyond our current framing of a situation. This is the way in which universal *concepts* or *symbols* need to function, inspiring, for instance, a scientific search for truth, a moral search for goodness, and an artistic search for beauty. At the very point of taking them seriously, we move beyond their absolutization. Thus we should not make the mistake of associating them solely with their top-down usage.

Ideas of universality in bottom-up usage are associated with an aspiration, so we can thus reasonably talk about universal aspiration. This aspiration functions for us merely by evoking a meaning, so it is not necessary to *believe* that any statement is 'true', or any act 'good' in a final rather than provisional fashion. The distinction between meaning and belief is thus crucial to the provisional use of the idea of universality. We find the terms meaningful, probably profoundly so, in the same way that we do characters in a novel: but the synaptic links that create that meaning do not need to extend to the kind of associations we would need to use them directly in action, or indeed in speech about action. Being meaningful without being an object of belief is not necessarily a lesser status or an undervaluing of the key archetypal symbols for universals (such as truth, goodness, or God): they can have a huge impact on our lives, be objects of veneration and worship, and be associated with life-changing experiences, without being taken 'literally' as objects of belief.

This point is connected to one of the key reasons why negative beliefs rejecting absolutization do not rid us of it. By substituting 'God does not exist' for 'God exists', for instance, we remain in the realm of belief, and we remain focused only on two alternatives. It is thus hardly surprising if atheism (in the sense of the belief that God does not exist) can be associated with all the features of absolutization just as theism can – proliferation, representationalism, projection, substitution, and so on. As with theism, we have to employ contextual judgement in interpreting statements by atheists, but if we take their statements of belief in the non-existence of God 'literally', they are clearly caught in the same framing, excluding further options, that theists are caught in. The example of God can illustrate a wider point here about universals – that denying a universal does not free you from universal beliefs, even if they are negative ones. Negative beliefs about universals can also be used in the same top-down fashion.

Universal aspiration, on the other hand, is a practical requirement for stretching our sense of responsibility, as discussed in 7.c. Without any concept of universality, it would be difficult to understand what we are stretching our judgements *into*, and to distinguish that stretch from any random extension. Our 'ought' has to come from 'somewhere', although the 'somewhere' is not a location except in the sense of synaptic connections creating possible meaning. This is where we need the concept of normativity, at least in an adaptation of the form it has been used in by moral philosophers. This will be discussed in the next chapter.

Universal aspiration also has a relationship with systems theory that will need to be explored, even if it is not common currency for systems theorists. The very process of understanding an object, not in a fixed, linear way, but as part of a system, arguably involves universal aspiration. When we then see one system in relation to other systems, and recognize that no system can be independent, we are also creating a universal aspiration, as I will discuss further in 8.c.

The final three chapters of this section all explore different dimensions of universal aspiration – in terms of groups, space, and time – and the differing impacts that these have in helping us to formulate the best available practical response to absolutization. In doing this it will become increasingly clear that those intellectual approaches that rely on relativism, nihilism, or other kinds of negative denial of the meaningfulness of universality, must be rejected for entirely practical reasons.

8.b. Normativity

> *Summary*
>
> Normative expectations of what we *ought* to do are needed to address the absolutizing tendencies either to rely on the fact-value distinction, or to idealized normativity. Normativity is not 'queer', but an aspect of embodied practice that needs a motivating prompt from archetypal universals to help us make more provisional judgements. When motivated it *stretches* what we can do slightly beyond our existing identifications.

Normativity, the positing of beliefs about how we *ought* to judge or act, is not some strange 'queer' property sitting outside the 'normal' range of what we talk about, as analytic philosophers have often portrayed it.[1] It's an entirely normal aspect of human experience. As organisms, we maintain ourselves by consuming and utilizing aspects of our environment, so we have desires. These desires, when generalized and justified in relation to our beliefs, become values. Values urge stretches of our beliefs, and these need to be scaffolded by meaningful *concepts* or *symbols* of what we 'ought' to do, which I call archetypes. We then need to be prompted towards *openness* in our judgements, so that we engage with more than the two options of absolutizing judgement. Symbols that prompt this openness need to be universal or infinite in scope whenever they are given a conceptual form, because values vary for each individual embodied situation, and we do not yet understand what specific forms our more developed values will take.

Far from depending on metaphysical beliefs (or alternatively being 'merely subjective'), then, normativity needs to be *provisional:* as soon as we slip back into the rigidity of absolutization, we are no longer doing what we *ought* to do by developing our judgement towards greater adequacy. Normativity thus does not consist in verbal formulae (such as moral rules) that absolutely represent what we ought to do, but in prompts for new moral possibilities that take us beyond absolutization. They do not need to (and indeed cannot) precisely describe how we should act, but they do something far more valuable – actually motivating us to judge and act in creative ways.

---

1   Most famously Mackie (1977) ch. 9.

However, all too often, academic approaches to the phenomena that comprise absolutization (such as those of psychology, other social sciences, cognitive science, many branches of philosophy, and even systems thinking) do not engage with our values (and thus our motives) because of a false neutrality based on the fact-value distinction. It is the fact-value distinction that generally leads philosophers to claim that 'facts' are or can be 'objective', whilst values are 'subjective', imposing a false dichotomy on our always uncertain judgements. The fact-value distinction is based on a merely logical distinction, when in actual experience facts and values are completely inseparable. Every time we select a 'fact' for attention we exercise our values, and every time we identify how we ought to act we assume 'facts'. Because academics working in a broadly scientific paradigm tend to over-inflate the significance of this logical distinction and try (unsuccessfully) to purge their work of values, academic writing often lacks an explicit *normative* dimension. What *we ought* to do or not do, what we judge to be good or bad or right or wrong (not just what we observe people to believe about these things, but what we actually feel *we* ought to do), is a dimension of our lives that is systemically inseparable from what we believe in other respects.

A common philosophers' response to criticism of the fact-value distinction is to claim that it is not treated absolutely, but that some sort of fact-value distinction is used in practice. They are correct about this in the sense that, even to criticize the fact-value distinction, I have to talk about 'facts' and 'values'. Our ability to distinguish between the *meanings* of each, however, is not the issue. Rather it is the *beliefs* about the absolute separation of facts and values that are assumed when philosophers and others make further deductions about ethics. Analytic philosophers constantly make subtle distinctions one minute and then fail to apply them the next, in this case forgetting the interdependence of facts and values as soon as they plunge into metaphysical discussion about 'naturalism', 'emotivism', and suchlike metaethical theories about what ethical language *'really means'*. If facts and values are really understood to be interdependent, there is nothing that value talk 'really means' distinct from meaning in general – which depends on association in our bodies. In this case, I am arguing that the associations we should be concerned with are those that prompt new options in our thinking beyond an absolutized framework.

The fact-value distinction is also responsible for the further distinction between 'descriptive ethics' and 'normative ethics', which plagues the social sciences, as well as philosophy, whenever ethics of any kind are discussed. 'Descriptive ethics' are supposed to be a neutral representation of facts about what people believe about ethics. That there can be no such thing in practice is obvious as soon as you identify the big normative assumptions (often reductive ones) in social scientific discussions of ethics. Jonathan Haidt, for instance, has done some really helpful work on the empirical basis of socio-political values that can be observed in different cultural contexts, but he then rushes on to reduce ethics (and even religious experience) to social evolutionary function – excellent scientific work undermined by crass philosophical assumptions.[2] In the process he sweepingly ignores the whole of individual experience of moral motivation and its significance. Throughout, of course, he assumes the normative value of developing a scientific understanding of these socio-political values, and he even goes on to apply this in helping polarized Americans to understand each other from either side of their political chasm – without once acknowledging that what he is doing is normative. The result of ignoring normativity in social sciences is of course that, repressed, it pops up again without being subject to critical examination, and meanwhile social science theory continues in its purely descriptivist delusions. This is the kind of failure to connect the dots that results from a combination of academic over-specialization, together with continuing philosophical failure to challenge its effects.

The only philosophical approach to normative ethics that I have found that in some measure gets beyond this absolutizing of the fact-value distinction is that of Mark Johnson,[3] which in some ways builds on the earlier account of John Dewey.[4] Both of these recognize that moral experience (which is not totally distinct from other sorts of experience) involves judgements that need to be weighed up against each other, and that thus become more effective when we consider a wider range of options. This also means that what I would identify as absolutizing judgements (that is, ones caught in habitual and conflicting modes) are inadequate. Neither of them, however, really offers any explanation of moral inspiration, and the

2   Haidt (2012).
3   Johnson (2014).
4   Dewey (1922).

helpful as well as unhelpful role that symbols with infinite scope might play in it. Both also identify with 'naturalism' – an identification that seems to me still enmeshed in representationalism of 'nature' at some level, perhaps a subtle but still unnecessary one.

Nevertheless, Mark Johnson's account of the opposite of moral growth could very well be an account of how absolutization lacks effective normativity:

> The sin of moral obtuseness (or failed perceptiveness) is the inability to appreciate all, or at least most, of what is going on in the situation you are facing. It is a failure to recognise the plurality of competing values, conflicting habits, incompatible desires, emotional responses, and emotional dispositions. It is also a failure of vision regarding the possibilities for reconstructive improvement of the present situation. The result of such a failure is dogmatic adherence to prior habits of feeling, thinking, and response that only reinforce what is problematic about the situation in the first place.⁵

The normative dimension is an aspect of our embodiment and of any adequate practical response to it. That is because the values we express in normative language (ought, good, etc.) are motivators as well as reminders of people's beliefs. When we have resolved to make a moral effort, the danger is that we simply forget our resolution, because we are not consistently aware enough of the conditions and feelings that prompted these motives. Normative moral language (when it is not just a group binding shortcut) prompts us to remember. In this sense, it is a crucial driver of practice that we speak normatively, and a widespread academic failure to do so in relation to the phenomena of absolutization thus leaves a gap in social understanding of the justification and motivation for practice.

To operate as a successful reminder over time, our sense of normativity also needs to be *sustained* beyond the values we may prioritize at any one particular point, so as to get beyond the mere flipping between opposed absolutes that may be our initial response to a recognition of absolutization. Much damage has been done by the deeply rooted absolutizing assumption that normative language that is sustained and universalized needs to be deduced from some metaphysical source. Instead, both factual claims and values are justified through *practice* that draws on an increasingly integrated range of our experience over time. The more we can apply either a factual or a value belief in a provisional space within our experience,

5   Johnson (2014) p. 201.

and the more we find that it supports practical progress in experience rather than absolutized shortcuts, the better justified it is.

A variety of philosophical, religious, and ideological traditions propose a normative ethics. As I have argued, however, in *Archetypes in Religion and Beyond*,[6] these traditions have strong projective and dogmatic elements running through them that have also distracted from their practice. In other words, they have often been corrupted by absolutization, to such an extent that many people now assume that religion is necessarily absolute. In mining the normative inspirations and practical riches of religious traditions, we are constantly faced with a critical task of separating the dogmatic from the practical elements in those traditions. This largely means that (with the exception of elements of Buddhism, perhaps) we need to look elsewhere for the tools with which to engage in this sorting process and then apply them to religions, rather than using religions as usually presented as our point of departure.

Similar points can be made about normative ethics as it has been presented in philosophical traditions. Aristotelian virtue ethics, for example, often sounds eminently practical and empirical, until we look more closely at its relationships both with universalized metaphysics and the conventions of ancient Greek society. The test here is not just that Aristotle invented the very term 'metaphysics', but also that he uses absolute logical deduction from what are taken to be the essential characteristics of humans as well as other kinds of object. His vision of normative ethics involves humans achieving happiness by attempting to fulfil their 'proper' function in distinctively rational human nature.[7] This is an idea that can be readily used to justify other absolutizations – including those that are culturally specific to Aristotle's context, but that he takes to be universal. Aristotle thus universalizes magnanimity as a virtue of his class,[8] and slavery as a social system.[9] Though those using him today might not make exactly the same mistakes, the unacknowledged absolutizations in their method could easily lead them into new ones.[10]

---

6   Ellis (2022).
7   Aristotle (1976) 1097b22–1098a20 (pp. 75–6).
8   Ibid. 1119b22 ff.
9   Aristotle (1905) I.4 (p. 31).
10 i.7.d & e; VIII.5.

The normative moral philosophies of the enlightenment – Kantianism and Utilitarianism – both offer critical perspectives on earlier ways of justifying practical judgement, and both also have a universal aspiration that helps us to challenge more limited or parochial values. However, neither sufficiently recognizes absolutization as a problem that might affect their own normative judgement procedures. Kant's approach to ethics is heavily reliant on representationalism, to formulate universal moral rules that are supposed to have a representational meaning based on a universal moral state of affairs. This creates an obvious problem of inflexibility, as the embodied meaning of the rule to someone in a particular situation is not taken into account: for example, Kant condemned all lying, even to save someone's life.[11] Any use of rules or principles clearly has to treat them more provisionally, given that their meaning is not simply a fixed state of affairs – which also means that other ways of assessing normative judgement are needed.[12]

Utilitarianism, on the other hand, makes use of empirical evidence to try to maximize the happiness of everyone affected by an action. This also ignores the embodiment of a person making a judgement, in other respects, by not taking into account the motives and mental states of people making such judgements in practice. Why should I be concerned with everyone's happiness, and how can I take into account my ignorance of how to actually bring it about in its massive uncertainty and complexity? Utilitarianism may thus provide a consensus decision-making procedure for socio-political decision-making, but is not at all practical for individual judgement. Its only response to the psychological factors distorting our judgement through absolutization is abstract idealization of the decisions we *ought* to make if we were in some God-like absolute position.[13]

No, to be properly normative, ethics needs to be practical. This point is indeed foreshadowed in an analysis of the requirement of ethics going back to Kant – that is the idea that *ought* implies *can*.[14] There is no sense, on this account, in which I *ought* to travel back to the fourteenth century to prevent the Black Death by introducing modern sanitation and medical treatment, because I can't. However

11   Kant (1996) pp. 605–15.
12   i.7.f; VIII.4.
13   E.g. in Railton (1984) and Brink (1986) – addressed in more detail in Ellis (2001) 3.k.iv. On consequentialism also see i.7.h & I; VIII.3.
14   Kant (1929) A548/576, p. 473.

morally desirable the action might seem, time travel is not available to me. One only needs to apply this insight to the psychological conditions of judgement to recognize that what I *ought* to do also needs to be within the bounds of *psychological* possibility, as well as other forms of constraining condition. I can no more sell all my goods and give the money to the poor (as Jesus unrealistically demanded of a young man) than I can time travel to retrospectively cure the Black Death. I could, however, *stretch* my practice from the point where I start, to identify less with my possessions, and perhaps be more generous with them. *Can* implies a practically realistic policy, which lies ambiguously between an impossibly idealized demand on the one hand and a deterministic excuse for total inaction on the other. Practicality implies the ethics of stretch.[15]

If normative ethics fails to provide adequately practical theory to tackle absolutization, then, one can turn instead to theoretical approaches that are framed as 'practical' rather than normative. These include more specific contextual types of practicality, such as professional practice, as well as more general pragmatic theories. However, one of the first questions one then needs to ask is whether such theory is also normative. Very often, normativity in modern discourse is disguised: for instance as professionalism, political correctness, economic desirability, rationality, mental health, or social adjustment. Any of these disguises, once penetrated, invites the question 'Why should I do that?', that is, a wider normative question demanding further context. Why should what an individual doctor or teacher ought to do as a professional be seen in isolation from the wider context of what they ought to do as an individual? Why, indeed, should other individuals be exempted from these normative demands being made on professionals? The limitation of specific types of practical theory, then, is that the goals of that practice may be taken for granted, and indeed become an absolutized form of group binding for the professional or other group concerned. For example, much can be learnt from models of therapeutic practice, but unless they are explicitly extended beyond that professional practice, its boundaries and shared assumptions may be implicitly absolutized.

Overall, then, any effective response to absolutization needs to be normative, but without either absolutizing normative claims,

---

15 VIII.1/2.

or fruitless attempts to avoid them on the grounds that they are assumed to be necessarily absolute. In some respects, then, the many other areas of discussion in modern life where normativity is deceptively and ineffectively avoided need to learn from normative philosophy, where at least normativity is discussed explicitly – but not from the fact-value distinction or other absolutizing assumptions made in these philosophical contexts. A new, practical understanding of normativity is needed that, I would suggest, makes use of the meaning of normative concepts to prompt us towards judgements that challenge absolutization. In the process we can get rid of the fruitless conflicts between positively absolute and 'relative' (i.e. negatively absolute) ethics, and the general ineffectuality of ethical discussion that merely appeals to impractical idealizations. All of these impediments to ethics, I want to suggest, are products of absolutization. By addressing absolutization as a whole we can liberate normative ethics into a valuable practical role, but only if we include it in the discussion to begin with.

8.c. Systematicity

> *Summary*
>
> Systems thinking also prompts a universal aspiration to motivate us to move from linear to complex thinking, whether on boundaries, categories, causal relationships, or goals, which form the basis of our factual understanding of a situation. This is reflected in the development of 'ideal' conceptual models as an aspect of problem-solving in soft systems methodology.

Systems theory offers an alternative way of understanding universal aspiration, because of the ways in which it requires us to face up to complexity. Whilst our normal practical way of understanding the world around us is simple and linear, the requirements of systems thinking (systematicity) challenge that normality. They do not do so, however, by merely offering us an alternative normality, but by requiring us to take into account possibilities beyond our current framework for understanding that normality. The scope of what they ask us to take into account is also open, with every system being nested in other systems, and no system independence (see 2.b). In this sense, the systemic thinking required to overcome absolutization also involves universal aspiration – requiring us to have an *understanding* of infinite possibilities at the level of meaning, but avoiding top-down beliefs that assume knowledge of systems as a whole.

The thinking involved could be analysed in these four terms:[1]

1. Normal practical thinking is dichotomous (either-or), but a systemic perspective requires us to see fluid boundaries and varied perspectives
2. Normal practical thinking involves static categories, but a systemic perspective requires us to categorize things in lots of different possible ways from different possible perspectives
3. Normal practical thinking involves linear causal relationships, but a systemic perspective requires us to see complex interrelationships and webs of mutual causality
4. Normal practical thinking involves a limited goal-oriented perspective, with our assumptions reflecting that perspective,

---

1   This is an adaptation of an analysis I have seen used in online discussion by Derek Cabrera.

whereas a systemic perspective requires multiple perspectives associated with different possible goals.

To change our understanding of boundaries, categories, relationships, or goals, new possible perspectives are required at every point. We need to be able to imagine those perspectives, and be motivated to consider them, in the same way as I argued in the previous chapter in connection with normativity. Just as we need an association with experience that takes us beyond our current perspective to remind us to make moral judgements considering alternatives from beyond that perspective, similarly in a more scientific context, we need associative prompts to adopt a systemic view when we would otherwise be inclined to resile back to a limited linear view. Limited linear views are not always absolutizations, but absolutization takes them for granted, and thus a systemic view followed through even-handedly will always challenge an absolutization.

As far as I'm aware, the challenges of maintaining the psychological conditions for systemic thinking in the wider population, in practical judgement, have not been a major preoccupation for systems thinkers. Yet systems thinking as a whole demands no less. People are themselves systems nested within other systems, and adequate thinking about oneself or about others requires a systemic approach. It is not sufficient, then, for academic scientists to use systemic thinking to illuminate psychology or other areas of thought that impact people's judgements from a standpoint that remains remote and abstract to others: people need to be able to adopt systems thinking for themselves. The wider the range of people who contribute to systems thinking, too, the more perspectives will become available to it, and the more genuinely systemic it will become. Yet at every stage such thinking poses challenges both of conceptual development and of motivation.

Let's take the example of an ordinary voter's attitude to climate change. Climate change is a complex systemic issue, requiring us to weigh up multiple causal factors to accept firstly that rising average world temperatures are caused by human activity, even though there are more limited linear explanations for smaller-scale changes within the climate. For example, some denialists have tried to explain rising temperatures as results of normal variations in the sun's activity. The sun's activity does have some impact on the climate, but is only one of a number of factors affecting global temperatures.² To accept anthropogenic climate change, one must look at a bigger picture in which a linear relationship between solar activity and world temperature is put in a wider context of other varied effects. These include the greenhouse effect caused by rising CO_2 and methane levels, which are impacted not only by human activity, but also increasingly by independent reinforcing feedback loops. In these feedback loops, melting ice at the poles reduces the albedo effect whereby the sun's rays are reflected back into space, and melting permafrost releases methane, another potent greenhouse gas.

An ordinary voter, coming across information online that focuses entirely on solar activity as an explanation of rising temperatures, may well absolutize this information, because it can apparently offer a line reinforced by wishful thinking. Its absolutization means that the voter will consider only solar activity as a total cause of climate change, lumping all other possibilities into the category of the mere negation of this position, and thus repressing more complex third alternatives. To move beyond this to recognizing climate change as a complex product of human activity in which solar activity plays only one of many roles, requires all four of the aspects of systemic thinking mentioned above. She would have to question the dichotomy of solar activity versus everything else, categorize the sources and causes of global warming in new ways, think in terms of complex interrelationships, and consider a wider range of possible perspectives on the issue. To do this requires a stimulus to the imagination with an impelling reason to look further.

An established way of applying this sort of thinking to a loosely-defined problem is found in *soft systems methodology*. This involves a process of establishing root definitions of the key terms in a problem, establishing a conceptual model of how these could work ideally, and then comparing this conceptual model with people's experience of what occurs. This does not create closely defined 'solutions' to the problem, but rather stimulates the stakeholders to consider possible structural, process, policy, or cultural changes needed to address the issue.³ It is the establishment of an 'ideal' model here that offers a normative stimulus with universal aspiration, even when the participants do not think of it as a 'moral' issue.

2   Benestad (2005).
3   Waring (1996) chs. 4, 8, & 9.

The whole of this book could be interpreted as a type of soft systems methodology, but this terminology is mainly used in the directly practical contexts of, for instance, workplace dysfunction.

Our normative stimulus to systemic thinking could come from a variety of possible sources in experience, such as a conversation with a friend or an article read. However, to make the difference it will need to have enough association with other occasions when the mind has been opened to stimulate a connection with new possibilities. That association might be symbolized by, say, a friend, a classroom, a book, or a Buddha. The prompt to systematicity, however, is no different from a prompt to normativity, and in both cases involves the development of a more universal view than was held before. Though scientists may not habitually think in terms of the values that inspire them to continue in the provisionality required in effective scientific investigation, those values are just as much aspirations to universality as any avowedly 'moral' position. They are, or can be, also symbolized archetypally just as much as moral positions.

Examples of archetypal symbols that might inspire greater systematicity are usually conceptual symbols, since concepts can act as such prompts regardless of whatever other functions they may have. The concepts of 'nature', 'reality', 'rationality', or 'truth' might all inspire systematicity by prompting provisional reflection on boundaries, categories, causes, and perspectives,[4] even though those same concepts can be taken metaphysically and form the basis of top-down universalist absolutizations. Everything depends on the practical context in which we interpret these potentially infinite concepts.

---

4   See Ellis (2022) section 6.

8.d. Universality across Groups

> *Summary*
>
> Universality across groups does not consist in similarity of moral rules, but in similarities in the ways absolutization can be overcome. These appear to be very similar across human populations. To access shared provisionality across group divisions, mediation processes promote mutual recognition of shared needs and conditions. Genuine universality thus comes from addressing psychological conditions rather than finding shared top-down prescriptions.

The kind of 'universality' that is most often sought in ethics is that of empirical consensus about moral rules across cultures.[1] Do all cultures forbid murder, it is sometimes asked, or do they promote the 'golden rule' of doing as you would be done by? This whole enterprise, however, involves an assumption that ethics consists only in rules or principles that attempt to represent things we should or should not do. This immediately falls apart once we reflect on the deficiencies of representationalism, for any similarities in moral rules do not necessarily reflect similarities in moral motivation or awareness. Moreover, the comparison of such rules without any consideration of whether they are right or not limits us to descriptive ethics without prescription, and the accompanying fact-value distinction discussed in 8.b. Instead, we need to look for cultural or group universality in *the similarities between methods of effective judgement*, that is, in *how* they judge, not *what* they judge. That also embodies the universality and makes it systemic.

These similarities create normativity in the same way for all humans, on the evidence so far at least, because the embodied structure of all humans is the same. For instance, we all have a functional specialization between left and right hemispheres (even though the functions are reversed in some individuals[2]), such that over-dominance of the left pre-frontal cortex creates absolutized beliefs, which can also be eased through more connection to the right hemisphere and its access to new information. Any racial differences in the extent of that specialization, as evidenced by differential hemisphere size differences, appear to be very marginal.[3] Similarly, we

1 E.g. Curry, Mullins, & Whitehouse (2019).
2 McGilchrist (2009) pp. 11–13.
3 Wang et al. (1999).

are all subject to the hijacking of our equanimity by the 'reptilian' brain, that can then lead us into hasty absolutized judgements. All our senses and perspectives are also limited, so we all have to deal with the same uncertainties as well as the same shortcuts. All of this, on the face of it, looks very unlikely to be affected by whether you are an Amazonian Indian, a Chinese factory worker, or an English vicar. Still, to avoid top-down ways of thinking about this, we still need to be open to new evidence about the possible effects of both genetic variation and culture on our capacity for absolutization.

Here one needs to distinguish the *capacity* for absolutization from the *probability* that one will absolutize. I have seen no evidence that any individual or group is exempt either from the capacity for absolutization or from the capacity to overcome it, but it is very likely that different individuals will vary a great deal in how *prone* they are to absolutization. That depends on the individual process of human development, which I intend to discuss in detail in a future volume of this series.[4] If we are capable of practice that reduces absolutization, we are also capable of making it less likely, and thus some individuals will absolutize less on average than others. That will also occur regardless of any genetic advantages or disadvantages in our starting points, which are much more debatable: Iain McGilchrist argues that oriental people may be less dominated by the left hemisphere,[5] and there may also be an argument that women are on average less prone to absolutization than men, particularly based on the evidence that conflicts decrease when women are given more social and political power.[6] However, these are matters for further empirical investigation (on which I have no firm opinion), and do not need to interfere with a wider recognition of everyone's *capacity* both to absolutize and to avoid doing so.

Nevertheless, there are obvious ethical conflicts between different human groups, from a big cultural level down to a disagreement between two neighbouring families. At the highest level, for instance, there is a continuing cultural conflict between the West and the traditional cultural practice of many African and Middle Eastern countries over female genital mutilation. At the immediate level, two neighbouring families anywhere could conflict over noise. This has often been attributed to different moral principles

4   III.5
5   McGilchrist (2009) pp. 452-9.
6   Pinker (2011) p. 827 ff.

being applied by different cultures or groups, but if we focus not on these but on the mental states in which the moral judgements are made, we can avoid the polarizing alternatives of relativism on the one hand and conflicting absolutized beliefs on the other. We are not necessarily simply stuck with such conflicts, when we also have the capacity to address them.

A focus on the provisionality of judgement creates the conditions for opposing judgements to be compared and discussed in relation to the experiences of those on both sides. A process of *mediation*, then, is what allows universality between groups to be constructed rather than imposed. Transformative mediation techniques, in recognition of this, often involve a mutual recognition element, with mutual acknowledgement from each side of the humanity and needs of the other.[7] If we allow our sensitivity and empathy towards others to operate, not absolutely, but a bit further, what they are saying can then become an option for us, rather than being shut out by a binary restriction to our current belief and its denial. Once alternative judgements become an option in practice, in a particular case, the groundwork may be established for the apparent principles to gradually change.

For instance, in the case of a noise dispute between neighbouring families, one of the starting points for a mediation process would be the noisy family acknowledging the need of the other family for quiet, and the quiet family acknowledging the need of the noisy family to make noise. In the case of female genital mutilation, there may be a process of convincing law-makers in a given country to prohibit it by law, but there is then a danger that the law will merely be cited to satisfy international criticism and not enforced. For cultural change, the judgements of individuals need to be engaged, for instance so that they start to recognize the negative long-term effects of female genital mutilation on its victims as morally important by comparison with traditional social values. Popular theatre can sometimes be effective in opening up such options for people, but in some cases there may be no alternative to many individual grassroots conversations, supported by an adequate educational basis in society. This is not the imposition of 'Western values' (which would be a top-down attempt to *impose* universality), but rather a development of

---

7   Baruch Bush & Folger (2005).

universality from the bottom up through provisionality that allows new value alternatives to emerge in experience.

The basic incompatibility between genuine bottom-up universality and power means that appeals to 'rationality', 'love', or even human rights as the basis of universality to bind conflicting human groups do not necessarily succeed. These values may be assumed by their advocates to imply forms of provisionality, but unless provisionality as a psychological state is developed as an inextricable part of these values, they can easily be interpreted as opposing absolutizations by those who do not start off with non-absolutizing experience of their application. In recent years we have seen many instances, particularly in the Islamic world, of characteristically Western universalized concepts being interpreted merely as attempts to impose power: for instance even vaccination programmes, motivated by ideals of a universal human right to health, have been the subject of conspiracy theories that interpret them as Western plots to instal surveillance microchips in Muslims.[8] Bewildering as such responses may seem to liberals, who may assume a degree of provisionality as a norm of judgement, the basic psychological explanation is surely that, for someone judging in absolutized ways, any new proposals must be fitted into a false dichotomy that is for the group or against it. Without addressing the psychological states that enable the genuine bottom-up advance of universality, we are unlikely to be able to extend it very far beyond its origins in a highly-educated Western elite.

---

8   https://www.dw.com/en/pakistan-conspiracy-theories-hamper-covid-vaccine-drive/a-56853397 (accessed 2021).

8.e. Universality across Space

> *Summary*
>
> Universality across space involves stretching from an embodied experience of space towards an idealized (universal) conception of it, also avoiding a parochial limitation of space. Our identification with spaces is deeply rooted, but requires stretch to address world-scale problems. The Middle Way as a metaphor stretches our bodily experience of moving through embodied space towards a goal in conceptual space.

'Space' is a concept in Newtonian physics, an abstract three-dimensional matrix in which everything could be located. However, it's also an aspect of human experience, because we move through space and identify people and things as located in a represented space. We are likely to be absolutizing if we assume that our represented space is completely equivalent to the abstract matrix, but nevertheless, the process of correcting and improving our understanding of spatial locations and relationships can be an aspect of stretching towards an aspired universality. To re-examine our spatial assumptions, we need to cease to interpret them absolutely and compare them to alternative possibilities.

The points where we have spatial beliefs are those about objects, people, and whole environments in relation to us, or in relation to the represented world where we have goals. Even if our goal was that of a new and more adequate theory of spatiality in theoretical physics, we would still have goals, and would be likely to make use of our observations in a located universe to support our background assumptions. The vast spatial environment we can construct conceptually, though, greatly outruns both the limited one our bodies are situated in, and the spatial environment we can actually stretch into. Both of these have far more practical significance than merely abstract space.

Top-down universality across space absolutizes by substituting a propositional understanding of what is taken to be generally true across the world (or even, in some cases, the universe), and assuming this to be the whole story, in place of an appreciation of the spatial limitations of our view. The Platonic interpretation of the status of mathematics is an example of this, assuming that mathematical claims are universally true solely because of their conceptual consistency, regardless of their dependence on cognitive models that are spatially localized in particular peoples' bodies and their limited perceptions.[1] Having a conceptual understanding of the space of the universe as a whole does not ameliorate this. The challenge of developing greater universality across space, then, is that of stretching to take into account more space whilst retaining provisional ways of thinking.

When we focus instead on our more immediate spatial environment, however, that also carries the reverse danger. Then our beliefs are likely to focus only on a very limited section of the universe – they become parochial. The internet has vastly increased our ability to make contact with people in other locations, but nevertheless we are still subject to such parochiality, as we construct a new 'parish' of similarly-minded people from around the world and ignore the rest. We assume that our experience in a particular limited sphere is generally true – for instance, that if we have always observed men and women behaving in ways prescribed by the culture in a particular area, this is the 'right' way to understand sexual differences and their implications, even if only 'right for us' in the relativist form.

Stretching the scope of our identification across space is an urgent matter. In the issue of climate change, for instance, a systemic global view is required to adequately understand the threatening conditions impacting on any given location. It is only by considering feedback loops of melting polar ice, melting permafrost, and reduced photosynthesis of heat-stressed vegetation (amongst other things), that we can understand why there is such an imminent threat (at the time of writing) to, for instance, the city of Miami or the agriculture of Bangladesh. Yet large numbers of people who are directly threatened continue to limit their awareness, and their political judgement, to parochial concerns. Understanding climate change does not require top-down beliefs about the whole earth so much as a willingness to piece together and synthesize different sources of information, whilst interpreting them in a systemic framework of relationships rather than as an isolated set of linear problems.

There is obviously an overlap between what is required to stretch our understanding across groups and to stretch it across space. People live in, and identify with, spaces. It is easy to overestimate our integration of groups when it is based only on conceptual communication, and not on crossing space to meet them in person and

1   See Lakoff & Nuñez (2000).

encounter the conditions they live in. It's also easy to underestimate our own connection to particular spaces: the houses we live in, the streets or fields or woods we walk in, the wildlife we see. Each of these aspects of our spatial environment helps to build up a set of neural associations of what we find meaningful, and thus of what perspectives need to be stretched for greater adequacy. The metaphor of a 'path' from one judgement to the next throughout our life (the basis of the Middle Way), closely maps onto our embodied experience of actually walking a path, and in both cases our path is unique to the conditions we begin with.

In terms of the embodied schemas recognized by George Lakoff and Mark Johnson, the Middle Way metaphorically incorporates the schemas of source-path-goal and those of balance.[2] Both of these are basic and early embodied experiences that get imprinted onto our neural associations, and then become a basis for *metaphorical extension*, which one could see as a form of stretching. Our schematic experiences involve moving through space *with a goal*, and thus following a 'path', which is just our relationship to that space as we pass through it. As we follow that path, too, we need to maintain balance, not toppling one way or the other, nor deviating too far from the path that will take us to our goal.

The metaphor of the Middle Way thus encapsulates effectively how we can stretch our perspective in relation to space (and by extension also to groups and time). We need to stay focused on our goal and not deviate too far from the path to it, but the goal itself is also provisional in the terms of the Middle Way. Our progress along that path involves a unique trajectory dependent on our starting point, just as our attempt to stretch towards universality in space is a move outwards from one particular point in it. At the same time we exert bodily effort to traverse space by walking, which includes an effort not only in covering distance, but also maintaining balance. To maintain an effective and adequate effort it needs to avoid obsession or wilfulness, requiring an integration of our motives around the goal so that it is not a matter for conflict. Just as a flow of bodily effort is required to keep walking and balancing, a flow of mental effort is required to keep extending our awareness of conditions outwards from our starting point.

---

2   Johnson (2017) pp. 101–2; Ellis (2019) 3.b.

To maintain that flow of effort without disruption, whether we are following a path alone or with others, also requires an aspiration to universality across time, which is the final (but in some ways the most important) aspect of stretch.

8.f. Universality across Time

> *Summary*
>
> Universality over time involves stretching our awareness from the present over time, without that awareness being substituted by absolutized conceptual beliefs about it. Such beliefs can be represented by temporal biases that absolutize past, present, or future over the other times. Such biases are not removed by reactions that completely deny the relevance of the other time, but require an integrative approach, extending our awareness of responsibility rather than imposing it.

An aspiration for universality over time begins with our capacity for awareness of the past and future, which provides a larger context for our current beliefs and identifications. Whether we currently believe in the completely evil nature of an object of anger, the totality of temporary suffering that we are going through, or the normality of our age, it is greater awareness of the past and future that is needed to avoid absolutization of our beliefs and desires in the current time. The kind of time we are talking about here, then, is phenomenological – time as we experience it. It is not Newtonian absolute time, even though a provisional belief in a shared time helps us to make social arrangements. Newtonian beliefs about time in the abstract used in a top-down way could be just as absolutized as other such beliefs, but a helpful universality that enables us to build up wider awareness from the bottom begins with a recognition of the limitations of our temporal awareness.

Those limitations are particularly obvious when we are in the grip of emotions such as impatience. In a state of impatience, we want to circumvent the progression of experience that our embodied situation requires, and go directly to some other idealized point in the future. Impatience absolutizes, because it adopts a rigid belief in the longed-for future event (let's say, the arrival of the bus) and creates a conflict between our obsessive concern with belief and our actual bodily situation and repressed awareness of that situation. Patience, on the other hand, involves accepting that progression, even welcoming and enjoying it, and a more mindful state can greatly improve our capacity for such patience. We are then able to extend our awareness from the present towards an anticipated future event without that anticipation proliferating and dominating our awareness. A relaxation and shift from impatience to patience when, say, waiting for a bus, or being stuck in a traffic queue, is a basic shift towards universality across time. Our desires and beliefs about the future are being taken into account in the context of the present, rather than being projected and usurping the present.

The same can be said about the integration of conflicting motives that we become aware of at different points in time. If I decide to avoid putting on weight by not eating cake at one moment, but then an hour later am overcome by an immediate desire to eat cake, one can see this as an immediate conflict across time, where our beliefs and desires at each time have become absolutized in relation to the other. The potential resolution of the conflict obviously involves not blocking our potential awareness of future craving at the time of abstentive resolution, and not blocking our awareness of the abstentive resolution when we are gripped by the craving. Our awareness of other times also needs to carry enough weight of meaning to motivate us, not to be an entirely abstracted merely left-hemisphere based 'intellectual' acknowledgement. In this way we can start to take responsibility for our past and future selves, rather than having only abstracted or alienated views of them.

The absolutization of idealized past, present, or future experience at the expense of integrating our experience across time can occur in a variety of ways that are well captured by the temporal biases identified in cognitive psychology. I have given a fuller account of these elsewhere,[1] and will return to them in a later book in this series, so here I will only briefly mention these. We can absolutize a view of the past, for example by appealing to history or not letting go of the effects of past efforts (sunk cost fallacy). We can absolutize a view of the present over the past, for instance in the survivorship bias that ignores the effects of past selection over our current experience. We can absolutize the view of the present over the future, for instance in procrastination. We can absolutize a view of the future over the present, for example in forecast illusion or neomania. Both optimism and pessimism can also be absolutized to ignore the complexity of probabilities regarding the past and future and focus only on what confirms our bias. In a more immediate context, we can absolutize what we experience at one moment even within a relatively short experience, and forget the rest – as for instance in the

---

1 iv.3.j & k; V.5.

primacy effect, where 'first impressions' trump our awareness of every other aspect of a person.

To avoid absolutization in relation to any such biases, we need to be neither taken in by the bias, nor react against it by embracing its negation as a total account. So, for instance, if I am gripped by neomania, in which I assume that the latest iphone will solve all my problems in an idealized future, it will not necessarily help to renounce all updates to technological devices on the assumption that they are always unhelpful, as the effect of this may be that I will be unable to use them at all when previous versions cease to work. My more immediate awareness of how far technological devices can actually enrich or impoverish my long-term experience as an embodied creature (including its effects on my attention) instead needs to be balanced and stretched to realistically assess the effects of new devices.

The same point applies to attributions of responsibility in the past. If people in the past believed in and practised slavery, should I treat the past as identical to the present by holding them just as responsible for this as a present person, or treat the past as wholly different from the present by judging them by wholly different standards? This became a matter of debate in 2020, for instance, when a crowd of protestors in Bristol tipped the statue of Edward Colston (a seventeenth-century philanthropist who was also involved in a company that participated in slave trading) into the harbour.[2] The assumption here seemed to be that Edward Colston should be judged by present standards rather than those of his own age, and that the continuation of his statue would signal public support for unacceptable past standards. The alternative, of course, is to treat the values of the past as exempt from those of the present, so that we do not apply any such current values to figures like Colston.

A bottom-up universality of normative judgement does not necessarily imply treating the past as judged by standards that are either wholly the same or wholly different to the present, but rather a recognition both that their judgement occurred in a different context and that it had some features in common with present judgements. The precise extent of our attribution of responsibility for judgements in the past is not a metaphysical one imposed dualistically from above, but one involving the extension of our awareness

---

2   https://www.bbc.co.uk/news/uk-52954305 (accessed 2021).

of responsibility into the past as far as it can be justified and is practically relevant. We thus need to ask questions such as how far someone who believed in slavery could have considered alternatives, what would have been the consequences for them if they had questioned that belief, and how they interpreted that belief. In this way we can extend our understanding of responsibility through time in relation to our understanding of wider conditions, rather than only making an absolutized judgement based on the imposition of freewill or determinism assumptions.

Overall, then, universality over time combines with universality between groups and across space, both systemically and normatively, to provide a criterion for any response to absolutization. Most importantly, *a relativist response to absolutization is not an adequate one*. The lack of justification for top-down universality does not justify us in the converse rejection of all universality. The distinction between meaning and belief, crucially, allows us to fully credit the value of maintaining universal *meanings* in archetypal form, even whilst we reject premature universal *beliefs*.

9. Criteria for a Response: Judgement Focus

9.a. Judgement as the Cutting Edge

> *Summary*
>
> Judgement is the cutting edge of our interaction with the world. Whether it is absolute or provisional determines the crucial *how* of justified judgement. Judgement focus helps us recognize our experience of building up responsibility for judgement through awareness of options maintained over time. It avoids both the opposed attractions of freewill and determinism, whereby we have total or zero responsibility for our judgements *a priori*.

What is judgement? I take it to be the point at which we respond to a stimulus with either an action or the formation of a belief. Actions imply implicit beliefs about the goals and background to those actions, whilst beliefs, though they don't necessarily result in immediate actions, alter our neural connections in such a way that we may act differently in future. Some of the stimuli we encounter are *meaningful* to us, creating new neural connections, without producing judgements, because they only add to the overall motives and resources that we might apply to possible future beliefs, without changing our implicit beliefs themselves. However, a judgement creates, confirms, or disconfirms a belief and involves a decisive response to our meaningful experience.

For example, if I am crossing a road and hear a roaring noise on one side, I *judge* that a car is approaching, which I then also start to *believe*. I then have to *judge* whether to move more quickly across the road because of the danger that it will hit me, or whether the speed of the car and the distance it has to travel mean that it is still safe. The first judgement here probably occurred almost simultaneously with the second one, and indeed might not be distinguishable in practice, as part of the meaning of the car for me is potential danger.

The judgement in that example is not one that will just be made by an isolated 'reason'. Rather my whole body is involved. In some circumstances I might panic, going into fight-or-flight mode and rapidly jumping out of the way in the conviction that the car is about to hit me: then my whole body will be quickly tensed by adrenalin. In other circumstances, I might remain relaxed, my startle response overlain by long habituation to traffic. Perhaps I might need to remind myself that there is no threat, or perhaps the judgement that there is no threat will be so habitual that I won't need to do this. In that case, though, it is the fact that my body remains relaxed that is crucial to the way I judge the situation.

As we can also see from that example, judgements can be large or small. Judgement is required when I choose one flavour of yoghurt over another, as also when I decide whether to accept a job or make a proposal of marriage. We should not assume that judgement is only exercised at the points when we are most aware of it, since we are constantly interpreting and responding to the world with differing degrees of awareness in relation to even the most trivial concerns. Even taking another step out of the thousands we may make on a given walk involves a judgement, which we may only become aware of when we decide not to make it, stopped in our tracks by an attraction or an obstacle.

Judgement needs to be central to our response to absolutization, because it is at the cutting edge of practice. At each point where we make a judgement, we interact with the conditions around us, and thus our path changes in some way. The idea of a 'path' here, by analogy with moving through space, consists of a movement from one judgement to the next, our experience of time in many ways formed by that progression. At each of those points we could potentially change that path by bringing more awareness to that judgement. The crucial difference in awareness, I argue, is whether the judgement is absolute or provisional. Each time we are able to recognize and move away from an absolutized judgement by considering alternative options apart from acceptance or rejection of an entrenched view, we are following the provisional Middle Way rather than absolutizing, *regardless of the content of the beliefs we arrive at.*

Judgement focus, then, involves working with the way in which we make our judgements so as to consider more options, *not* just accepting one view rather than another according to its content. Of course, for practical reasons we also have to weigh up *what* we believe in the circumstances, but it is vital not to assume that *what* we believe is what makes the difference to overcoming absolutization. This is because, as I have noted in many places in this book, absolutization operates by constantly distracting us away from the *how* of judgement to the *what*. This can be seen, for instance, in its assumed system independence, in its representationalism, in its obsession with (and inflation of) metaphysics and deductive logic, and in its psychological mechanisms of projection and substitution, which take us away from awareness of our processes always to examine only the objects of belief. We do need to pay attention to the objects of belief, but considering these *in the context of the process of judgement* is a crucial move in de-absolutizing the beliefs we arrive at.

This slippage from *how* back to *what* can be seen in many contexts where traditions have started to focus on *how* to varying extents, but then been distracted back to *what*. Religion, philosophy, and psychology all provide lots of instructive examples of this, which I will explore further in the next chapter.

Two twin absolutes are waiting ready to hijack any attempt at provisionality of judgement focus: freewill and determinism. If we are hijacked by freewill ideology, we will start to assume that judgements are entirely under our control, and that we have total responsibility for them. Perhaps we just need to have sufficient faith, or sufficient enlightenment, to be able to wrest total control over our judgements. Perhaps we just need to follow the master's instructions more fully. When we inevitably fail to judge in a way that we have idealized that we should, a new conflict is set up that can readily divert our energies into new absolutizations. We may then feel unhelpfully guilty because we 'should have' judged differently. For instance, the smoker who is convinced that she can decide to give up right now, throwing her cigarettes in the bin, sees her subsequent judgement to take them out of the bin again as a 'failure of willpower'. She then gets caught up in a reinforcing feedback loop of idealization and guilt, in which absolutization continues to dominate.

If, on the other hand, we are hijacked by determinism, we assume instead that we have no control over our judgements, and zero responsibility. There is then no point in attempting to act differently: we surrender to our compulsions, to the 'Will of God', to the pressure of conditions. This can be rationalized in all sorts of ways, including the philosophical belief that determinism can be a 'truth' independent of our response to it – a focus for more intricate arguments that I pursue elsewhere.¹ As far as I am concerned, though, there is no *practical* difference between determinism and fatalism. Either we implicitly believe in determinism in a way that changes our judgements, or we avoid doing so. Practical determinism can be illustrated by an addict who surrenders to their addiction, or a parent of conjoined twins who refuses to have them separated because it is 'the Will of God'. The position is self-deceptive (or inauthentic, as existentialists would say) because a judgement has been made 'not to make a judgement' – to rule out options from consideration that are potentially available in our imaginations. The conditions that 'make' us act in one way rather than another are then a rationalization of absolutization.

Between our judgement being completely under our control, and it being pre-ordained by the conditions around us, is the potential for influencing the total set of conditions that affect our judgement to varying degrees. In some cases, conditioning effects seem very slight – I can just 'choose' the strawberry yogurt rather than the cherry yogurt for instance, even if some sort of far-fetched deterministic explanation for the choice could be assembled (for instance, I developed more favourable associations with strawberries as a young child). In others, the determining effects of conditions seem overwhelming – as with heroin addiction, perhaps triggered by traumas and lack of self-esteem. Yet even heroin addicts can 'turn round their lives': for instance, when help is offered in rehabilitation, they can make judgements that accept it and use it, or shrink from it and reject it.

Philosophers have similarly argued for 'doxastic involuntarism' – that we have no choice about the beliefs we adopt – for instance, I see a book, so I have to believe that it is a book. Yet we know that in certain circumstances people might believe that the book is a booby trap or a concealed message from God. We are never entirely free from the potential of judgement to change over the long term what may seem inevitable over the short term, and the over-fast distinctions made by analytic philosophers between long- and short-term judgements² do not show even our immediate responses to be completely determined.

1   iv.4.c; VI.3.
2   E.g. Clarke (1986).

To illustrate our ambiguous degree of control, Jonathan Haidt offers the example of riding an elephant:[3] we cannot simply steer the elephant as we would a car, because it has a mind of its own and a lot of momentum, but we can control the elephant by thinking ahead and influencing it to go in the direction we want to go. An alternative image might be that of an oil tanker that takes several miles to slow down – you can't just race your oil tanker into port and then expect to brake it to a standstill. These images point to the importance of integration of our judgement over time – that is, that a provisional judgement is capable of being changed in awareness of new conditions, relative to a past one. Our responsibility *develops* as we are able to identify with our judgements at other times more fully. As discussed in 7.c, that responsibility is best seen as encompassing all forms of judgement, including even our interpretation of the world around us.

The way in which judgement is often filtered through the absolutized freewill-determinism dichotomy is closely associated with focusing on *what* rather than *how* we judge. If you look at judgement as an object, it seems that you either identify a connected chain of causes – from conditions, to motive, to belief or action, and perhaps to consequences – or you don't. When we identify a chain of causes but think representationally, as though that chain is not part of a complex system, we think we have the whole picture and thus that there must be an explanation of our judgements as determined. When we don't identify such a chain of causes, though (easier in ignorance of the operation of the brain), our judgement appears to emerge *ex nihilo*, like the world when created by God (and often attributed to a Godlike essence in ourselves). An understanding of judgement as a part of a system that we don't understand in its entirety begins to point us at least towards agnosticism on freewill and determinism. If we focus on the *how* of judgement rather than the *what*, though, the practical value of assuming neither freewill nor determinism also becomes clearer, because the *way* in which we judge involves *developing* a sense of agency, not assuming either the presence or absence of one to begin with.

Judgement, then, is both the cutting edge of our experience and (at the risk of mixing metaphors) also the point of growth. Each judgement is an experimental application of our body in the world,

---

3   Haidt (2012) ch. 3.

enabling feedback that we can then take into account to hone our subsequent judgement. Each piece of feedback creates more neural connections that add to the complexity of meaning that we can draw on when judging in future. Judgement is thus also where absolutization is continued or avoided from moment to moment, and if we fail to focus on it effectively, we are in great danger of merely continuing around the same reinforcing loops.

9.b. Diversions from Judgement Focus

> *Summary*
>
> Whilst the most obvious diversions from judgement focus are blatantly metaphysical, the nearer and more practically damaging distractors involve representationalist assumptions introduced into investigations that appear to be addressing absolutization in some respect. The spurious claim to be focusing on facts without values undermines the value of academic work in, for instance, Buddhist Studies, cognitive psychology, and moral philosophy, by entrenching the omission of crucial elements of the context in each case.

The flip side of judgement focus is the avoidance of irrelevant distraction, where the criterion of relevance is a lack of practicality. At the extreme such distraction obviously consists of metaphysics, where claims are made and defended that have no possible relationship to practical judgement at all: for instance, claims about God's existence or non-existence. In other cases, a point that is helpful in a particular case is made into a metaphysical claim. For example, there may be an attempt to impose a particular moral rule that would stretch some people helpfully in some circumstances (like a ban on drinking alcohol) into a universal rule.

There are also other less obvious cases that in practice may have a greater effect in diverting those who might have focused effectively on judgement from actually doing so. This involves cases where distracting claims are relevant to some conditions, but the top-down universality with which the claims are framed makes them into absolutizing impositions in other circumstances. In such cases, the claims involved may possibly be provisional ones, and the diversion a matter of degree. We can choose to focus our energy primarily on what makes a difference, or we can choose to focus it on things that are very unlikely to make any difference, perhaps with an implicit absolutizing belief in the background that makes our focus an end in itself. For example, even a provisional theory about governmental corruption may in some circumstances act mainly as a distractor from corporate corruption and foreign influence, when there is a greater weight of evidence for the latter. The more strongly one then defends one's choice of focus against the weight of evidence, the more likely it is to start containing elements of absolutization. The most obvious dimension of such absolutization that shows itself here is representationalism: we are diverted by the assumption that we are capable of representing the world 'as it is', and that this should be our overriding goal.

The Buddha's teaching to Malunkyaputta, discussed in 1.a, gives an example of the kind of diversion that is imbued with absolute assumptions, not because of obvious claims of infinite scope, but instead because the diversionary process of information-gathering has become an end in itself. This is also known as the information bias – the assumption that more information will necessarily always help us to make better judgements. As Nassim Nicholas Taleb points out, beyond a particular point of optimum practicality, more information can merely increase the ratio of meaningless 'noise' to meaningful material.[1] Although it may be desirable to try to stretch the amount of information we take into account in our judgements, this is not achieved through the top-down method of trying to process an unfeasibly large amount of information that it is currently beyond our ability to find helpful significance in. Whilst computers have greatly extended our data-processing abilities, they have also in the process extended our capacity for drawing premature conclusions from untypical patterns, by cherry-picking, fishing expeditions, the Texas sharpshooter fallacy (drawing a target around your bullet-holes),[2] and a number of other statistical fallacies.

It is an extension of the information bias problem to create theoretical explanations that are meaningful and perhaps provisional but have only a remote probability of being practically relevant. The Buddha's example of the type of bird from which the feather of the wounding arrow has come would fit this. Yes, it is very remotely possible that the type of arrow could influence the way that the arrow buried itself in the man's flesh, and thus how the doctor should go about pulling it out or treating the wound – but hard even to imagine how. In the context of the man being wounded by an arrow, then, speculation about the species of bird that the feather came from is very probably 'noise', just as (to use Taleb's example), detailed variations in stock-market figures over only one hour are very unlikely to tell you anything decisive about the direction of prices and thus whether you should buy or sell the stock.

---

1   Taleb (2012) p. 126.
2   http://www.fallacyfiles.org/texsharp.html (accessed 2021).

Yet much academic research is also 'noise' in this way, in relation to the practical applications of that research. For instance, I have long been frustrated by this aspect of Buddhist Studies, which confines itself to descriptive or causal research into the phenomena of the Buddhist tradition as identified through textual, sociological, or historical evidence. Through a narrow application of the fact-value distinction, eschewing normative discussion, Buddhist Studies fails to be relevant to anyone's motives for practising Buddhism. I don't meditate because that's what the forest monks in Thailand do, I do it because it is helpful. I don't read about the Buddha in order to find out the historical facts of his context, I read for inspiration. Yet when I put forward a practically-focused account of the Buddha in my book *The Buddha's Middle Way*,[3] one of the common reactions was to dismiss it because I had deliberately not concerned myself with whether the account was historically justified. The goals of Buddhist Studies, aside from being developed under the influence of the fact-value distinction, involve deliberate insulation from the cutting edge of Buddhist experience in practice, focusing only on the *what* instead of the *how*. In the course of this, as humans, obviously scholars of Buddhism do not even succeed in avoiding expressions of their values, which are liable to emerge implicitly in the way they frame supposedly neutral accounts of Buddhist phenomena. Indeed, its focus on decontextualized representation inadvertently makes Buddhist Studies quite effective propaganda for the most conservative forms of Buddhism: it creates a conservative normative effect by constantly focusing on authoritative sources rather than experiential criteria.

Another example of a diversion from judgement focus (in an area very much adjacent to understanding judgement) is the psychological study of biases. Here, a focus on theories about the *causes* of biases in human prehistory in the sub-discipline that has become known as 'evolutionary biology' is highly reminiscent of the Buddha's arrow example. Biases are causing a great many pressing social, political, and psychological problems here and now across the globe, yet evolutionary psychology diverts from this by focusing on historical theories about how biases were actually good adaptations to a previous environment. That might be a potentially helpful source of understanding if we then contrasted it to the modern environment

---

3   Ellis (2019): see pp. 4–5 for discussion of this approach.

in which biases are clearly unhelpful: for example, an instinctive suspicion of those in another group (ingroup/outgroup bias) may have served us well when we were hunting in scattered, autonomous tribes with distinctive, homogeneous cultures, in a way it does not when walking down an average street in New York today. As one source on evolutionary psychology of biases puts this, xenophobia is an 'error management bias', reducing 'net costs' because a less costly error is made: 'the costs of falsely assuming peacefulness on the part of an aggressor were likely to outweigh the comparatively low costs of elevated vigilance about aggression'.[4] What is alarmingly *not* mentioned at this point is that the error costs of this strategy are likely to be reversed in the multicultural, globalized context of a modern city, where elevated vigilance against anyone of a different race or culture is likely to produce both chronic stress and social dysfunction.

By focusing only on past explanation without any contextualization in relation to the present, evolutionary psychology thus lends itself to defending or excusing biases through an implicit determinism, offering a ready rationalization to anyone who wants to indulge their biases that they can't help it. The more a focus on *what* is insulated from the *how* of immediate contemporary experience, the harder it is to integrate with that experience. The spurious neutrality of the fact-value distinction merely increases that insulation, and opens up the opportunities for exploitation by absolutizing ideologies.

A third example of a diversion can come from philosophy: namely the supposed ethical debate about what is known as 'the trolley problem'.[5] This is a thought experiment, and thought experiments can open up new ways of thinking – but this merely reinforces old ones. The thought experiment has many variants, but the most common one is to imagine that a train is careering towards five people tied onto a railway track who will die when the train hits them. However, you are standing by a lever which can divert the train onto another track where only one person is tied, and thus only one person will die instead of five if you pull the lever. It's very tempting to get sucked into discussion of what is 'right' or 'wrong' in this situation, and thus this is a very effective

---

4   Haselton, Nettle, & Murray (2015).
5   First prominent in Foot (1978).

diversion from discussion of what is actually right or wrong in an embodied context. The situation is, of course, not totally impossible but extremely unlikely, not only in the way the effects of different options have been lined up, but also in the ways that the person making the decision is assumed to have perfect information and certainty, and that the person is also supposed to be 'rational' in their decision-making, even under intense stress and time pressure. The judgement made in any actual likely scenario remotely resembling this would depend, not on calculations about how many people we 'know' will die if we do x or y, but on *how* the judgement was made. Would the person act automatically or in a panic, perhaps dependent on very imperfect information about the effects of their actions? Or would they have the capacity to reflect quickly but effectively on the information available, questioning any entrenched assumptions in the process? If the latter, we don't have to worry about whether they have made the 'best' decision from a false God's eye view that nobody has – they will have made the best decision they could have made in the circumstances. The idea that these kinds of philosophical problems constitute 'ethics' is itself a diversion from helping people act ethically.

I have selected those three examples because they are all *adjacent* to effective responses to absolutization in different ways. Of course, there could be lots of other possible examples that are not likely to be so easily mistaken for effective responses to absolutization: for instance, just distracting yourself from it with a computer game, or declaring an absolute war on absolutization. It cannot be completely ruled out that Buddhist Studies, evolutionary psychology, or utilitarian thought experiments might still contribute to a response to absolutization by in some ways helping to make people aware of different ways of thinking. Nevertheless, it is the 'near enemies' of an effective response that are most likely to divert from it those who might contribute to it. They become less likely to contribute to it as a particular absolutizing perspective is implicitly adopted in the background that has the effect of diverting them from what might initially seem to be part of an effective response. These background absolute assumptions are, for instance, those of the fact-value distinction, or the belief that one particular normative ethical theory could completely represent the correct moral response to a situation where embodied humans have to make judgements.

In urging a judgement focus, then, I am suggesting a more refined and subtle criterion, beyond practicality and an aspiration to universality, that can help us to differentiate what is needed for an effective response to absolutization. It is a *focus*, not a proposed ban on all factual investigation that is not judged relevant by some prior criterion, nor a proposed ban on 'pure science'. We do not 'know' what will definitely not help us, but we can get a good idea of the probabilities of what will. Rather, it is a question that I think we need to ask ourselves before we conclude that a particular approach is an effective response to absolutization: namely, 'Does it focus on *the process* of judgement?'. Whilst this may be too demanding a criterion to apply to judging the worth of every kind of source, if absolutization is to be avoided, it needs to be particularly applied to all sources that in any way claim to be addressing absolutization, whether from the angle of Buddhism, psychology, philosophy, or any other related approach.

10. Criteria for a Response: Error Focus

10.a. Falsification and Error Focus

> *Summary*
>
> Error focus is a more effective approach than positive focus for avoiding confirmation bias as a dimension of absolutization. It suggests that we make incremental progress towards objectivity, not by eliminating absolutely false claims, but by identifying absolutizations as the erroneous *how* of judgement. This is reliably but not absolutely available to us from reflection on individual experience of past judgements, and applies equally to all kinds of judgement – individual or social, scientific or moral.

The final criterion of the four is necessitated by the long shadow of confirmation bias, which leads us so often to positively idealize in ways that have infinite scope and thus turn into absolutizaton. The error focus is a response to this that draws on the inspiration (but not all the details) of Karl Popper's falsification. Popper recognized the problem of induction, indicating that we cannot justify a positive generalization based on a finite number of examples.[1] He also recognized the effects of confirmation bias, leading to the infinite rationalization of claims with infinite scope, as discussed in 4.d. Popper described this as *ad hoc* reasoning:[2] rather than letting go of a positive theory that we identify with, we move the goalposts that we specify for justifying it. In this way, he identified some aspects of absolutization, although he eschewed all exploration of its psychological dimension.[3] His solution, falsificationism, also offers some key ways forward in avoiding absolutization. The key insight of falsificationism is that we can justify our identification of errors better than we can justify our positive theories, and we thus make *incremental* progress towards objectivity from the bottom up, by ruling out things we should not believe rather than making top-down deductions from generalizations that we should believe.

1   Popper (1959) ch. 1.
2   Ibid. p. 42.
3   Ibid. ch. 2.

One common misunderstanding of falsificationism should be headed off from the start. It did not, even in Popper's hands, involve any claim about the absolute justification of falsifications. Of course, if we rely on an observation to falsify a belief (for instance, that all swans can't be white because we have discovered a black swan), we could still be mistaken about our observation. The black swan could have been a fake, for instance, being originally white but having had all its feathers carefully dyed by a hoaxer – we can't totally rule out that possibility. Nevertheless, falsifications are *more* justifiable than positive claims about a theory, and the reason for this depends only on the comparison of infinite scope with finite scope. Only one falsification is needed to require us to modify a generalizing theory, whereas no finite number of positive observations will positively prove that theory (rather than merely making us more confident of it). The more aware we are of the limitations of our perspective as embodied humans, the more we can become aware of how much arrogance is required to take a set of observations from the one infinitesimal piece of the universe we have observed, and claim that they are generally true of all of it.

Popper's critics have been correct to point out that scientific theories are not cleanly falsified.[4] Popper's successors in the philosophy of science, Lakatos and Kuhn, have drawn more on the history of science to show how in practice, it is only the most general assumptions made in whole 'research programmes' or 'paradigms' that may eventually be rejected because of their lack of fruitful testing potential.[5] Aristotelian astronomy, for instance, was never proven wrong so much as being found untestable compared to a more testable Copernican version, where the predicted orbits of planets around the sun were (broadly) verified by observation. We can only ever weigh up explanations of the world against alternatives, not in absolute terms as finally correct or incorrect. Kuhn's work also begins to recognize the *psychological* conditions for objectivity that are then required in this situation, talking about the 'puzzle solving ability' of scientists that has not only enabled them to work within established paradigms to solve problems, but also enabled them to move on from one paradigm to another when necessary, and thus underlies scientific progress.[6]

4   E.g. Ayer (1971) p. 19.
5   Lakatos (1974); Kuhn (1996).
6   Kuhn (1996) p. 205; Ellis (2001) 2.b.iii.

If we apply Popperian insights to our response to absolutization, however, we can become much clearer about the necessary psychological element that Kuhn was suggesting. Scientists, like anyone else, hang on to their theories because they absolutize them as the whole story, and their ability to switch paradigms at the crucial point depends on their provisionality – crucially, their ability to consider alternatives in a light that makes them not merely negations of the view they have held hitherto. If they can consider alternative theories in this light, they are then in a position to investigate the ways in which they are supported by evidence, and the ways in which this may be superior to the support given for theories they have previously been attached to. Since science is conducted by embodied human beings, its degree of success can hardly be understood in isolation from human judgement in general.

This means that the way these Popperian insights can be applied to our response to absolutization needs to be in accordance with the judgement focus – falsifying the *how* of judgement, not the *what*. If the basic problem we are trying to avoid is confirmation bias, then provisionality is the effective response, but provisionality is about *how* we judge, not *what* we judge. Provisionality involves considering *more than two* alternatives, without being able to prescribe exactly how many are optimal for each judgement. It is the development of the capacity for such judgement that can enable us to move on from one paradigm to an alternative, without thinking of the alternative as merely a negation of the old paradigm.

The *error focus*, then, is a focus on identifying absolutization as the problematic element in the process of judgement, rather than the supposedly correct content of judgements. Whilst we will need to continue to maintain provisional beliefs about *what*, errors are specific to *how*. Such errors are not easily ascertained at the moment we are engaged in them, but can be identified with much greater clarity at a later time when we subsequently recognize that our judgement was constrained. Here the features of absolutization can help us to identify when an error has taken place: for instance, proliferation, reinforcing feedback loops of thought, states of craving and hatred, a lack of body-awareness or any other kind of contextualization, metaphysical claims, circular justifications, conflict, binding group identification, projection, and substitution.

Such error focus is also an implication of *practicality*, because it is the most effective way to train ourselves to reduce absolutization in practice. Whilst in theory we may be attached to a particular positive explanation, in practice this will at best prove applicable within a limited sphere of application. Similarly, then, to be universal we need to adopt an error focus, so as not to be taken in by the confirmation bias of belief in a particular positive theory in a particular group, place, and time. The products of absolutization are in one sense or another parochial, but the practical identification of absolutization as an error is a practical universal that it appears could be used at least by all human beings.

Unlike Popper's falsification, error focus obviously does not only apply to science with its shared theories, but just as much to individual judgement on all matters, and to value judgements as much as factual judgements. Absolutization helps us identify errors just as easily in these areas of individual judgement as it does in science. The lack of the formal procedures employed to help identify errors in science, such as peer review, though, places much more of an emphasis on the effectiveness of individual practice to help us identify absolutization when it has occurred. The habitual boosting of awareness levels through mindfulness or similar practices, the development of the imagination through the arts and education, and the development of a critical perspective through critical thinking skills, can all contribute to creating the conditions whereby individuals can more readily become aware of error. Error focus, then, as a criterion for response to absolutization, does not mean that we should only be *directly* concerned with errors: rather we should try to combine awareness of errors with a positive cultivation of the conditions that help us to identify errors. Nevertheless, the avoidance of errors provides a more consistent justification for our longer-term practical preparation than does any positive general belief.

Error focus also implies that we should remain strictly provisional in any other wider theories we may adopt. The beliefs that we need to employ at this time cannot be a total commitment. For instance, a particular scientific account may need emphasis at present – for instance during a pandemic people need to understand how viruses are passed on. However, at another time a scientist may possibly find herself engaged in research that involves questioning the accepted view of how viruses are passed on. A particular political situation – say, one in which the incomes of ordinary people have been static or falling for around forty years, but those of the very rich continue to multiply rapidly – requires a political commitment to social justice, and thus perhaps voting for a left-wing party, that more equitable times would not necessarily require. By adopting a theoretical or ideological view as though it was the whole story for ever, though, we leave ourselves open to the likelihood of absolutization as we start to defend that view in circumstances where it does not have all the answers.

This emphasis does raise some other questions that I will need to address in the remaining chapters of this section. One of these is about the implications of labelling absolutization 'error': do we thus regard it as 'wrong'? There is a potential revolutionizing of our view of evil in this approach that I will explore in the next chapter. A further issue is about the relationship between error focus and our need for positive inspiration – wouldn't it be discouraging to focus on things that we do wrong all the time? This point also deserves a full discussion in the following chapter.

10.b. Refining Shadow Avoidance

> *Summary*
>
> A focus on avoiding error is an avoidance of evil in the sense of threats from absolutized human judgement, that we have learned to recognize in 'evil' characteristics. This is the most practically important part of our response to the shadow, which also includes 'natural' evils. It is better targeted than the identification of evil as sociopathic character, which involves the projection of one variable feature as necessary to a character as a whole.

To understand the significance of error in relation to our wider avoidance strategies as embodied beings, I find the Jungian concept of the shadow archetype very helpful. This does not require any speculations about the 'collective unconscious', but only observations of human threat-avoidance connected to those of how we use the concept of evil. As we will see, the idea of avoiding absolutization as an error is merely a refinement of the ways that our archetypal symbolization of evil helps us to avoid threats – a refinement that avoids the projection of that archetype. Here I summarize an account of evil as the shadow archetype, and as absolutization, that I have elaborated in more detail elsewhere.[1]

I suggest that there are three different forms that 'evil' can take in our experience. In some ways this distinction follows the traditional theological distinction between 'natural' evil and 'moral' evil, with a further distinction within 'moral' evil.

1. Evil as the object of any instinctive response to avoid threats. We thus tend to regard anything associated with threats, such as volcanoes, disease, or snakes, as evil.
2. Evil as the human tendency to make absolutized judgements – and thus strictly limited to judgement. This rightly associates evil with absolutization.
3. Evil as the *projection* of the human tendency to make absolutized judgements. This associates the properties of absolutized judgement with individual people, groups, ideologies, traditions, etc.

The first kind of evil is the basis of the shadow archetype, and makes it clear why we have a basic embodied need to identify

[1] iv.3.n; V.2; Ellis (2022) 2.i & 4.e.

'natural' (i.e. non-human) evil. We are primed to vigilance against threats by a sensitivity to associations between what we have experienced as threats and whatever might produce a future threat, so we react strongly to a rustle in the undergrowth that might be a snake, are afraid of the dark, mistake mossy trunks for bears, and so on. For the same reason, the symbolization and conceptualization of threats helps us to guard against them, whether that is a reading of a textbook about disease or the retelling of stories about the slaying of monsters.

However, the function of the shadow archetype obviously extends not just to non-human evil but also to the potential threats in other humans. As we have moved gradually from the palaeolithic environment in which non-human threats loomed larger, to a modern environment in which human threats are larger, it has become increasingly important to prime ourselves against human threats instead. However, human threats are harder to identify than non-human ones. A smiling diplomat from another tribe might suddenly reveal a weapon and attack, or a person from one's own tribe might even become crazy and go on a killing spree. To identify human threats, we need to be primed to small differences in behaviour that may be associated with unreliability. As absolutization is normally required to override feelings of human solidarity, it is thus the signs of absolutization that we have come to identify with evil.

Table 3. Features of evil correlated with dimensions of absolutization.

Features associated with evil	Dimensions of absolutization
Lust for power, despotism	Group-binding, repression
Egoism, greed, megalomania	Mental proliferation, craving, reinforcing feedback loops, denial of embodiment, foundationalism (with regard to oneself)
Cruelty	Mental proliferation, hatred, reinforcing feedback loops, denial of embodiment, repression and conflict, projection (with regard to others)
Deception, manipulativeness	Representationalism, assumed system independence, metaphysics
Defensiveness, rigidity	Fragility, conflict, confirmation bias, exclusion of options
Impatience, short-termism	Exclusion of options, representationalism (over time)
Literalness, false emotion, despair	Representationalism, denial of embodiment (especially left hemisphere over-dominance)

These signs consist of a whole set of qualities that we associate with evil and that are also associated with absolutization. For instance, we are likely to associate evil in humans as qualities like despotism, egoism, cruelty, manipulativeness, rigidity, impatience, and despair. All of these can be clearly correlated with dimensions of absolutization as described earlier in this book. Some of the correlations are illustrated in **table 3**.

This is, at present, just a theoretical analysis. I invite you to compare your experience of every villain you have seen or read about with these features. Look at the representations of the shadow, especially where it appears in a relatively concentrated form in popular depictions of evil, such as those in J.R.R. Tolkien or J.K. Rowling, and I think you will find these features. They are the result, of course, of differentiation between general human features and those specific to a particular culture, but need to be subjected to scrutiny in relation to possible exceptions in other cultures. The associations, at least in the West, could easily be checked by psychological testing, but I have yet to find any studies on this. Once you accept that these features are generally associated with evil, their relationship to absolutization should also be evident.

Of course, we tend to visualize these evil features as features of *character* rather than of *judgement*, because character is far easier to differentiate than judgement. Even psychological discussions of evil have tended to see it as a matter of character, by for instance associating it with psychopathy and sociopathy (as a long-term condition affecting an individual).[2] However, individuals vary a great deal in their judgements, and (as the stories tell us) may be corrupted or may reform, so it is *judgement* that needs to be identified as the sphere in which evil may operate. A cruel or impatient judgement, for instance, does not necessarily make a cruel or impatient person, let alone a cruel or impatient group. It is the third type of evil, the projected form, that leads us to identify these features of evil with over-generalized objects.

The projected form of evil is the one that we most often identify in conflict: for instance, assuming that our enemy in a war, or in a quarrel, is evil, or believing that Satan exists as a supernatural force rather than as an archetype. This is an absolutization of the results of our capacity to detect absolutizations.

---

2   E.g. Baron-Cohen (2011); Lobaczewski (2007).

The error focus, then, needs to be understood as a focus on recognizing evil as found specifically in judgement. Primarily that means our own judgement, although, as discussed in the next chapter, this needs an overall positive emotional context. Our attempts to identify evil in others' judgement are subject to contextual misinterpretation of the kind discussed in 3.d, so need to remain provisional – even though there are some circumstances where we can have a very high degree of confidence that an absolutization is being employed, because of the explicit use of features of absolutization.

Within those limitations, however, the error focus requires a revolutionary reconsideration of our understanding of evil. Instead of good being the prior concept, and evil being a privation of good (as it is defined, for instance, by St Augustine[3]), evil becomes the most readily identifiable element in the form of error. Rather than applying an absolute conception of good and seeing the shadow as its ill-defined opposite, then, we can identify error, and at each point where we identify it, gradually proceed in the direction of an assumed good that we can only identify archetypally.

The *refining* of shadow avoidance, then, is the shaping of the basic instinct of avoiding threats that is an aspect of our embodied situation. That instinct becomes associated with symbols of what might possibly constitute a threat, but the complexity of modern human civilization makes it increasingly difficult to differentiate actual threats. The error focus, concentrating on absolutized judgements, allows us to do this, much more effectively treating these threats as parts of a complex system rather than as fixed 'evil' entities.

---

3   St Augustine (1945) 11.9.

10.c. Emotionally Positive Context

> *Summary*
>
> Although logical negativity is conventional and reversible, the idea of error may still have emotionally negative associations for us. These can be put in a wider positive frame by a growth mindset that puts error in the context of wider success, so are not a sufficient argument against error focus. The development of a growth mindset may be aided by mindfulness, imagination, and critical thinking practices.

An error focus might seem to be a 'negative' one, but before leaving this topic it is worth considering exactly what we might mean by 'negative' in this context. To be helpful to our response to absolutization, does an approach have to be 'positive', and if so why? Is it just a matter of representation?

At first it does seem to be a matter of representation – of a kind that can be changed without loss in the function of the language. Any statement that is *logically* negative can easily be rephrased to be logically positive, and vice-versa. For instance 'The dog has not eaten' can be rephrased as 'The dog has fasted', or 'There is one king' can be rephrased as 'There is not more than one king'. There are subtle distinctions in meaning between these pairs, but in most situations they could serve the same communicative purpose. If we are avoiding representationalism, we should also avoid the assumption that 'negative' statements tell us something 'negative' about the world: they merely use a negative form to represent or express a meaning for us that is not necessarily either positive or negative.

However, of course the meaning for us can be *emotionally* negative or positive in a way that is not necessarily connected to the logical form. I may be very happy that the dog has not eaten, for instance, so that it can immediately have a life-saving operation that it having eaten would have precluded. However, when it comes to error as a logically negative form, we can't avoid the likelihood that it will also often have an emotional negativity attached to it. That's likely to be because we experience 'error' as a bad thing. It interferes with our fulfilment of a goal with which we identify, or perhaps means social disapproval.

Whether we experience error like that, though, is entirely a matter of context. One of the reasons that a *growth mindset* differs from a *fixed mindset* in the influential educational research of Carol Dweck,[1] is that those with a growth mindset are able to contextualize error as part of a path for growth. Those with a fixed mindset, however, are unable to perceive error as anything other than an evil undermining their confidence. This also suggests that the fixed mindset reflects absolutization, particularly through the absoluteness of the negation offered by failure in one respect. Those subject to it are unable to reframe failure in one respect as part of potential success in another, larger respect, because alternative interpretations have been excluded. The interpretation of error as emotionally negative, then, is an effect of absolutization. The challenge of interpreting the error focus in an emotionally positive way cannot be separated from the challenges of responding to absolutization in general.

However, the danger of interpreting error focus in an emotionally negative way can hardly be a justifiable reason for rejecting error focus as a criterion. We need the error focus because of the overwhelming problem created by confirmation bias as an aspect of absolutization, and the danger that a 'positive' focus will simply be a delusive one. The challenge is thus making sure that an emotionally positive framing of error is part of our understanding of how to respond to absolutization.

We cannot create that positive framing from nowhere for those who lack it, but it is worth noting that there are a variety of ways to develop it. Mindfulness, the imagination, and critical thinking can all play this role.

Mindfulness can help to offer a positive context for error through body awareness, and indeed the practice itself can be seen as a repeated balancing feedback loop of recognizing error, re-contextualizing, and going back to the practice. In addition, our most basic confidence and self-esteem provide a positive emotional context that grows out of our capacity to do basic physical tasks of increasing complexity. Mindfulness taught to children at school from an early age can thus be a powerful way of supporting a growth mindset.

The development of the imagination can help to provide new options apart from immediate success and failure, particularly if imaginative associations keep linking us back to a wider vision of potential success despite immediate failure. I argue that this role

1   Dweck (2012).

is taken by *archetypal symbols*, as discussed in 5.f. For example, a symbol that has a heroic archetypal function, who might just be 'my hero' from a book or film, can become associated with the long-term success that can follow from repeated learning from failure. Reading or watching stories with heroes can thus make an important contribution to helping us contextualize error and develop a growth mindset.[2]

Critical thinking can also help us to contextualize error by encouraging reflection on our beliefs about it and their limitations. Cognitive behavioural therapy is an example of a therapeutic approach that can help people to overcome problematic patterns of fixed thinking through such reflection (whether this is induced by oneself or by a therapist). 'Disaster thinking' in which errors are exaggerated as failures is a recognized pattern of unhelpful thinking in this context: as Aaron Beck comments about depressed patients, they 'expect deprivation or defeat to continue permanently'.[3] Often simply labelling these tendencies and identifying them when they arise can provide a bigger context to help reverse a negative reaction to error.

Whatever our means of finding a larger positive context for error, the challenge of doing so can hardly be separated from the error focus as a more general aspect of our response to absolutization, particularly for those who have not already made a growth mindset a habitual part of their response to challenges. Recognizing absolutization raises particular challenges when compared to any other type of error (just making a mistake in a calculation, for instance), because the recognition has the potential to re-trigger the absolutized mental state in which the error occurred. To avoid this, we need all the help we can get from awareness of past positive framing, prompts from others, and the contextualization offered by the body.

---

2   See Ellis (2022) 4.c.
3   Beck (1976) p. 117.

Conclusion: Criteria for the Middle Way

This book has provided an account of the necessity for the Middle Way and of some basic criteria for the form it needs to take. It has done this firstly by showing the interrelationships between the 23 dimensions of absolutization. Secondly, this has aimed to show that a *connected* response to these dimensions is required to address them all. Past partial responses to some of the dimensions have been inadequate because of a failure to appreciate their synthetic relationship with the others.

Whilst absolutization might have been avoided in some limited respects, then, by such limited responses, remaining absolutized assumptions in the responses are likely to seed new sources of absolutization. For example, Buddhist practice that attempted to undermine greed, hatred, and delusion has had limited success because of its continuing dependence on metaphysical rather than provisional theorizations (such as the appeal to discontinuous enlightenment). Embodied practice has had a limited application if it is interpreted in terms of relativist absolutizations and excludes the aspiration to universality (for instance, merely practising yoga to reduce one's stress levels, without attempting to change the conditions of one's job that cause the stress). Western philosophical formulations of the ethical good have had very limited success in changing behaviour because of their dogmatic exclusion of psychological states of judgement (for instance, identifying gluttony as a 'deadly sin' does little to address bulimia).

I want to argue that any effective response to absolutization must take a form that I would call *The Middle Way*, because it cannot consist only in either the assertion or rejection of belief in an ideal. For the same reason it is neither entirely religious nor entirely secular, neither solely scientific nor solely artistic, neither 'rational' nor 'emotional', neither solely normative nor solely descriptive. These are only a few of the pairs of opposed absolutes that need to be reconsidered and reframed as part of any adequate response to absolutization. This is because the absoluteness of negation and the exclusion of alternative options are structural features of absolutization itself, and one fails to avoid absolutization by merely negating and thus remaining within a binary framework. The challenges of this point alone are vast.

The Middle Way is not a description of one particular approach or technique, so much as a general description of any effective approach or technique to avoiding absolutization and its effects. The parameters of any such approach are offered by the four criteria:

1. Practicality – including embodiment, responsibility, and effectiveness
2. Universality of aspiration – normatively and systemically over groups, space, and time
3. Judgement focus – focus on *how*, not *what* we judge
4. Error focus – refining shadow avoidance and framing with emotional positivity

Without *practicality*, our theoretical formulations for human life are never actually tested against active experience: they are likely to remain caught up in a reinforcing feedback loop of psychological states and circularity of reasoning. Factual beliefs become of merely abstract interest, and normative beliefs become institutionalized failures. The failure to integrate theoretical insights with practicality for individual (not just professional) practice is one of the major shortcomings of academia, and where Buddhist and similar groups in the West have led the way.

Without *universality of aspiration*, rejections of idealized beliefs are liable to remain in the same framework of assumptions as those they reject, maintaining an absoluteness of negation. For this reason, relativist standpoints that fail to identify a Middle Way need to be avoided, although these are common in secularist reactions to religion, parochial responses to universalism, and postmodern reactions to modern globalization. These at best may have some value as transitional states prior to recognizing the Middle Way.

Without *judgement focus,* even movements that start off with practicality and universality of aspiration can easily be diverted into beliefs that are not relevantly applicable in every context. Our obsession with describing states of affairs easily becomes a substitute for improving our judgement about any given state of affairs. I gave examples of how this can happen from metaphysical Buddhism, evolutionary accounts of biases, and abstracted normative ethics.

Without *error focus*, even the idea of the Middle Way can turn into an absolutized positive that is continually subject to confirmation bias. Thus, even though our theorizations of a helpful path may start off avoiding absolutization, the need to keep stoking our positive view rather than seeking falsifications may lead us into *ad hoc* thinking designed to maintain our positive theory. A common example of this involves commitment to a political ideology whose values we believe to be the correct ones in all contexts, rather than merely appropriate for a particular context. We need to keep looking for ways that other possible values are more appropriate for new contexts, avoiding representationalism of our values as somehow equivalent to a moral 'reality'.

The Middle Way can take all kinds of forms, using different kinds of language according to the cultural and traditional context it is being discussed and applied in. However, I have put the four criteria in this way, and tried to show how they are required in order to respond adequately to absolutization, in order to provide as universal a description as possible. They are *criteria*, in the sense that they can be used to try to test whether a claimed Middle Way approach is consistently so. Provisionality, of course, also requires me to note that this list of four criteria may not be complete.

These criteria can be used to provide at least an initial test of whether a claimed Middle Way approach in the context of a particular tradition is genuinely so, and thus whether it is practically compatible with similar Middle Way approaches in other traditions and able to resolve framing conflicts with those other traditions. I have already written in other books about the Middle Way in the context of three other traditions: Buddhist,[1] Christian,[2] and Jungian.[3] These only provide examples of how the criteria could be applied. They do not imply, of course, that the whole of the tradition, or even what some regard as 'essential' to that tradition, is compatible with the Middle Way. However, if one can interpret a given tradition in terms that are practical, universal in aspiration, focusing on judgement, and focusing on error then I would contend that a genuinely Middle Way interpretation of that tradition is possible, making it possible to practise the Middle Way whilst staying in touch with

---

1 Ellis (2019), and to a lesser extent also (2020a).
2 Ellis (2018).
3 Ellis (2020b).

the cultural heritage, symbols, social structures, and practical techniques of that tradition.

As an example, let me briefly discuss the application to Christianity, since this seems to be amongst the least obvious applications for many. Here are the four criteria applied in that context:

1. *Practicality:* Looking for positive aspects of Christian tradition that support embodiment (e.g. Christocentrism, some aspects of mysticism – especially Simone Weil's work), felt responsibility (linking of ethics with spirituality), and effectiveness (confidence through spirituality, linked to awareness of limitations in humility).
2. *Universality of aspiration:* Christian tradition is strongly universal and normative throughout. The challenge here is to avoid top-down dogmatism: critical theology may help.
3. *Judgement focus:* Being clear that we are focusing on *how* people relate to God, not *what* they are relating to and whether it 'exists' (or whether they 'believe' that it 'exists'). Drawing on the agnostic approaches in Christian mysticism, and treating God and Christ as archetypes.
4. *Error focus:* Relating positively to the discussion of *sin* in Christianity as reflecting people's experience of the effects of absolutization. Placing sin in the larger Middle Way context of the tension between divine ideal and human limitation, and interpreting atonement as integration rather than a magical shortcut.

Such applications of the criteria can be made in any other complex human tradition, though of course some are more amenable to such interpretation than others. This can be applied to philosophical, political, disciplinary, and artistic traditions as well as religious ones, provided we are able to avoid essentialism in the definition of those traditions that makes them necessarily opposed to the criteria. Obviously there will be more opposition to such an interpretation in some traditions and sub-traditions than in others: it is very hard to envisage a Middle Way Fascism, for example, because that tradition is so dominated by obvious absolutizations. In other kinds of Middle Way interpretation one will need to very carefully distinguish a Middle Way interpretation of that tradition from a mere appropriation of the Middle Way by that tradition. I am pretty sceptical of claims to Middle Way Platonism, for instance, but there is plenty of complexity and ambiguity in Plato's dialogues, and in their neoplatonic interpretation, that could form the basis of it, provided the rationalist absolutization that has become synonymous with Plato is clearly avoided.

Apart from revealing inadequate pretensions to the Middle Way, the four criteria can also be used more positively to help identify versions of it, or moves in its direction, that have not been articulated as such. That these are common should already be suggested by my use of the five starting points that structure my account of the dimensions of absolutization in this book: Buddhism, systems, embodiment, philosophy, and psychology. The ways in which these five starting points can take us a long way towards an effective response to absolutization, but still fall short because of an insufficient synthesis, should be clear from the discussion throughout: for example that Buddhism generally scores excellently on practicality and universality of aspiration, but not sufficiently on judgement focus and error focus.

There is, however, a distinction between these criteria, which are intended to be used primarily to help identify the Middle Way at a philosophical or ideological level, and the principles that are needed to help articulate a full adequate response in practice at individual or socio-political levels. My intention is that the next book in this series, called *The Five Principles of Middle Way Philosophy*, will provide a more adequate structure for identifying how our outlook needs to develop to practise the Middle Way. These five principles do have an interdependent relationship on the four criteria, but not a simple relationship. I will outline them here only in order to provide a link to that forthcoming book, with its bridge from the analysis of the problem in this book to the fuller account of its solution in the next. They are as follows:

1. Scepticism: the recognition of uncertainty in human experience
2. Provisionality: the maintenance of options in human judgement
3. Incrementality: the interpretation of qualities as a matter of degree
4. Agnosticism: the deliberate avoidance of polarized framing
5. Integration: the overcoming of conflict through practice, at both individual and socio-political levels

Of these, *scepticism* (carefully interpreted in an even-handed way) helps us to identify error and supports judgement focus. All too often, sceptical arguments are used selectively to try to elevate one absolutization over another, but when applied as much to negative absolutizations as to positive ones, they can help to free us of belief in those absolutizations. This even-handedness in the application of sceptical argument is also an aspect of universality of aspiration, so that we move beyond the parochiality of only recognizing the uncertainty of some views but not others. Scepticism is thus entirely compatible with practicality, and has the effect of extending our range of practical engagement but promoting critical awareness of its limitations.

Provisionality helps to overcome the absoluteness of negation by enabling mental states in which further options can become available to us in judgement. As such, then, it has a particular relationship with judgement focus, but also draws on the other criteria.

Incrementality (or continuity) is particularly concerned with overcoming discontinuity as a feature of absolutization. It also has a close relationship with the idea of ethical *stretch* as discussed in 8.b. If we can understand our practice of the Middle Way itself in continuous terms, rather than as a discontinuous conformity with an ideal or a mere description of our limitations, one of the important aspects of bottom-up universality is addressed.

Agnosticism is an important aspect of error focus, and consists of taking a confidently and deliberately even-handed approach to polarized absolutes, not accepting the dualistic framing but instead insisting on a reconsideration of the terms in a way that enables the conflict to be resolved. Without to some extent understanding the nature of absolutization, and the ways it can seduce us or goad us into joining in fruitless conflicts, it is very difficult to practice the Middle Way.

Integration is the long-term resolution of unnecessary conflict (whether psychological or socio-political) created by absolutized opposition and repression. It involves taking a long-term view based on an understanding that conflict is not resolved by 'winning' – rather by getting the 'opponent' on your side. It is this principle that has the closest relationship with practicality amongst the criteria, because actually resolving conflict depends on dealing with its embodied conditions. Much Middle Way *practice* is primarily focused on integration, although it will also involve the other principles.

Integrative practice is what creates the long-term conditions for addressing absolutization. It does this primarily by *contextualizing* absolutization in a wider form of awareness of one kind or another, and by setting up the habit and the expectation of being able to contextualize. That contextualization can happen at the basic level of body awareness, so that emotions from the 'reptilian brain' can be diluted and gradually cease to dominate our responses. It can happen at the level of the imagination, where we can have a wider context of *meaning* in which to place our beliefs, and thus have access to more options for new possible beliefs. It can also happen through critical thinking at the level of belief, so that our current beliefs occur in a wider intellectual context, in which we remain aware of their limitations and of the alternative possibilities.

Practices such as mindfulness, the arts, and critical thinking, then, already widely recognized as beneficial, can be given a new importance and wider purpose in the context of Middle Way practice. This, in the end, then, is the most important reason for understanding absolutization as a connected phenomenon. Intellectual understanding of it as a phenomenon can help us to begin to address it, but it does not go very far by itself. It is only when understanding of absolutization helps to motivate and support Middle Way practice that it comes into its own.

Appendix

Table 4. The 23 dimensions of absolutization.

Dimension	Main source(s)	Example evidence	Example implications
1. Mental proliferation	Buddhism, mindfulness	Meditation hindrance, addiction	Mind subject to reinforcing loops (5)
2. Interdependence of craving, hatred, and delusion	Buddhism, psychology	Motivated reasoning, reason/emotion interdependence	Avoid fact/value distinctions in Western thought
3. Absoluteness of negations	Buddhism	Conventionality of negation, association phenomena	Even-handedness in treatment of absolutes
4. Excluding the options	Buddhism, informal logic	Conflict resolution, evolution	Optionality as aspect of provisionality
5. Reinforcing feedback loops	Systems theory	Autopoiesis, mental proliferation	Balancing feedback loops
6. Assumed system independence	Systems theory	Representationalism (8), metaphysics (12)	No justification for special 'cognitive' status
7. Fragility	Systems theory	Conversion phenomena, mental illness	Long-term perspectives
8. Representationalism	Embodied meaning theory/ neuroscience	Popular essentialism, conflict over meaning	Non-justification of metaphysics
9. Denial of embodiment	Embodied meaning theory	Mindfulness, neuroscience	Fragility (7), contextual interpretation (11)
10. Discontinuity	Neuroscience	Hemispheric differences, organic continuity	Discontinuity as easy absolutization test
11. Contextual interpretation	Embodied meaning theory	Sociology of religion	Archetypal function (23)
12. Metaphysics	Western philosophy	History of philosophy and religion	Foundationalism (14)
13. Absoluteness of deductive logic	Western philosophy	Linguistic evidence	Contingency of logic

14. Foundationalism and circularity	Western philosophy	Appeals to authority	Defensive rationalizations
15. Infinite rationalizations of experience	Western philosophy	Problem of evil, intractability of metaphysical disputes	Imperviousness to observation or probability
16. Claim that metaphysics is inevitable	Western philosophy, cognitive psychology	Critical systems heuristics	Contingency of metaphysical claims
17. Inflation of metaphysics and logic	Western philosophy/critical thinking	Social function of fallacy avoidance	Decoupling fallacy from logic
18. Repression and conflict	Psychoanalysis/ mindfulness/ political history	Cognitive dissonance phenomena, mental illness	Suppression and reframing
19. Projection	Psychoanalysis/ religious history	Idolatry, biases	Integration of projections
20. Confirmation bias	Cognitive psychology	History of science	Other biases, effects on scientific method
21. Substitution	Cognitive psychology	Fast/slow thinking effects	Practical training facilitates slow thinking
22. Group binding	Cognitive psychology	Group bias effects	Balanced individuality
23. Archetypal function of contextualized absolutes	Jungian psychology	Benefits of religious practice, inspirational effect of symbolism	Complexity of religion and its effects

The Old and New Middle Way Philosophy Series

Although this book can stand alone as an account of the nature of absolutization, it is also the first of a planned series of at least eight books on Middle Way Philosophy, to be published by Equinox over the next few years. These books will together form a highly interconnected argument for the Middle Way as a practical philosophy. In the process they will synthesize various different sources of insight, and challenge various entrenched assumptions about human judgement, its justification and motivation. This series is in turn a substantial development, rewriting, and updating of an earlier series of four volumes.

While the new series is in the course of being written, I will need to refer the reader at a number of points to supporting and connecting arguments in both the old series and the new series. I suggest referring to the new series if possible, but using the old series if the required volume of the new series has not been published yet. To distinguish between them, I have used lower case Roman numerals (i, ii, iii, iv) in references to the books of the old series, and upper case Roman numerals (I, II, III, etc.) to refer to the planned books of the new series. Both series are listed below.

Old series (Robert M. Ellis, 2012–15)

This has been published both as four separate volumes and as an omnibus edition by Lulu, Raleigh. This series is referred to using lower case Roman numerals, followed by section and chapter numbers.

  i. *Middle Way Philosophy 1: The Path of Objectivity* (2012)
  ii. *Middle Way Philosophy 2: The Integration of Desire* (2013)
  iii. *Middle Way Philosophy 3: The Integration of Meaning* (2013)
  iv. *Middle Way Philosophy 4: The Integration of Belief* (2015)

Middle Way Philosophy: Omnibus Edition (2015)

New series (Robert M. Ellis, 2022 onwards)

Absolutization is the first book in this planned series to be published by Equinox. This series is referred to using upper case Roman numerals. Obviously, references to books that have not yet been written (at the time of writing this book) must be approximate. I have given an indicative section number, but otherwise you will need to use the contents and index of the relevant book in the new series to locate a reference.

I. *Absolutization: The Source of Dogma, Repression, and Conflict*
II. *The Five Principles of Middle Way Philosophy: Living Experientially in a World of Uncertainty*
III. *A Systemic History of the Middle Way: The Biology, Developmental Psychology, and Cultural Change behind Integrative Practice*
IV. *Embodied Meaning and Integration: Overcoming the Abstracted Grip on Meaning in Theory and Practice*
V. *Bias and the Integration of Belief: The Psychology of Absolutized Judgement and the Middle Way*
VI. *The Practice of Agnosticism: Overcoming False Dualities across Human Thought*
VII. *Mindful Beauty: Aesthetics as Gathering Attention*
VIII. *Middle Way Ethics: Stretching across the Gap between Relative and Absolute Values*
IX. *The Middle Way Manifesto: Combining Radical Change with Political Effectiveness*

Bibliography

Ackerman, Joshua, Nocera, Christopher, & Bargh, John (2010) 'Incidental haptic sensations influence social judgments and decisions' *Science* 328:5986, pp. 1712–15. https://doi.org/10.1126/science.1189993

Adams, H., Wright, L., & Lohr, B. (1996) 'Is homophobia associated with homosexual arousal?' *Journal of Abnormal Psychology* 105:3, pp. 440–5. https://doi.org/10.1037/0021-843X.105.3.440

Allan, Lorraine & Jenkins, Herbert (1980) 'The judgement of contingency and the nature of the response alternatives' *Canadian Journal of Psychology* 34:1, pp. 1–11. https://doi.org/10.1037/h0081013

Aquinas, St Thomas, trans. Fathers of the English Dominican Province, ed. Knight (2008) *Summa Theologica*. http://www.newadvent.org/summa

Aristotle, trans. Jowett (1905) *Politics*. Oxford University Press, Oxford.

Aristotle, trans. Thomson (1976) *Ethics*. Penguin, London.

Asch, Solomon (1956) *Studies in Independence and Conformity: 1. A Minority of One against a Unanimous Majority*. Psychological Monographs. https://doi.org/10.1037/h0093718

Augustine of Hippo, St, trans. Healey (1945) *City of God*. Dent, London.

Ayer, A.J. (1971) *Language, Truth and Logic*. Penguin, London.

Baggini, Julian (2016) *The Edge of Reason: A Rational Skeptic in an Irrational World*. Yale University Press, New Haven.

Baron-Cohen, Simon (2011) *Zero Degrees of Empathy: A New Theory of Human Cruelty*. Allen Lane, London.

Baruch Bush, Robert & Folger, Joseph (2005) *The Promise of Mediation*. Jossey-Bass, San Francisco.

Beck, Aaron (1976) *Cognitive Therapy and the Emotional Disorders*. Penguin, London.

Benestad, R.E. (2005) 'A review of the solar cycle length estimates' *Geophysical Research Letters* 32:15. https://doi.org/10.1029/2005GL023621

Bezuidenhout, Anne (2002) 'Truth-conditional pragmatics' *Philosophical Perspectives* 16, pp. 105–34. https://doi.org/10.1111/1468-0068.36.s16.5

Blackburn, Simon (1998) *Ruling Passions: A Theory of Practical Reasoning*. Oxford University Press, Oxford.

Bodhi, Bhikkhu (1999) *A Comprehensive Manual of Abhidhamma*. Buddhist Publication Society, Kandy, Sri Lanka.

Bodhi, Bhikkhu (2000) *The Connected Discourses of the Buddha: A New Translation of the Samyutta Nikaya* (2 vols). Wisdom Publications, Boston.

Boom, Jan (2009) 'Piaget on equilibration' from *The Cambridge Companion to Piaget*. Cambridge University Press, Cambridge. https://doi.org/10.1017/CCOL9780521898584.006

Bradley, Darren (2017) 'Carnap's epistemological critique of metaphysics' *Synthese* 195, pp. 2247–65. https://doi.org/10.1007/s11229-017-1335-x
Brink, David (1986) 'Utilitarian morality and the personal point of view' *The Journal of Philosophy* 83:8. https://doi.org/10.2307/2026328
Chabris, Christopher & Simons, Daniel (2010) *The Invisible Gorilla*. HarperCollins, New York.
Chalmers, Alan (1982) *What is This Thing Called Science?* Open University Press, Milton Keynes.
Clarke, Murray (1986) 'Doxastic voluntarism and forced belief' *Philosophical Studies* 50:1, pp. 39–51. https://doi.org/10.1007/BF00355159
Cook, Norman (1984) 'Callosal inhibition: The key to the brain code' *Behavioral Science* 29:2 pp. 98–110. https://doi.org/10.1002/bs.3830290203
Cupitt, Don (1989) *The Long-Legged Fly: A Theology of Language and Desire*. SCM Press, Norwich.
Curry, Oliver, Mullins, Daniel, & Whitehouse, Harvey (2019) 'Is it good to co-operate? Testing the theory of morality as co-operation in 60 societies' *Current Anthropology* 60:1. https://doi.org/10.1086/701478
Dawkins, Richard (1989) *The Selfish Gene*. Oxford University Press, Oxford.
Dawkins, Richard (2006) *The God Delusion*. Black Swan, London
Dennett, Daniel (1993) *Consciousness Explained*. Penguin, London. https://doi.org/10.2307/2108259
Descartes, René, trans. Sutcliffe (1968) *Discourse on Method and the Meditations*. Penguin, London.
Dewey, John, ed. Boydston (1922) *Human Nature and Conduct*. Southern Illinois University Press, Carbondale Illinois.
Drake, Stilman (1978) *Galileo at Work: His Scientific Biography*. Dover, Mineola New York.
Dreyfus, Hubert (1991) *Being in the World: A Commentary on Heidegger's 'Being and Time' Part 1*. MIT Press, Cambridge Mass.
Dweck, Carol S. (2012) *Mindset: Changing the Way You Think to Fulfil Your Potential*. Robinson, London.
Edmonds, David (2020) *The Murder of Professor Schlick: The Rise and Fall of the Vienna Circle*. Princeton University Press, Princeton. https://doi.org/10.1515/9780691185842
Ellis, Robert M. (2001) 'A Buddhist theory of moral objectivity'. PhD thesis, Lancaster University. https://ethos.bl.uk/OrderDetails.do?uin=uk.bl.ethos.289002
Ellis, Robert M. (2012–15) *Middle Way Philosophy series:* see section preceding bibliography.
Ellis, Robert M. (2016) *Parables of the Middle Way*. Lulu, Raleigh.
Ellis, Robert M. (2017) 'Reason is not objectivity: A response to Julian Baggini's narrowly rational criteria for objectivity' https://www.researchgate.net/publication/313696637_Reason_is_not_objectivity_A_response_to_Julian_Baggini's_narrowly_rational_criteria_for_objectivity
Ellis, Robert M. (2018) *The Christian Middle Way*. Christian Alternative, Winchester.
Ellis, Robert M. (2019) *The Buddha's Middle Way: Experiential Judgement in His Life and Teaching*. Equinox, Sheffield.

Ellis, Robert M. (2020a) *The Thought of Sangharakshita: A Critical Assessment.* Equinox, Sheffield. https://doi.org/10.1558/isbn.9781781799284

Ellis, Robert M (2020b) *Red Book, Middle Way: How Jung Parallels the Buddha's Method for Human Integration.* Equinox, Sheffield. https://doi.org/10.1558/isbn.9781800500082

Ellis, Robert M. (2022) *Archetypes in Religion and Beyond: A Practical Theory of Human Integration and Inspiration.* Equinox, Sheffield.

Ellis, Robert M. (forthcoming) *Middle Way Philosophy series:* see section preceding bibliography.

Fazio, Russell & Zanna, Mark (1978) 'On the predictive validity of attitudes: The roles of direct experience and confidence' *Journal of Personality* 46:2, pp. 228–43. https://doi.org/10.1111/j.1467-6494.1978.tb00177.x

Festinger, Leon (1957) *A Theory of Cognitive Dissonance.* Stanford University Press, Stanford.

Festinger, Leon, Riecken, Henry, & Schachter, Stanley (1956) *When Prophecy Fails.* University of Minnesota Press, Minneapolis. https://doi.org/10.1037/10030-000

Foot, Philippa (1978) 'The problem of abortion and the doctrine of the double effect' from *Virtues and Vices.* Blackwell, Oxford.

Fox, Michael & 5 others (2005) 'The human brain is intrinsically organized into dynamic, anticorrelated functional networks' *Proceedings of the National Academy of Sciences USA* 102:27, pp. 9673–8. https://doi.org/10.1073/pnas.0504136102

Frege, Gottlob (1966) 'On sense and reference' from Geach & Black, ed., *Translations from the Philosophical Writings of Gottlob Frege.* Blackwell, Oxford.

Freud, Sigmund & Breuer, Joseph, trans. Luckhurst (2004) *Studies in Hysteria.* Penguin, London.

Friederici, Angela (2002) 'Towards a neural basis of auditory sentence processing' *Trends in Cognitive Sciences* 6:2, pp. 78–84. https://doi.org/10.1016/S1364-6613(00)01839-8

Gandhi, Mohandas K. (1939) Article in *Harijan* 64, dated 25/3/1939.

Gardner, Helen (2003) *The Metaphysical Poets.* Penguin, London.

Gilbert, Paul (2010) *The Compassionate Mind.* Constable, London.

Gould, Stephen J. (1999) *Rocks of Ages: Science and Religion in the Fullness of Life.* Ballantine Books, New York.

Hacker, P.M.S. (1972) *Insight and Illusion.* Oxford University Press, London.

Haidt, Jonathan (2012) *The Righteous Mind: Why Good People are Divided by Politics and Religion.* Penguin, London.

Hamilton, J. Paul, Farmer, Madison, Fogelman, Phoebe, & Gotlib, Ian (2015) 'Depressive rumination, the default-mode network, and the dark matter of clinical neuroscience' *Biological Psychiatry* 28:4, pp. 224–30. https://doi.org/10.1016/j.biopsych.2015.02.020

Harrington, Deborah, Haaland, Kathleen, & Knight, Robert (1998) 'Cortical networks underlying mechanisms of time perception' *Journal of Neuroscience* 18:3, pp. 1085–95. https://doi.org/10.1523/JNEUROSCI.18-03-01085.1998

Harris, Sam (2007) *Letter to a Christian Nation.* Bantam Press, London.

Hart, H.L.A. (1968) *Law, Liberty and Morality.* Oxford University Press, Oxford.

Haselton, Martie, Nettle, Daniel, & Murray, Damian (2015) 'The evolution of cognitive bias' from *The Handbook of Evolutionary Psychology*. John Wiley. https://doi.org/10.1002/9781119125563.evpsych241

Hebb, Donald (1949) *The Organization of Behavior*. John Wiley.

Heidegger, Martin, trans. Macquarrie & Robinson (1962) *Being and Time*. Blackwell, Oxford.

Hobbes, Thomas (1909) *Leviathan*. Oxford University Press, Oxford.

Hume, David (1975) *An Enquiry Concerning Human Understanding and Concerning the Principles of Morals*. Oxford University Press, Oxford. https://doi.org/10.1093/actrade/9780198245353.book.1

Hume, David (1978) *A Treatise on Human Nature*. Oxford University Press, Oxford.

Ireland, John D. (1990) *The Udana: Inspired Utterances of the Buddha*. Buddhist Publications Society, Kandy, Sri Lanka.

James, William (1981) *Pragmatism*. Hackett, Indianapolis.

Janis, Irving L. (1982) *Groupthink: Psychological Studies of Policy Decisions and Fiascos*. Houghton Mifflin, Boston.

Johnson, Mark (2007) *The Meaning of the Body*. University of Chicago Press, Chicago.

Johnson, Mark (2014) *Morality for Humans*. University of Chicago Press, Chicago.

Johnson, Mark (2017) *Embodied Mind, Meaning and Reason*. University of Chicago Press, Chicago. https://doi.org/10.7208/chicago/9780226500393.001.0001

Johnson, Mark (2018) *The Aesthetics of Meaning and Thought*. University of Chicago Press, Chicago. https://doi.org/10.1017/S275390670000259X

Johnston, E.H. (1972) *The Buddhacarita or Acts of the Buddha*. Oriental Reprint, New Delhi.

Jones, Edward & Harris, Victor (1967) 'The attribution of attitudes' *Journal of Experimental Social Psychology* 3:1, pp. 1–24. https://doi.org/10.1016/0022-1031(67)90034-0

Jones, Edward & Nisbett, Richard (1971) 'The actor and the observer: Divergent perceptions of the causes of behavior' from Valins & Weiner (1987) *Attribution: Perceiving the Causes of Behavior*. Lawrence Erlbaum, Hillsdale New Jersey.

Jung, Carl Gustav, trans. Baynes (1946) *Psychological Types*. Kegan Paul, London.

Jung, Carl Gustav, trans. Hull (1966) *The Practice of Psychotherapy* (Collected Works 16). Routledge, London.

Kahneman, Daniel (2011) *Thinking, Fast and Slow*. Penguin, London.

Kant, Immanuel, trans. Kemp Smith (1929) *Critique of Pure Reason*. Macmillan, London.

Kant, Immanuel, trans. Gregor (1996) 'On the supposed right to lie from philanthropy' from *Practical Philosophy*. Cambridge University Press, Cambridge.

Kegan (1982) *The Evolving Self: Problem and Process in Human Development*. Harvard University Press, Cambridge Mass. https://doi.org/10.4159/9780674039414

Kierkegaard, Søren, trans. Hannay (1985) *Fear and Trembling*. Penguin, London.

Kolk, Herman & Heeschen, Claus (2007) 'Adaptation symptoms and impairment symptoms in Broca's aphasia' *Journal of Aphasiology* 4:3, pp. 221–31. https://doi.org/10.1080/02687039008249075

Körner, S. (1967) 'The impossibility of transcendental deductions' *The Monist* 51:3, pp. 317-31. https://doi.org/10.5840/monist196751325

Korzybski, Alfred (1993) *Science and Sanity: An Introduction to Non-Aristotelian Systems and General Semantics*. Institute of General Semantics, New York.

Kruglanski, Arie (2004) *The Psychology of Closed-Mindedness*. Psychology Press, New York.

Kuhn, Thomas (1996) *The Structure of Scientific Revolutions*. University of Chicago Press, Chicago.

Lakatos, Imre (1974) 'Falsification and the methodology of scientific research programmes' from Lakatos & Musgrave, ed., *Criticism and the Growth of Knowledge*. Cambridge University Press, Cambridge.

Lakoff, George (1987) *Women, Fire and Dangerous Things: What Categories Reveal about the Mind*. University of Chicago Press, Chicago. https://doi.org/10.7208/chicago/9780226471013.001.0001

Lakoff, George and Johnson, Mark (1999) *Philosophy in the Flesh: The Embodied Mind and its Challenge to Western Thought*. Basic Books, New York.

Lakoff, George and Nuñez, Rafael (2000) *Where Mathematics Come From: How the Embodied Mind Brings Mathematics into Being*. Basic Books, New York.

Langer, Ellen (2014) *Mindfulness*. Da Capo Press, Boston.

Le Duc, Jollyanne, Fournier, Phillipe, & Hébert, Sylvie (2016) 'Modulation of prepulse inihibition and startle reflex by emotions: A comparison between younger and older adults' *Frontiers in Aging Neuroscience* 8:33. https://doi.org/10.3389/fnagi.2016.00033

Leibniz, Gottfried, trans. Duncan (1890) *The Philosophical Warks*. Tuttle, Morehouse & Taylor, New Haven.

Lewis, Marc (2015) *The Biology of Desire: Why Addiction is Not a Disease*. Public Affairs, New York.

Lobaczewski, Andrew, trans. Chciuk-Celt (2007) *Political Ponerology*. Red Pill Press, Frome.

Lyotard, Jean-Francois, trans. Bennington & Massumi (1984) *The Postmodern Condition: A Report on Knowledge*. Manchester University Press, Manchester. https://doi.org/10.2307/1772278

MacIntyre, Alasdair (1981) *After Virtue: A Study in Moral Theory*. Duckworth, London.

Mackie, J.L. (1977) *Ethics: Inventing Right and Wrong*. Penguin, London.

Maturana, Humberto and Varela, Francisco (1980) *Autopoiesis and Cognition*. D. Reidel, Dordrecht.

Maturana, Humberto & Varela, Francisco (1987) *The Tree of Knowledge: The Biological Roots of Human Understanding*. Shambhala, Boston.

McGilchrist, Iain (2009) *The Master and His Emissary: The Divided Brain and the Making of the Western World*. Yale University Press, New Haven.

Meadows, Donella (2008) *Thinking in Systems: A Primer*. Chelsea Green, White River Junction, Vermont.

Merton, Robert (1957) 'Bureaucratic structure and personality' extracted from *Social Theory and Social Structure* (Free Press, Glencoe Illinois) at https://web.archive.org/web/20121227113532/http://www.sociosite.net/topics/texts/merton_bureaucratic_structure.php

Morrison, Robert (1997) 'Three cheers for tanha' *Western Buddhist Review* 2. www.westernbuddhistreview.com/vol2/tanha.html

Nagel, Thomas (1986) *The View from Nowhere*. Oxford University Press, New York.

Ñanamoli, Bhikkhu & Bodhi, Bhikkhu (1995) *The Middle Length Discourses of the Buddha: A New Translation of the Majjhima Nikaya*. Wisdom Publications, Boston.

Nicol, Valérie (2011) *Social Economies of Fear and Desire: Emotional Regulation, Emotional Management, and Embodied Autonomy*. Palgrave Macmillan, New York.

Panksepp, Jaak (1998) *Affective Neuroscience: The Foundations of Human and Animal Emotions*. Oxford University Press, Oxford.

Payutto, P.A., trans. Dhammavijaya & Evans (1994) *Buddhist Economics*. Buddhadhamma Foundation, Bangkok.

Pettigrew, Thomas (1979) 'The ultimate attribution error: Extending Allport's cognitive analysis of prejudice' *Personality and Social Psychology Bulletin* 5:4, pp. 461–76. https://doi.org/10.1177/014616727900500407

Piaget, Jean (1985) *Equilibration of Cognitive Structures*. University of Chicago Press, Chicago.

Pinker, Steven (2011) *The Better Angels of Our Nature: A History of Violence and Humanity*. Penguin, London.

Piyadassi Thera (2006) *The Three Basic Facts of Existence: Wheel Publication 202–4*. Buddhist Publications Society, Kandy, Sri Lanka. https://www.accesstoinsight.org/lib/authors/various/wheel186.html

Plato, trans. Guthrie (1956) *Protagoras and Meno*. Penguin, London.

Plato, trans. Lee (1974) *The Republic*. Penguin, London.

Plato, trans. Tarrant & Tredennick (1993) *The Last Days of Socrates*. Penguin, London.

Polt, Richard (1999) *Heidegger: An Introduction*. UCL Press, London.

Popper, Karl (1959) *The Logic of Scientific Discovery*. Hutchinson, London. https://doi.org/10.1063/1.3060577

Railton, Peter (1984) 'Alienation, consequentialism, and the demands of morality' from Scheffler, ed. (1988) *Consequentialism and its Critics*. Oxford University Press, Oxford.

Rorty, Richard (1989) *Contingency, Irony and Solidarity*. Cambridge University Press, Cambridge. https://doi.org/10.1017/CBO9780511804397

Rosenberg, Marsall (2002) *Nonviolent Communication: A Language of Compassion*. Puddledancer Press, Encinitas California.

Ross, Lee, Greene, David, & House, Pamela (1977) 'The false consensus effect: An egocentric bias in social perception and attribution processes' *Journal of Experimental Social Psychology* 13:3, pp. 279–301. https://doi.org/10.1016/0022-1031(77)90049-X

Sartre, Jean-Paul, trans. Mairet (1980) *Existentialism and Humanism*. Methuen, London.

Schaefer, Michael & 8 others (2018) 'Incidental haptic sensations influence judgment of crimes' *Scientific Reports* 6039. https://doi.org/10.1038/s41598-018-23586-x

Scott, Sophie, Blank, Catrin, Rosen, Stuart, & Wise, Richard (2000) 'Identification of a pathway for intelligible speech in the left temporal lobe' *Brain* 123:12, pp. 2400–6. https://doi.org/10.1093/brain/123.12.2400

Siegel, Daniel (2011) *Mindsight*. Oneworld, London.

Solomon, Robert C. (1972) *From Rationalism to Existentialism*. University Press of America, New York.

Sperber, Dan & Baumard, Nicholas (2012) 'Moral reputation: An evolutionary and cognitive perspective' *Mind & Language* 27:5, pp. 495–518. https://doi.org/10.1111/mila.12000

Storbeck, Justin & Clore, Gerald (2007) 'On the interdependence of emotion and cognition' *Cognition and Emotion* 21:6, pp. 1212–37. https://doi.org/10.1080/02699930701438020

Sunstein, Cass R. (2005) 'Moral heuristics' *Behavioural and Brain Sciences* 28:4, pp. 531–542.

Swinburne, Richard (2004) *The Existence of God*. Oxford University Press, Oxford. https://doi.org/10.1093/acprof:oso/9780199271672.001.0001

Taleb, Nassim Nicholas (2010) *The Black Swan: The Impact of the Highly Improbable*. Penguin, London.

Taleb, Nassim Nicholas (2012) *Antifragile: Things that Gain from Disorder*. Penguin, London.

Taylor, Donald and Doria, Janet (1981) 'Self-serving and group-serving bias in attribution' *Journal of Social Psychology* 113:2, pp. 201–211. https://doi.org/10.1080/00224545.1981.9924371

Ulrich, Werner (2005) 'A brief introduction to critical systems heuristics': *ECOSENSUS project website*, The Open University. http://projects.kmi.open.ac.uk/ecosensus/publications/ulrich_csh_intro.pdf (accessed 2020)

Valore, Paolo (2017) 'A note on the indispensability of metaphysics' *Metaphysica* 18:2, pp. 231–6. https://doi.org/10.1515/mp-2017-0006

Van der Knaap, Lisette & van der Ham, Ineke (2011) 'How does the corpus callosum mediate interhemispheric transfer? A review' *Behavioral Brain Research* 223:1, pp. 211–21. https://doi.org/10.1016/j.bbr.2011.04.018

Varela, Francisco, Maturana, Umberto, & Uribe, R. (1974) 'Autopoeisis: The organization of living systems, its characterization and a model' *Biosystems* 5, pp. 187–96. https://doi.org/10.1016/0303-2647(74)90031-8

Walshe, Maurice (1995) *The Long Discourses of the Buddha: A Translation of the Digha Nikaya*. Wisdom Publications, Boston.

Walton, Douglas (1987) *Informal Fallacies: Towards a Theory of Argument Criticisms*. John Benjamins, Amsterdam.

Walton, Douglas (2011) 'What is a fallacy?' from Van Eemeren et al., ed., *Across the Lines of Disciplines*. De Gruyter, Berlin.

Wang, Yi-Xiang & 4 others (1999) 'Cerebral asymmetry in a selected Chinese population' *Australasian Radiology* 43:3, pp. 321–4. https://doi.org/10.1046/j.1440-1673.1999.433683.x

Waring, Alan (1996) *Practical Systems Thinking*. Thomson, London.

Wason, P.C. (1960) 'On the failure to eliminate hypotheses in a conceptual task'. *Quarterly Journal of Experimental Psychology* 12:3, pp. 129–40. https://doi.org/10.1080/17470216008416717

Williams-Nguyen, Jessica & 8 others (2016) 'Antibiotics and antibiotic resistance in agroecosystems: State of the science' *Journal of Environmental Quality* 45, pp. 394–406. https://doi.org/10.2134/jeq2015.07.0336

Wittgenstein, Ludwig, trans. Anscombe (1967) *Philosophical Investigations*. Blackwell, Oxford.

Wootton, Raymond & Allen, David (1983) 'Dramatic religious conversion and schizophrenic decompensation' *Journal of Religion and Health* 22:3, pp. 212–20. https://doi.org/10.1007/BF02280627

Yang Jisheng, trans. Mosher & Guo Jian (2021) *The World Turned Upside Down: A History of the Chinese Cultural Revolution*. Swift Press, London.

Zięba, Wlodzimierz (2008) 'Metaphysics as an inevitable dimension of cognition' *Dialogue and Universalism* 18:1/3, pp. 81–5.
https://doi.org/10.5840/du2008181/399

Index

a priori 9, 107, 116, 167, 172–3, 236
Abhidhamma 19, 271
abortion 139, 273
Abraham 199–200
absolutization **1–2** and *passim*
activity 70, 73, 112, 169, 179, 182, 201, 203–4, 207
ad hoc reasoning 2, 32, 88, 105, 107, 110–11, 113, 180, 190, 248
ad hominem 126
adaptation 29, 46, 53, 58, 133, 179, 244
addiction 2, 16, 239, 267
aesthetics 14, 76, 94, 161–2
Africa 225
agency 240. See also responsibility
Aggañña Sutta 20
agnostic 95, 191, 263
agnosticism 24–5, 28, 95, 191, 240, 263–4, **265**
albedo 40, 222
alienation 47, 70, 196
Allen, David 55, 278
amygdala 27
analogy 13–14, 35, 79, 237
analytic philosophy 64, 67, 71, 91, 95, 137, 212–13, 239
analytic psychology 130. See also Jungianism
anatta see non-substantiality
anicca see impermanence
anima/animus archetype 161
annihilationism 19
antibiotics 59
antifragility 53, 57–8
anxiety 15, 26, 55, 58, 105, 157, 169
appeal to history 233
appropriation 5, 28, 72, 122, 263
Aquinas, St Thomas 108, 114, 271

archetype 9, 70, 78, 86–7, 121, 139–40, **160–2**, 177, 180, 190, 194, 196, 199, 210, 223, 235, 253–5, 259
Archetypes in Religion and Beyond 139, 161, 216, 273
Aristotelianism 36–7, 102, 108, 114, 216, 249, 275
Aristotle 107, 216, 271
art 34, 46, 120–1, 154
arts 66, 88, 190, 206, 251, 266
asceticism 18, 23, 31, 56–7, 134
Asch, Solomon 156–7, 271
aspiration to universality see universal aspiration
astronomy 249
asymptosis 119
atheism 25, 28, 111, 210
attribute substitution 149
Augustine, St 256
authority 13, 26, 58, 106, 150, 156, 159, 202, 268
autonomy 192
autopoiesis 32, 40, 44
Ayer, A.J. 93, 249, 271

background assumption 117
balancing feedback loops 5, 39, **40–1**, 43, 45–6, 59, 149, 161, 205–6, 230, 258
basic level categories 62, 75
Bayesian reasoning 115
Beck, Aaron 259, 271
Being and Time (Heidegger) 93, 274
belief 2, **5–7** (nature of absolutized ~), 12, **14** (proliferation of absolutized ~), 16, **18–22** (~ and desire), **23–8** (opposing ~s), 29, 31, 35, 39, **41–7** (biology of ~), **48–52** (assumed independence),

53–60 (fragility of ~), **61–3** (~ and meaning), 64, 66, 68, 70, **77** (absolute ~ v confidence), 82, **84–8** (interpretation of ~), **91–2** (provisionality of ~), 99, **101–2** (logical relationships between ~s), **105–6** (foundational), 109, **110–15** (imperviousness of absolute ~), **116–19** (need for relevance of ~), **120–4** (inflation of absolute ~), 128, **131–8** (conflicting ~s), **142–8** (defensiveness of ~), **150–1** (substitution by abstract ~), 153, **155–7** (dominance in group), 160–1, 163–4, 168, 170–1, 173, 180, **182–3** (theoretical and practical ~), **187** (confusion with 'truth'), 191–2, 199, 201–2, 205, 210, **212–3** (normativity of all ~), 215, 226, **232–5** (temporal dimension of ~), **236** (~ and judgement), 238, 240, 242, 246, 249, 251, 260, 265–6
belief disconfirmation paradigm 144
bhava-tanha see craving for existence
bias 2–4, 7, 27, 32, 43, 46, 49–50, 107, 129, 136, 139, **143–7**, 148–9, 151, 155–7, 164–6, 168, 177, 180, 185, 191–2, 234, 243–5, 248, 250, 254, 258, 261–2, 268
bigotry 163, 190
'bigots' 190
biology 39, 100. See also systems, neuroscience
black swan 58, 93, 250
body scanning 193
boundaries 44, 48, 64, **78–82**, 100, 118–19, 156, 161, 184, 203, 218–21, 223
Bradley, Darren 95, 272
brain 6, 15–16, 22, 26–7, 48, 50–1, 61, 63, 66, 78–9, 103, 130, 132, 169, 177, 225, 240, 266, 272–3. See also amygdala, balancing feedback loops, Broca's Region, left hemisphere, left pre-frontal cortex, neural connections, reinforcing feedback loops, 'reptilian' brain, right hemisphere, striatum
brain hemispheres see left hemisphere, right hemisphere, brain
Broca's Region 51, 63, 65
Buddha 4, 12–14, 18, 19, 23, 30–1, 34–5, 37–8, 56–7, 59–60, 77, 102, 134, 165, 174, 185, 223, 243–4
Buddhism 2, 4–5, **12–38** *passim*, 59, 79, 89, 91, 164, 171, 174, 176–7, 180, 182–3, 200, 216, 244, 246–7, 260–2, 264, 267
Buddhist Studies 242, 244, 246
Buddhist tradition 4, 5, 20, 25, 164, 182, 244. See also Buddhism
Bush, George W. 35

Carnap, Rudolf 94, 272
Cartesian circle 106
Cartesian theatre 74
categories 31, 62, 76, 89, 135, 220–1, 223
categorizations 62, 153, 188
Catholicism 31, 106, 108, 114, 116, 137, 151, 190
catuskoti (fourfold logic) 37, 102
causal relationships 64, 103–4, 108, 141, 220
causation 120, 128
certainty 2, 99, 108, 122–3, 127, 205, 246
character 77, 100, 152, 253, 255
Charybdis 24
cherry-picking 243
China 204
Chinese Cultural Revolution 55, 278
Christ 162, 198–9, 263
Christianity 34, 54, 62, 68, 106, 162, 180, 198–9, 262–3
Christocentrism 263
circular argument 105
circularity **105–9**, 168, 177, 261, 268
clear and distinct perceptions 106
cliché 151
climate change 40, 46, 221–2
Clore, Gerald 22, 277
cognition see belief, meaning and related terms

cognitive behavioural therapy 259
cognitive dissonance 110, 113
cognitive linguistics see embodied meaning
cognitive modelling 167
cognitive psychology 129, 242
combat 133
community 67-8, 199, 207
concentration 18, 53, 169
concepts 70-2
conceptual space 79, 82, 228
conditionality 39, 84-5, 90, 112, 123, 155, 159, 168
confidence 10, 53, 57-8, 68, 70, 77, 192, 201, **204-7**, 256, 258
confirmation bias 107, **144-8**, 248, 251. See also bias
conflict 3, 7, 14, 21, 23-4, 29, 32, 48-9, 54-5, 66-7, 76-8, 84, 93, **129-38**, 141, 145, 148, 153, 155, 157, 159-60, 163, 168, 173, 178-80, 196, 201-3, 207, 219, 225-6, 230, 232-3, 238, 250, 254-5, 262, 264-5, 267-8
conspiracy theory 52, 148, 227
constitution 3
contextualization 78, 146, 250, 259, 266
continuity 34, **79-83**, 168, 265, 267
conversion 17, 53-5, 162
Conway, Kellyanne 123
Copernican astronomy 108, 249
corpus callosum 51, 70, 132
craving 4-5, 13-15, **18-21**, 23, 26-7, 30, 34, 107, 147, 164, 182, 233, 250, 254, 267
craving for existence 20
credibility 106, 126-7, 160
Critical Systems Heuristics 118
critical thinking 29, 35, 103, 153, 257, 258, 259, 266, 268
cruelty 255
cult 113, 119
culture 1-2, 98, 120, 128, 172, 224-6, 229, 245, 255
Cupitt, Don 96, 272

dairy farming 59
Dalits 135
Dawkins, Richard 42, 115, 272
De Chirico, Giorgio 121
decontextualization 50-2, 79, 184, 244. See also contextualization
deductive logic 6, 70, 75, **99-104**, 105, 116-17, 120, 124, 127-8, 136, 147-9, 152-3, 167, 172, 193, 208-9, 216, 238, 267
default mode network 169
deformátion professionelle 165
delusion 4-5, 13-14, 18, **20-1**, 23, 26-7, 30, 34, 50, 60, 72, 84, 96, 100, 103, 128, 168, 182, 260, 267
demonization 1. See also projection
denial 6, 19, **23-8**, 31, 37, 69-78, 127, 134, 139, 142, 179, 188, 190, 211, 226, 254
denialism 221
Dennett, Daniel 74, 272
depression 55, 130
Descartes, Rene 73, 104-6, 272
description 72-3, 179, 184, 261-2, 265
descriptive ethics 214
desire 12, 14, 16, 18-22, 26, 37, 49, 70, 76, 129, 131-5, 136, 140-2, 202, 212, 215, 232-3. See also craving
despair 254-5
despotism 254-5
determinism 28, 103, 119, 185, 188, 191-2, 200, 235-6, 238-40, 245
Dewey, John 73, 214, 272
dhyana 162
diachronic standpoint 167, 169
dialectic 95, 148, 173
dialetheism 102
dialogue 97, 119, 152, 187
diet 100, 200
directionality 203
disaster thinking 259
discontinuity 6, 34, 35, **79-83**, 168, 267
disequilibrium 56
dogma 2, 20, 92-3, 95, 151, 157, 160, 163-4, 192

dogmatic religion 163
dominance 27, 51, 70, 79, 81, 87, 114, 132, 135–6, 168, 224, 254. See also repression
Donne, John 121
Doria, Janet 156, 277
double-blind testing 148
doxastic involuntarism 239
dualism 4, 23, **25**, 26, 29, 31, 36, 89
Dweck, Carol 258, 272

echo chamber effect 157
economic exploitation 47
education 56, 89, 120, 122, 133, 153, 185, 203, 251
effectiveness 77, 157, 176, 179, 181–3, 192, **201–7**, 251, 261, 263
effort 15, 19, 58, 70, 77–8, 113, 133, 137, 150, 152, 154, 184, 203, 215, 230–1
ego 130–1
egoism 255
Eightfold Path, Noble 18, 182
elephant 71, 165–6, 240
embodied meaning 5–6, 22, 26, 50, **61–3** (defined), **64–88** *passim*, 93, 115, 151, 167, 174, 199, 217
embodiment 6, 42, 63, 65, 69, **70–8** (denial of ~), 79, 89, 97, 100–2, 122, 126–8, 134, 139, 140, 168, 176–7, 179–83, **188–93** (implications of ~), 206, 215, 217, 254, 261, 263–4, 267. See also embodied meaning
emergence 9, 45, 130, 167, 168–70
emotion 14, 16, 21–2, 26, 28, 51, 65, 77, 103, 114, 121, 149, 150, 158, 172, 200, 215, 232, 254, 256–8, 260, 261, 266–7. See also fact-value distinction, values
emotive meaning 57, 62, 66–7, 74
emotivism 213
empirical knowledge 105
empiricism 49, 74
energy 7, 12, 15, 17, 20–1, 45, 59, 77–8, 132–4, 145, 147, 149–50, 165, 169, 183, 202–3, 242
enlightenment 20, 30, 77, 180, 217, 238, 260

entailment 99, 101, 125. See also deductive logic
environment 3, 27, 33, 39–40, 42, 45–6, 53–4, 60–2, 73, 132, 184, 201, 204, 212, 230, 244
epistemic adequacy 197
epistemology 91–3
equanimity 200, 225
error focus 10, 177–8, 180, 248, **250–2**, 256–8, 261–5
escalation 39, 45–6
essentialism 34, **66–7**, 122, 199, 263
eternalism 18, 31
ethics 6, 31, 65, 76, 94, 103, 153, 172, 179, 182, 195–6, 200, **212–19**, 224, 246, 261, 263
even-handedness 28, 95, 264–5
evil 13, 110–11, 113, 139, 232, 252, **253–6**, 258, 268
evolution 33, 185, 214, 261, 277
evolutionary psychology 244–6
excluded middle 36–7
excluding the options see restricting the options
exercise 57, 98, 193, 199–200, 213
existence 6, 19, 20, 25, 82, 90, 97, 100, 104–6, 111, 114–15, 120, 162, 199, 210, 242
existentialism 239
extremism 47

facts 10, 21–2, 70, 123–4, 153, 194, 197, 199, 208, 213–14, 242, 244. See also fact-value distinction
fact-value distinction 94, **197**, 212, **213–15**, 219, 244–5. See also values
faith 70, 205, 238
fallacy 2, 7, 29, 35, 99, 102, 120, **124–8**, 144, 147–8, 197, 243, 268, 277. See also formal and informal fallacy, and specific named fallacies
fallacy of composition 209
false consensus 155–7, 276
false dichotomy 4, 5, **35–6**, 63, 74, 213, 227. See also restricting the options
false dilemma see false dichotomy

Index

false neutrality 213
falsehood 91, 179, 209
falsification 28, **248–51**
Fascism 263
fast thinking 32, 113, 145, 149, 205–6
fat tails 204
fatalism 239. See also determinism
fear 23, 26–7, 29, 49, 57, 140, 145–7, 162. See also anxiety
feedback loops see balancing feedback loops and reinforcing feedback loops
female genital mutilation 225, 226
feminism 137
Festinger, Leon 113, 144, 273
film 87
fishing expeditions (evidence) 243
Five Ways (Aquinas) 108
fixed mindset 258
flip 53, **54–7**, 58, 68, 86, 132, 142, 242
force 103, 142, 147, **201–3**, 255
Forest (in life of Buddha) 19, 56, 139
forest monks 244
formal fallacy 125–6
foundationalism **105–6**, 150, 177, 254
fourfold logic (*catuskoti*) 37, 102
fragility 5, 39, **53–60**, 68, 88, 132, 142, 147, 157, 158, 190–1, 202, 205
framing 17, 24–5, 29, 35, 37, 49, 56, 58, 82, 89, 111, 113–14, 117, 135, 141, 158, 164, 166, 171, 173–5, 209–10, 258, 261–2, 264–5
freedom 31, 119
freewill 30, 90, 111, 188, 191–2, 200, 235–6, **238–40**
Frege, Gottlob 71–2, 74, 273
Freud, Sigmund 130–2, 273
Freudianism 129
friendship 207
fundamental attribution error 191
fundamentalism 1, 118, 203
future 15–16, 23, 110, 115, 117, 119, 121, 225, **232–5**, 236, 241, 254
fuzzy logic 102

Galileo Galilei 107, 110, 272
Gandhi, Mohandas 137, 273
gender 153. See also sex

generality 127, 182–4
generalizations 45, 151–2, 209, 248
genetic inheritance 82
geometry 172
gestalt 33, 173
global warming see climate change
goals 10, 21, 26, 30, 70, 72–3, 76–8, 81, 114, 131–4, 140, 147, 169, 176, 185, 187, 197, 201–2, 207, 218, 220–1, 228, 236, 244
God 6, 30, 71–2, 78, 82, 87, 104, 106, 108, 111, 113, 115, 118, 120, 142, 154, 161–2, 180, 197–9, 210, 217, 238–40, 242, 263
God's eye view 70, 72, 93, 246
Goebbels, Josef 138
golden rule (Aristotle) 224
Gould, Stephen 153, 273
group 1, 7, 23, 40, 52, 55, 57–8, 66–8, 82, 88, 107, 123, 129, 135, **155–60**, 187, 191, 198, 202, 203, 206, 215, 218, 224–5, 227, 245, 250–1, 255. See also false consensus, group binding, groupthink, ingroup-outgroup bias, social proof
group binding 55, 129, **155–60**, 215, 218
group consciousness 156
groupthink 155–6
growth mindset 257–9
guilt 194, 238

Haidt, Jonathan 214, 240, 273
hallucinations 55
haptic sensations 49
hatred 4–5, 13–15, **18**, 21, 26, 30, 34, 147, 164, 168, 182, 250, 254, 260, 267
Hebb, Donald 15, 274
Hegelianism 165
Heidegger, Martin 89, 92–3, 272, 274, 276
Heraclitus 91
hero 96, 161, 259
hierarchies 136
Hinduism 135, 174
Hobbes, Thomas 158, 274
holism 92

homophobia 54
Honeyball Sutta 13
human nature 145, 158, 216
human rights 227
Hume, David 21, 99–100, 105–6, 274
hypothesis 41, 45, 50, 99
hypothetical beliefs 41, 45

idealization 86, 183, 217, 238
ideology 3, 28, 36, 78, 136, 141, 154, 158, 160, 163, 202, 216, 238, 245, 252–3, 262, 264
idling 169
idolatry 142
illusion of control 191
imagination 39, 44, 79, 192, 194, 221–2, 243, 245, 251, 257–8, 266
impatience 126, 232, 255
impermanence 34
imperviousness to observation 115
impracticality 184–5
impressions 106, 234. See also sense data
income 153
incremental 77, 80, 82, 99
incrementality 34, 35, 77, **79–83** (as continuity), 99, 120, 122–3, 127, 147, 153, 191–2, 194, 248, 264, **265** (as Middle Way principle)
independence 42, **48–52**, 60, 67, 69–70, 93, 97, 105, 134, 157, 168, 220, 238, 254, 267
India 83, 102
individuation 130
induction 70, 75, 99–100, **101**, 127, 149, 152–3
inequality 46
infinite scope 54, **110**, 111–12, 162–3, 215, 243, 248–9
infinity 12–13, 27–8, 30, 33–4, 54, 65–7, 79–81, 85, 104, 108–13, 115, 117, 119–20, 129, 132, 136, 142, 145, 161–3, 187, 188, 190–2, 198–9, 212, 215, 220, 223, 243, 248
inflation 102–3, **120–8**, 136, 145, 148, 189, 195, 197, 205, 238
informal fallacies 126–8

information 2, 26, 40, 43, 45, 47, 51, 62, 73, 81, 85, 107–9, 114–15, 125, 128, 132, 136, 144, 146, 152, 198, 205, 222, 224, 229, 243, 246
information bias 243
ingroup-outgroup bias 155, **156**, 245
inspiration 9, 78, 120–1, 139, 141–2, **161–3**, 190, 194, 199, 214, 244, 248, 252
institutions 157
integrated development 70, 77
integration 21, 56–7, 78, 120–1, **130** (in general), 135, 137, 139, 141, 162, 194, 204, 229–30, 232–3, 240, 263, 264, **265** (as Middle Way principle), 268
integration model **21**, 137
integrative practice 266
interdisciplinarity 2
interpretation 1, 16, 21, 32, 37, 39, 42, 74, 75, 82, **84–8**, 91, 99, 111–12, 117, 121, 128, 143, 159, 167–8, 172, 194, 198–9, 228, 240, 258, 264, 267
intuition 51, 90–1, 154, **173**
invalidity 124–5. See also deductive logic
irony 97
Islam 1, 17, 106, 142, 227
Islamic State 1–2, 86, 118, 145
Islamism 1

James, William 85–6, 187, 274
Janis, Irving 156–7, 274
Johnson, Mark 5, 61–2, 70, 73, 75–6, 103, 214–15, 230, 274–5
judgement *passim*. See especially **236–41**
judgement focus 10, 178, 185, **236–41**, 242, 244, 246, 250, 261, 263–5
Jung, Carl 74–5, 130–2, 140, 161, 274
Jungianism 9, 129, 253, 262, 268
justice 31, 113, 163, 252
justification 1, 4, 35, 49, 52, 54, 57–8, 77, 92, 93–4, 97, 99, **101–2**, 105–9, 118, 120, 123–4, 126–8, 159, 165,

Index

170-1, 173, 176, 183, 195, 198, 205, 215, 235, 249, 251, 267, 269
justified true belief 122

Kahneman, Daniel 7, 27, 32, 50, 145, 149-50, 274
Kampfmittel (source of conflict) 93
Kant, Immanuel 172, 217, 274
Kantianism 172, 217
karma 19-20
Kierkegaard, Søren 197, 274
knowledge 6, 23, 30, 35, 41, 64, 73, 79, 90-2, 96, 105-6, 114, 119-21, **122-3**, 125, 209, 220
Kruglanski, Arie 56, 81, 201, 275
Kuhn, Thomas 92, 108, 148, 249-50, 275

Lakatos, Imre 92, 108, 148, 249, 275
Lakoff, George 5, 61-2, 75-6, 103, 229-30, 275
Langer, Ellen 85, 275
language games 68, 97
law 194-5
Law Book of Manu 136
law of logic 36
leadership 136, 154-5, 180, 202
left hemisphere (of brain) 51, 63, 70, **79-81**, 114, 132-3, 151, 168, 254
left pre-frontal cortex 27, 32, 51, 63, 132, 224
legal naturalism 195
legal positivism 195
Leibniz, Gottfried 103-4, 275
Lewis, Marc 16, 132, 275
liberal democracy 97
linearity 39, 53, 95, 118, 170, 201, 211, **220-2**, 229
linear causality 39
linguistics 2, 5, 61, 64, 174. See also meaning
literalism 70, 76
livelihood 18, 196
logic 7, 21, 23, 28-9, 35-7, 51, 75, 87, 90, 93, 95, **99-104** (absolutization of ~), 105-8, 116, 120, **124-8** (inflation of ~), 136, 141, 145, 147, 149, 152, 168, 197, 213, 216, 221, 248, 257, 267-8. See also deductive logic, induction
logical positivism 89, **93-5**, 124
long-legged fly 96
love 86, 142, 159, 162, 227
Lyotard, Jean-Francois 96, 275

Malunkyaputta 12-14, 30, 243
manipulativeness 254-5
Marvell, Andrew 121
Marxism 31, 155, 165
materialism 24, 31, 50, 105
mathematics 75, 77, 100, 103, 150, 152, 172, 228
Maturana, Humberto 32, 39-42, 44, 61, 122, 275, 277
maturation 56
McGilchrist, Iain 32, 51, 63-4, 79-80, 132, 224-5, 275
Meadows, Donella 40, 45-6, 48, 53, 59, 131, 275
meaning 4-6, **36** (false dichotomy in ~), **41-2** (in living systems), 44, 49-50, 57, **61-9** (representationalist v embodied accounts), 70, **71-2** (conceptual substitution for embodied ~), **74-5** (sign substitution for symbolic ~), **75-6** (schematic ~), **76-7** (metaphorical ~), 78, 84, **86-8** (~ distinguished from belief), 90, 93-7, **99-102** (neglect of ~ in absolute logic), 110, 112, **114-15** (imperviousness of absolute ~), 117, 120-3, 125, 137, 141, **150-1** (prototypes in), 153, 155, **161-3** (archetypal ~), 167-8, **171-3** (synthesis of ~), 174, 176-7, 179-80, 182, 187, **199** (responsibility for ~), 200, 202, **210** (~ evoked in inspiration), 213, 217, 219-20, 233, 235, **236** (role in judgement), 241, 257, 266-7
meaning-focus 84, **86-7**, 90
mediation 224, 226
meditation 18, 96, 104-5, 134, 182, 183, 244. See also mindfulness
meditative state 57

meme 42
men 86, 134, 152, 165, 225, 229
mental health 218
mental illness 130–1, 267–8
mental proliferation 4, **12–17**, 21, 30, 37, 39, 45, 59, 96, 146, 168, 169, 184, 191, 232, 254, 267
mental states 10, 46, 121, 194, 200, 217, 226, 265
metaethics 213
metaphor 34, 51, 62, 70, 76, 93, 96, 103, 121, 151, 161, 199, 228, 230, 240
metaphorical extension 230
metaphysical beliefs see metaphysics
metaphysical speculation 10, 13
metaphysics 2, 6–7, 9, 14, 31, 34, 73, 82, **89–98** (absolute nature of ~), 105–7, 110, **116–19** (claimed inevitability of ~), **120–4** (inflation of ~), 128, 136–7, 146, 148, 151–2, 158, 164, 168, 170, 177, 180, **189–90** (impracticability of ~), 195, 212, 216, 238, 242, 254, 267
metonymy 76
Middle East 225
Middle Way 3, 4, 9–11, 13–14, 17–18, 21, 23–4, 28–9, 37, 58, 86, 134, 164, 174, 176–7, 184, 189, 228, 230, 237, 244, **260–6**
Middle Way Philosophy 3, 24, 264
mind-body monism 36
mindfulness 12, **14–15**, 18, 50, 79, 98, 133–4, 187, 192–3, 200, 206, 251, 257–8, 266–8. See also meditation
modal logic 102
model 21–2, 68, 70, 73–7, 80, 82, 85, 87, 92–3, 99, 129–30, 138, 151, 183, 206, 218, 220, 222, 228
monism 89, 174. See also mind-body monism
moon 107, 111, 113
moral absolutism 95
moral evil 253
moral philosophy 242. See also ethics
moral principles 195, 225
moral rules 212, 217, 224, 242
morality 18, 21, 31, 46, 76, 195, 197. See also ethics
moving the goalposts see *ad hoc* reasoning
multidisciplinarity 2–3, 185. See also interdisciplinarity
multiple personalities 130
myth 161

Nagarjuna 25
Nagel, Thomas 72, 276
narrative 95–7
narratives 97
natural evil 253
Natural Law 116
naturalism 70, 72–3, 76, 174, 213, 215
naturalness 141
negation 4–5, 17, **23–8**, 29, 54, 56, 79, 82, 147, 168, 177, 179, 222, 234, 250, 258, 260–1, 265, 267
negative absolutizations 22–8
negativity 28, 129, 257
neomania 233–4
nervous system 41, 61, 63, 66, 78, 130
neural connections **15**, 133, 149, 152, 172, 174, 211, 230, 236
neuroscience 2, 6, 15, 32, 48, 79, 129, 132, 267
Newtonian physics 201, 228, 232
Nigeria 2
nihilism 19, 31, 97, 211
nirvana fallacy 96
no true Scotsman 110. See also *ad hoc* reasoning
non-existence 25, 242
non-linearity 53. See also systematicity
non-substantiality 34
Non-violent Communication 32
normative ethics 214, 216, 219
normativity 174, 177, 179–80, 211, **212–19**, 221–4, 234, 244, 246, 260–1, 263. See also ethics
novels 87
numbers 76, 188, 229, 269. See also mathematics

objectivity 5, 248–9, 272

observation 5-6, 22, 50, 57, 73, 92-3, 100, 110, **112-15**, 133, 141, 170-1, 228, 249, 268
Ockham's Razor 149
Odysseus 24
Oedipus Complex 130
omnibenevolence 111
omnipotence 106, 111
omniscience 111
ontological argument 104
ontology 73, 90, 92. See also metaphysics
openness 161-2, 212
optimism 233
optionality 29
oriental studies 174
oriental people 225
over-specialization 94, 164, 214

Palace (in life of Buddha) 19, 23, 56
palaeolithic 45, 254
Pali Canon 4, 13, 34-5, 37
papañca see mental proliferation
paradigm 22, 92, 108, 148, 213, 249-50
paradox 98, 176
Parmenides 90
parochialism 10, 204, 208, 228-9, 251, 261
particularity 10, 68, 73, 92
passivity 65, 70, 73-4
past 72, 145-6, 154, 194, **232-5**, 240, 245, 248, 259
path 11, 15, 18, 24, 62, 75, 114, 161, 182-3, 200, 230-1, 237, 258, 262
patience 232
Paul, St 54-5, 68
pedantry 122
perception 16, 106, 113, 139, **140-1**
perfection 100-1
perspective 3-4, 6, 9, 15, 17, 31, 33, 37-8, 48-9, 55, 59, 63, 69-70, **72**, 73-5, 77-9, 97, 131-2, 136, 148, 153, 171, 174, 176, 180-1, 183-4, 188, 190, 193, 206-8, 217, 220-3, 225, 230, 246, 249, 251, 267
pessimism 233
Phaethon 24

phenomenology 93, 185, 232
philosophy 2, 4, 6-7, 10, 22, 26, 51, 64-5, 71, 85, **89-128** *passim*, 153, 160, 171, 174, 177, 179, 182, 184-5, 187, 189, 213-14, 219, 238, 245, 247, 249, 264, 267-8
philosophy of science 89, 91
phobia 58, 245
physicalism 185
Piaget, Jean 56, 271, 276
Plato 77, 152, 264, 276
Platonism 24, 76, 101, 112, 152, 228, 263
polarization 47, 178
political correctness 67, 84, 218
politics 6-7, 15, 17, 42, 47, 54-5, 67, 76, 84, 90, 129, 135-7, 153, 154-5, **159-60**, 162-3, 177, 179, 190, 202-4, 214, 217, 225, 229, 251-2, 262-5, 268
pope 106
Popper, Karl 110, 140, 177, **248-51**, 276
positivity 28, 121, 261
postmodernism 89, 93, **95-7**, 124, 261
practical religion 163
practicality 3, 10, 84-5, 90-1, 112, **176-81** (~ of argument), **182-7** (as general criterion), **188-93** (as embodiment), **194-200** (as responsibility), **201-7** (as effectiveness), 208-9, 218, 242-3, 247, 250, 261, 263, 265
pragmatics (in linguistics) 64, 271
pragmatism 85-6, 96, 177, 184, 187, 197, 218
prayer 162
prayers of intercession 142
prejudice 152
Pre-Socratics 90
primacy effect 234
Primeval Horde (in Freud) 130
principle of charity 84
principle of sufficient reason 103
principles 1, 10, 34, 48, 76, 80, 86, 217, 224, 226, 264-5
private languages 66
probabilism 58, 99, 101

probabilistic evidence 58
probability 27, 58, 99, 101, 110, **115**, 125, 146, 150, 178, 225, 233, 243, 247, 268
problem of evil 111
procrastination 133, 233
professionalism 103, 218
profundity 120, 121
projection 2, 7, 9, 78, 103, 105, 108, 129, 136, **139–43**, 157, 167, 173, 177, 180, 238, 250, 253–4
proliferation see mental proliferation
proof text 106
prophecy 113
propositions 50, 61, **65–7**, 74, 84–5, 87, 93–5, 99, 101, 112, 162–3, 168, 190, 196
proprioception 51
prototypes 149–50
provisionality 7, 56–7, 72–3, 75, 77, 82, 84–5, 90–2, 95, 97, **98** (as non-metaphysical), 106, 115–19, 123–4, 127, 132–5, 147–8, 151, 153–5, 157, 159, 161, 167, 176, 182, 184–5, 187, 192, 195–6, 200–1, 203, 205, 209–10, 212, 215, 223–4, 226–7, 229–30, 232, 236–8, 240, 242–3, **250** (considering alternatives), 256, 260, 252, 264, **265** (as Middle Way principle), 267
prudence 76
psychiatry 169
psychoanalysis 7, **129–31**, 137, 143, 268
psychological states 84, 164, 172, 227, 260
psychology 2, 5, 7, 10, 22, 26, 32, 65, 68, 81, 94, 110, **129–63** *passim*, 171, 177–8, 191, 201, 213, 221, 233, 238, 247, 264, 267–8
Psychology of Closed-Mindedness 81, 275
psychopathy 255
psychosis 53, 55, 130
psychotherapy 9, 129, 177, 185, 200
pure science 247
puzzle solving ability 249

Pyrrhonism 91

Qur'an 1

race 153, 245
racism 82
rationalism 95, 100, 105, 108, 197
rationality 21–2, 27, 58, 76, 99, **102–3**, 120, 128, 145, 149–50, 199, 216, 218, 223, 227, 246, 260, 268. See also fact-value distinction
rationalization 85, 88, 91, **110–15**, 132, 136, 144–5, 245, 248
reality 5, 50, 55, 61, 64, 75, 81, 86–7, **89–93**, 95, 97, 99, 101, 105, 119, 121–2, 147, 157, 168, 170, 180, 197, 199, 209, 223, 262
reasoning 32, 75, 100–2, 109, 116, 125, 127, 141, 149, 152, 172–3, 248, 261. See also deductive logic, induction
rebirth 20
recreation 193
reductionism 49–50, 73
reference (in Frege) 72
reincarnation 31
reinforcing feedback loops 5, 9, 16, 27, 32, **39–47**, 51, 53–5, 58–9, 78, 93, 97, 105, 107, 128, 132, 136, 139, 141, 147, 149, 151, 157, 161, 202–3, 222, 238, 241, 250, 254, 261, 267
relationships
  human: 3, 15, 46, 155, 162, 168
  justificatory: 102, 167, 170
  logical: 66, 87, 98–104, 141
  spatial: 228
  systemic, including causal: 39, 48, 64, 75, 99, 103–4, 141, 153, 216, 220–1, 229
relativism 10, **97–8**, 123–4, 137, 179, 187, 211, 226, 229, 235, 260, 261
relaxation 14, 193, 232
religion 2, 6, 10, 54, 78, 85–7, 94, 96, 105, 111, 120, 139, 153, 161, **163**, 178, 199, 216, 238, 267–8, 273, 278
religious experience 7, 71, 115, **120–1**, 162–3, 173, 190

representationalism 5, 9, 50, 57, **61-9**, 70, 75, 92-7, 99, 115, 122, 147, 176-7, 179-80, 197, 210, 215, 224, 238, 242-3, 254, 257, 262
repression 2, 7, 9, 21, 32, 54-5, **129-38**, 147, 155, 157, 159-60, 196, 202-3, 254, 265
repression model 21
'reptilian' brain 26-7, 132, 225, 266
Republic (Plato) 77, 276
research programmes 249
resilience 5, 53, **58-9**
responsibility 132, 158, 174, 176, 178-9, 182-3, 188, 192, **194-200**, 204-5, 210, 232-6, 238, 240, 261
restricting the options 4-5, 17, **29-38**, 79, 85, 168, 179, 267. See also false dichotomy
revelation 106, 108, 114, 173
right action (in Buddhism) 18
right aspiration (in Buddhism) 18
right effort (in Buddhism) 18
right hemisphere (of brain) 51, 70, **80-1**, 114, 132, 152
right view (in Buddhism) 18
rigidity 44, 83, 134, 136, 212, 254, 255
Rorty, Richard 96-7, 187, 276
Rosenberg, Marshall 32-3, 276
Ross, Lee 157, 276
Rowling, J.K. 255
rumination 169

'saints' 188, 190
Sartre, Jean-Paul 197, 276
sassatavada see eternalism
Satan 255
scepticism 89, **91**, 92-3, 101, 113, 117, 122, 126, 173-4, 188, 206, 263-5
schema 56, **62**, 70, 75-6, 93, 230
science 6, 31, 65, 72, **91-2**, 94, 104-5, 120, 122, 148-9, 153-4, 166, 167, 171, 172, 177, 198-9, 203, 205, 213, 249-51, 268. See also biology, neuroscience, psychology, systems
scientific method 92, 148, 174, 268
scientific observation 63
scripture 106, 190, 198

Scylla 24
self help 178
self-censorship 157
self-esteem 70, 239, 258
self-serving bias 191
semantics 64
sense (in Frege) 71-2, otherwise see meaning, sense data, senses
sense data 74, 114
sense organs 72
senses 7, 43, 51, 67, 79, 91, 107, 122, 124, 157, 171, 188, 194, 225
sequencing (in time) 79-80
sex 150, 161. See also gender
sexuality 150, 151
shadow 64, 140, 161, 177, **253-6**, 261
short-termism 10, 254
Siegel, Daniel 129, 277
signs 43, 70, 74, 100, 102, 125, 190, 254-5
slavery 83, 216, 234, 235
slow thinking 32, 145-6, 149, 268
social functions 35-6, 39, 42, 46, 50, 54, 57, 64, 76, 85, 90, 97, 113, 118, 129, 135-6, 148-9, 151, 153, **155-60** (group binding), 165, 168-9, 177-8, 185, 187, 194-6, 197, 199, 206, 213, 215-16, 218, **224-7** (universality of ~), 232, 244-5, 252, 257, 263
social media 133, 157, 169
social proof 155-6
social sciences 39, 90, 165, 213-14. See also politics, psychology, social functions
social signalling 76
social status 114, 136
sociopathy 253, 255
Socrates 77, 152-3
Socratic questioning 152
soft systems methodology 222-3
solidarity 155-6, 190, 207, 254
soul 12-13, 31
space 33-5, 72, 74, 79-80, 82, 117, 177, 178, 188, 211, 222, **228-31**, 230, 235, 237, 261
spatiality 228

specialization 63, 153, 165, 182, 185, 203, 224
speech 13, 18, 35, 63, 210
statistics 58, 104, 147, **152-3**, 243
Storbeck, Justin 22, 277
stress 27, 47, 113, 153, 157, 200, 245-6, 260
stretch 183, 192, **195-6**, 200, 207, 210, 212, 218, 228-31, 242-3, 265
striatum 27, 132
structural couplings 40, 41
Studies in Hysteria (Freud) 130, 273
suboptimization 131
substitution 7, 9, 27, 32, 70-2, 74-6, 78, 97, 103, 106, 108-9, 120-1, 136, 144, 146-7, **149-54**, 155-6, 168, 183, 205, 210, 228, 238, 250
suffering 6, 56, 90, 111, 113, 232
sunk cost fallacy 233
Sunstein, Cass 150, 277
supernaturalism 70, 78, 105
suppression 135, 159
survivorship bias 233
sustainability 41, 141, 202
syllogism 100, 125
symbol 9-10, 26, 62-4, 67, 70, **74-5**, 76, 78, 84, 87, 94, 121, 161-2, 190, 199, 205, 209, 210, 212, 215, 223, 256, 259, 263
synaptic connections see neural connections
syntax 63, 65-6
synthesis 2, 9, 51, 143, 145, 166, **171-5**, 181, 185, 187, 260, 264
synthetic argument 166
systematicity **220-3**. See also systems
systems 2, 4-5, 22, 26, 32, **39-60** *passim*, 62-3, 69, 70, 80, 100, 102, 105, 114, 118, 125, 131, 151, 153, 165, 171, 174, 177, 203, 211, 213, 220-3, 264, 267, 268. See also balancing feedback loops, fragility, independence, reinforcing feedback loops, systematicity

tai chi 193
Taleb, Nassim Nicholas 5, 57-8, 204, 243, 277

Taylor, Donald 156, 277
technology 50, 188, 203
temporal biases 232, **233-5**
Texas sharpshooter fallacy 243
Thailand 244
theatre 74, 226
theism 25, 87, 111, 210
theology 85, 93, 106, 108, 114, 153, 263
therapeutic practice 171, 218
Theravada Buddhism 19
Thinking Fast and Slow (Kahneman) 145
thought experiment 245
Threefold Path 182
time 2, 15-16, 23-4, 27, 29-30, 34-5, 50-2, 54, 58, 62, 72, 74, **79-81** (continuity over ~), 82, 94, 111, 117, 129, **130-1** (emergence of repressed beliefs over ~), **161-2** (inspiration over ~), 167-9, **170** (evidence over ~), 171, 177-8, 189, 192, 199-200, **201-4** (sustained effectiveness over ~), 205, 211, 213, 215, 230, **231-5** (universality across ~), 236-7, 240, 246, 250-1, 254, 261, 270
tipping points **53-7**, 80, 142
Todd, Chuck 124
Tolkien, J.R.R. 255
training 34-5, 89, 102-3, 133, 153, 165, 194, 203, 268
transcendental deduction 172
transversal approach 2
true dichotomies 35-6
Trump, Donald 123, 124, 146
truth 6, 19, 35, 37, 49, 52, **64-5** (~ and representationalism), **72-3** (~ and naturalism), **90-2** (as metaphysics), 99, **105-6** (in foundationalism), 112, 120, **122-4** (inflation of ~), 125-6, 137, 142, 144, 159, 162, 173, 179-80, 182, **187** (in pragmatism), 199, **209-10** (archetypal use of ~), 223, 238
truth-conditionality 64
Tversky, Amos 7, 27, 32, 145
two-stage judgement process 23

ucchedavada see nihilism
Ulrich, Werner 118–19, 277
ultimate attribution error 191
uncertainty 39, 41, 49, 77, 91, 93, 98, 101, 108, 112, 126, 142, 206–7, 217, 264–5. See also scepticism
unconscious 44, 49, 114, 130–1, 253
unholy alliance 25, 89, 158
universality 19, 172, **208–11** (top-down v bottom-up ~), **212–19** (normative ~), **220–3** (systemic ~), **224–7** (across groups), **228–31** (across space), **232–5** (across time), 242, 247, 260, 261, 264, 265
universal aspiration 10, 124, 177, 178, 180, 204, **208–11**, 217, 220, 223, 232, 247, 261, 263–5
universe 30, 34, 48, 58, 65–7, 101, 103–4, 108, 110, 112, 120, 208–9, 228–9, 249
unreality 91. See also delusion, reality
utilitarianism 32, 195, 217, 246

vaccination 198, 227
vagueness 44, 110
validity 125–7, 147, 273
values 1, 16, 18, **21–2** (false dichotomy with facts), 49, 55, 68, 70, **76–7** (substitution for desires), 161, 179–80, 194, **196–7** (responsibility for facts and ~), 199, 208, **212–19** (normativity of ~), 223, 226–7, 234, 242, 244, 262. See also ethics
van der Ham, Ineke 51, 277
van der Knaap, Lisette 51, 277
Varela, Francisco 32, 39–42, 44, 61, 122, 275, 277
verifiability 93, 95
verification 28, 94
Vienna Circle 93, 272
violence 136
Virgin Mary 162
virtue ethics 216

Weil, Simone 263
Wheel of Samsara 18
wisdom 24–6, 120, 182
Wittgenstein, Ludwig 64, 66, 68, 123, 278
Wittgensteinianism 64, 97
women 225, 229
Wootton, Raymond 55, 278

Yeats, W.B. 96
yoga 193, 260

zeugma 172

www.ingramcontent.com/pod-product-compliance
Lightning Source LLC
Chambersburg PA
CBHW050553170426
43201CB00011B/1677